Information Technology and Globalisation
by *D.K. Gupta*

This edition is published by Rajat Publications
4740/23, Ansari Road Daryaganj,
New Delhi - 110002

ISBN: 978-81-7880-097-4

Edition 2026

Printed and bound in India

RAJAT
PUBLICATIONS

4740/23, Ansari Road, Daryaganj,
New Delhi- 110002 (India)
Mob:- +91-9811484973, +91-9811105389
E-mail: rajat_publication@yahoo.com

Preface

Nature and its evolution mechanism is an analogue process based on complex multilevel interactive matrixes. The nearest natural event that resembles a digital evolutionary step are large scale environmental phenomenons or disasters. Man is part of the analogue evolution and is in itself an analogue machine, consequently "Scientific and Technological" developments for the greater part of human existence tended to be of the same nature. The advent of electricity changed that tendency in a drastic way and opened up new scientific horizons in a very short historical period of time.

The fact that we are now witnessing a digital revolution is not in doubt, what is more difficult to pinpoint is whether the emergence of a single event or digital technology has acted as the catalyst.

To build a global community in which the people of neighbouring countries view each other not as potential enemies, but as potential partners, as members of the same family in the vast, increasingly interconnected human family.

Information technology has emerged as the most decisive, valuable and critical resource for individuals, enterprises, societies and countries. Barriers to trade and travel are being demolished, economics are getting globalised and communications are becoming instantaneous.

This book will see as a guide to students policy makers, business managers and is specially designed to help the reader an authentic knowledge provide on information technology.

Author

Contents

1
Information Highways

The information highways as a tool for a multipersonal game whose players have their own particular goals but may not be conscious of the goals of other participants. Hence, the ethics of using information highways can be considered as a set of general rules imposed on it for a common interest. The free right to express independent opinions, to do research, obtain and spread information and opinions without any restrictions and by all means, has been stated as one of the basic rights in the Universal Declaration of Human Rights of the United Nations Organization. The further development of the right for information can be found in art. 27 of the Declaration, stating the human right to use the achievements of art and science and to protect moral and material advantages resulting from any human activity in the field of science, literature or art.

It has been stated though (art. 29 of the Declaration), that every human being, in spite of his rights and freedom, undergoes certain restrictions imposed by law, and resulting from the necessity to protect the same rights and freedoms for all people, moral norms, requirements of public order, and welfare of the democratic society.

When the Universal Declaration of Human Rights was proclaimed, nobody expected such a rapid development of computer era (there were only a few computers of the first generation existing). In many countries public television has not been known yet, mass communication media were only press and radio, and individual communication media were: telephone, telegraph, and mail. In spite of that, both the basic, affirmative, and the final, restrictive, parts of the Declaration have not, for the 50 years, become outdated.

Still, the further years have shown that the range of the accepted restrictions imposed on the commonly accepted general human right for information according to the legal systems of particular countries can be interpreted in various ways. As time passed, the differences in interpretation of the right for information between the countries of different political systems and different levels of social and economic development were increasing.

It became clear at the beginning of the seventies, when the project of UNESCO Declaration was discussed, concerning the regulations of using satellite broadcasts (the Declaration was approved during the XVII Session of the UNESCO General Conference in 1972). The communist countries, as well as many countries of the Third World, were not going to stop restricting free information flow by technical and legal means.

Although the arguments about protection of moral values and personal properties of the individuals were used, it was clear that the core of the argument was concerning free distribution of political information. It should not be assumed, though, that legal regulations restricting access to information can completely stop the flow of information. It only means that in some countries, including Poland, in certain historical periods, a very high price had to be paid for the access to information. That is why nowadays, when democratic rules of political life have returned, the society so reluctantly accepts the necessity of restricting the access to information or controlling it for the sake of some superior goals.

The societies are able to understand and accept the need of introducing ethical and legal norms which do not allow for violating personal properties (including intellectual values or economic interest) through unlimited flow of information, but they are against the unlimited control of the state over establishing such norms. Any slogans which suggest introducing, in more or less hidden form, of the moral preventive censorship in press and other publications, are highly unpopular. But it does not mean society is favourable to pornography. It rather means the society would like to participate in deciding what is permitted, and what is forbidden in its own interest. Poland is one of those countries which began to apply computer technology relatively early. Research started at the beginning of the fifties, and by the end of the fifties several original constructions of the first generation computers were already existing. By the end of the sixties trade versions of the second generation computers were applied in economy, science, and didactics.

At the beginning of the seventies attempts were made to elaborate a long-term programme of computerization of economy and state administration. For the first time the concepts of computer network based on countrywide network of data transmission ("information highway") appeared. They aimed at improving the centralized system of managing economy, and as such have originally met the approval of the authorities. But the concepts disregarded technical and economic limitations, at thus the programme of their realization was considerably restricted.

Studies over the systems which were to be constructed at that time have shown the range and significance of the legal problems which appear in connection with building systems of central planning, electronic census, state statistics, scientific and technical information, etc. At that time the state had not only the monopoly in deciding about import, production, and distribution of computers, or about development of telecommunication network in the country, but also, as the programme of information systems development started, in deciding on kind of information stored and processed by the central and local systems, on the suppliers of the information, its users, etc. In some circles the first moral and legal doubts have appeared concerning the unlimited right of the state to store personal information about its citizens, the compliance of the scientific and technical information systems with the copyright law, etc. Still, there was no escape from the informatics era. After the first stage of development, in which only very few people knew what the computers were and what their possible applications could be, the society entered the next stage, in which the knowledge about where and how computers and computer networks can be used became common.

This common knowledge about computers is due, to a high degree, to introducing computer science at secondary schools and universities. Poland's experience shows that the popularization of computer science is one of the prerequisites for common access to information, as it is understood by the Universal Declaration of Human Rights. This commonness, though, requires not only the common knowledge on computers, but also the common access to computers or terminals. The real progress in this field has occurred in Poland only in the last few years, and has been connected with social and economic changes which resulted in market economy development. In that time both computer hardware and software markets have rapidly developed.

The recent years are also the period of multimedia databases market quick expansion. It is very advantageous that the majority of buyers are university and secondary students. The programme of countrywide computer network (NASK - Scientific Academic Computer Network) covering all the major academic centres has been realized for the last few years. NASK subscribers are also connected to Internet. The estimated number of Internet subscribers in Poland is about 500 000. At the same time general purpose networks - metropolitan range (MAN) are built, and many local networks (LAN) cooperate with them. Within a few years, the basic restrictions: administrative (control of the number of computers sold), financial (drop of prices of personal computers), and technical (development of communication network) disappeared. Computers became commonly used tools in offices, companies, R&D institutions, universities, schools and even private homes, which still at the eighties seemed to be utopia. This apparently optimistic trend has some negative aspects though.

The fast development of knowledge and fascination with computers and possibilities they create, especially among the youth, is not accompanied by the awareness that computer technology requires not only professional but also moral qualifications from the users. With the rapid development of hardware and software market illegal software trade appeared. To certain extent it was due to the lack of the appropriate regulations in Polish law, which could have restricted this phenomenon. Only in February 1994, Polish Parliament proclaimed the act, mainly based on the EU legislation, regulating intellectual property protection, including computer software. It enables counteracting against illegal software and databases trade by administrative legal means. It cannot however stop copying both databases and software for private, non-commercial use.

So far Poland has been the country with a small number of typical computer offenses like breaking into classified databases or their destroying for criminal reasons. It is more common that computer viruses are being implemented through the infected media; still the scale of this phenomenon should not worry. Open access to computer systems due to their connection with MAN or WAN networks creates the possibility for growth of the number of such undesirable cases. It is necessary to fight these phenomena with both technical and legal means. It also seems crucial to create and promote the model user of computer systems: honest, responsible and professional. So far the users have been trained in technical skills, and moral and legal issues have hardly been mentioned. Considering the spontaneous growth of interest in computer technology among both young and middle-aged generations, the idea of honest use of computers will meet general approval.

The easy access to computer networks and information services creates problems which can hardly be expressed in moral categories regarding human behaviour. Commonly accessible regional, countrywide or global computer network is a universal means which enables individuals, professional groups, institutions etc. realization of the particular, predetermined by them, goals. These goals are sometimes secret, and if not contradictory, usually they are at least not quite common. The institution presenting itself through Internet WWW pages usually tries to create a positive image, neglecting its weak points.

The user looking for prospective trade partners would like to have information about their weak points. The computer network operator who invested certain financial means would like to achieve the highest possible profitability, paying no attention to the quality of information sent through the network. For the users of databases placed in the network the easy access is as important as the fact they are credible and updated. The authors of information included in databases would like the users not to violate the copyright while using the database. Computer technology, as any other technology, is in a way morally neutral. It is human behaviour, supported by technology, that can be evaluated from the moral point of view. It could be assumed that all subjects involved in the process of creating, storing, processing, sending, rendering, or using information through computer network realize their own goals, and the problem lies only in easy, common access to the network and its efficiency.

The advocates of such liberal attitude should be reminded that not all the partners playing "common access to information" game, have the same chance to win, and thus the play is not fair. Usually the user is the weaker partner and more often he becomes a looser. He must accept: financial terms of using the network and its resources, technical and formal constraints (e.g. restricted access to some databases), language barriers, etc. At the same time the users are usually not informed if the information provided is updated, complete, credible, precise, etc. They must take into account that the information could be irrelevant or exceeding their current needs.

On one hand, as the factor positively influencing global communication, the development of information services through computer networks is undoubtedly a positive phenomenon. On the other hand, it makes it possible to influence individuals or groups which are not always aware of it or willing to be influenced by others. The following list of morally doubtful or even illegal activities can be made:

a) imposing the unwanted information (advertising, propaganda, etc.) over the users;

b) spreading the false information (e.g. economic forecasts, address databases, wrong advisory services, etc.), which can cause losses;

c) providing low quality information which can substitute the competent one (e.g. encyclopedic entries, information on museum resources etc.);

d) spreading information violating personal interests of individuals, economic interests of companies, legally protected secret information, etc.;

e) spreading information violating moral or social order (promoting pornography, racism, offending religious or patriotic feelings, etc.).

Only in the last two cases the interests of the users as well as the other people whom the information concerns are protected by law. The first three cases can undergo moral evaluation but they are not regulated by legal acts. The question arises how to restrict the scope of these undesirable activities effectively.

Theoretically speaking, it is possible to fight the above mentioned undesirable phenomena using one of the following means:

i. technical,

ii. financial and organizational,

iii. legal and administrative,

iv. educational and social.

They will be explained successively.

i. The range of technical solutions is quite limited. Computers do not understand the information they process, and research over semantic analysis of texts and images are still in the initial stage. That is why the computers cannot evaluate the merits and select the information. Technical means can only: assure (though not in 100%) the confidentiality of the information chosen and restrict the access to the network nodes, databases, etc. to the particular groups of users, select information according to easily recognizable formal or, to certain extent, topical criteria. Thus technical solutions can only support the other ones. The development of international standards, especially those concerning the protection of confidential information sent and stored in databases, as well as securing databases from illegal access, can play a significant role in the field of technical solutions.

ii. Organizational solutions are based on different access levels to the resources and to the services of the networks granted to various categories of users divided according to their rights. A similar, selecting role can be played by financial solutions, e.g. properly calculated scale of charges for services rendered by computer networks. Price reductions can help to stop the development of software black market. In fact these are preventive activities, contrary to the idea of common access to information. Introducing such solutions causes many problems: to make them effective they must be connected with technical solutions, they cannot be contradictory to law, e.g. to constitutional civil rights. Restrictions in access to resources and services of the computer network bring another problem: who should grant or refuse the rights, supervise if they are obeyed, judge the possible litigations, etc. Experience of Central and East European countries, including Poland, where the state claimed such powers, has been negative. What is more, it proved that the more restrictions in access to information or means of its spreading introduced, the stronger the trend to avoid or break them is. Breaking the rules becomes an entertainment, a challenge, a revenge for restrictions imposed, the matter of specifically understood honour of the user.

iii. On the contrary to organizational solutions, which are aimed against certain categories of potential users, the legal and administrative solutions concern particular individuals or organizations, who violated legal acts and thus have to bear responsibility through administrative or judicial procedure. These are proper and obvious solutions in democratic countries, where the law is based on the balanced interests of individuals and society. The problem appears, though, because civil (especially copyright) and criminal law in many countries is not precise yet in the cases concerning new phenomena which occur in connection with development of global means of communication and spreading information. For example, in Poland legal regulations exist forbidding to spread pornography, but no regulations state clearly what pornography is. Global range of computer networks makes it desirable to unify the law on criminal exploitation of computer networks in as many countries as possible. International organizations could play an important role here, popularizing the best legal solutions. It should be mentioned, though, that law does not regulate certain activities which can be called a "gray zone" of the undesired phenomena.

iv. Educational and social solutions are mainly preventive. They inform about inappropriateness or social harmfulness of some ways of using computer networks, even if they are not strictly forbidden by law. A positive role could be played by internationally proclaimed and approved Chart of Ethical Use of Common Information Exchange Means. The Chart should be widely promoted, and included in teaching programmes of secondary schools and universities if they are only anyhow connected with computer sciences. The atmosphere of acceptance for the Chart rules should be created among computer specialists and users, and, at the same time, of disapproval for individuals, institutions and companies which break those rules. Scientific, social and professional organizations could create a system of competitions and awards for those users and operators of computer networks who distinguish themselves with ethics, high quality of the information services offered, etc. In catalogues of network resources the databases characterized by the high quality level of the merits could be specially marked. In other words, the metainformation could be included in the resources of the network, which would enable the user to find the proper quality information at first. Constant observance of such procedures will gradually restrict the influence of worthless or harmful information.

A legal and economic aspect of the doctrine has been assessed to clarify whether the current international intellectual property system works for balanced economic and socio-cultural development in the global marketplace. Especially based on the economic characteristics and type of information goods, various specific criteria (such as specific classroom exemption, implied permission, interactive transmission rule, and market dynamics among players) are examined to figure out the appropriate level of protection for the copyrighted material across nations.

No one denies that intellectual products have been becoming an increasingly important component of national and international economies & socio-political development. That is, information and information-based products are not only valuable economic essentials in and of themselves: their use also increasingly affects the performance of other economic, and socio-cultural factors. It is very certain that information industry is becoming more and more important to the world economy and culture.

However, it is not rare to observe that only highly developed countries have earned profit from the development of electronic information markets. This is mainly because that developed countries are not only the producers of information but also effective users of information in fulfilling their economic and socio-cultural achievement. They are usually major owners and controllers for information distribution industry. Being an information rich country no longer means only the right of access to information but also the chance to produce, distribute and sell information. To the contrary, developing countries do not have sufficient manpower and information infrastructure for the efficient production and dissemination of information for their national development. In this vein, it might be inevitable and necessary to say that developing countries, rather than trying to produce their own but somewhat primitive information, would rather use of the information developed from other advanced countries as much as possible.

However, while their dependence on imported information from the developed countries is getting increased, people in developing countries have to pay more than used to be just for the access to the information they want. In other words, as the degree of copyright protection in the global marketplace becomes higher and higher, accessing to wanted information becomes costly to many developing countries. It is not much surprised to see that people in developing countries are complaining of excessive copyright protection for the intellectual material in the global marketplace. Developing countries even argue that they are having hard time in developing their own information based on the copyrighted material of the advanced countries, due to severe restrictions and unduly expenses required for the access to the information. As a result, they believe that the gap between the developed and developing ones is widening rapidly in terms of information-handling capacity, losing the chance of balanced development across nations.

Various measures have been suggested to resolve the situation. A need for New World Information Order in the information society has been raised. Among them, international intellectual property system that seems to be mostly in favor of the copyright owners needs to be reexamined especially in terms of fair use doctrine, for the doctrine sometimes en facto provides useful defense mechanism against copyright infringement claims, leading to viable dissemination of information in the global marketplace.

Based on the rationale mentioned above, this chapter is designed to evaluate the validity of the 'fair use doctrine' as a way of assessing the appropriate level of protection for copyrighted material in the information society. To this end, a legal and economic aspect of the doctrine has been introduced to figure out whether current international intellectual property system works for balanced economic and socio-cultural development among nations, especially between the developed and developing ones. Integrated legal & economic viewpoint is useful to assess the validity of legal stipulation based on the analysis of its impact on marketability of copyrighted material. Cooter & Ulen (1988), in their book law and Economics, also support the usefulness of integrated perspective of economics and law in clarifying the validity of legal code. For the systematic study, this study will firstly investigate the nature and applicability of the fair use doctrine on the basis of type of copyrighted material flowing across nations. Then, several policy directions for the revision of international copyright system will be suggested especially in terms of applicability of fair use doctrine in the global marketplace.

Fair Use Doctrine in the Global Marketplace

Before discussing about the fair use doctrine in the global marketplace, we need to realize that the copyright is not an inevitable right that confers on authors the absolute ownership of their creations. Rather it is designed to stimulate activity and progress in the arts and science for the intellectual enrichment of the public . Therefore, unlike patents, copyright law does not protect ideas, only their expression of the work in fixed form. The doctrine of fair use should be also understood in a direction to serve the nature of copyright mentioned above.

Until mid 20th century, the question of whether the defendant's conduct constituted a "fair use" was not clearly clarified at all for the conceptual ambiguity. The concept of "fair use" seems to be still dubious and not formulated at all. These days, interactive technologies' enormous power to copy, disseminate, manipulate electronic information makes even difficult to gauge the proper application of fair use in the marketplace. Leval (1990) argued that throughout the development of the fair use doctrine, courts has failed to fashion a set of governing principles or values. However, to certain point, it seems to be natural not to have any formula for fair use, for its judgment should be basically tailored to individual cases which may contain endless variety of situations. Having a standardized formula for fair use doctrine is not easy and even undesirable in terms of its legal flexibility in interpretation. Nonetheless, since Judge Story listed four factors for fair use judgment in Folsom v. Marsh, in 1841, the factors have been frequently cited in many cases. In approximate order of importance, the factors are : (1) impact on the potential market; (2) the purpose of uses; (3) the nature of copyrighted material at the time of the copying; and (4) amount of copying. In addition to the factors, customary practice without simple malice can be considered useful in determining whether copying of the copyrighted material without permission is within fair use domain or not.

The Court also identified four objectives that the doctrine of fair use ought to serve: (1) advancing social utility by increasing the supply of intellectual products and facilitating their distribution; (2) enforcing an author's natural right to a reasonable portion of the fruits of his labor; (3) protecting an author's interest in controlling the way in which his creations are presented to the world; and finally (4) aligning the law with custom and popular conceptions of decent behavior .

Several landmark court cases relating to the fair use doctrine have been made over time. They are: Folsom v. Marsh (1841) ; Basic Books, Inc. et al. v. Kinko's Graphics Corporation (1991) ; Princeton University Press v. Michigan document Services, Inc. (1992) ; Harper & Row, Publishers, Inc. v. Nation Enterprises (1985) ; Campbell v. Acuff-Rose Music, Inc. (1994) ; Frank Music Corporation v. CompuServe, Inc. (1995).

Deciding whether copying of intellectual material flowing across nations can be "fair use" should be also examined based on the considerations mentioned above.

Besides, various types and characteristics of copyrighted material in the global marketplace need to be also analyzed to estimate if the current level of protection for the copyrighted material is appropriate. Basically the characteristics of intellectual material such as films and sound recordings flowed across nations can be defined as follows:

1) Nature/type of information: The nature of information is so important in deciding whether it is for fair use. As mentioned earlier, one of the functions of the fair use doctrine is to serve "advancing social utility" by increasing the supply of intellectual products. Accordingly if copying of information is for advancing social utility such as education or pure academic research for public interest, it is more likely to fall into the area of fair use than copying for commercial use. Types of information (entertainment/educational, commercial/non-commercial) is also useful to assess the appropriateness of fair use. In general, copying of information with substitutability is more likely to have a broader scope of fair use than information with monopolistic influence in the market. It seems to be necessary to empower the copyright owners to charge fees for the privilege of using information, and to acknowledge that mutually exclusive right of copyright holders for a certain period might cause monopoly losses, which vary between types of copyrighted material.

2) Characteristics of information goods: Information is basically public goods. Therefore it has the characteristics of non-excludability (in consumption) and non-rivalry (in terms of utility). Accordingly

copyright law forbidding users from unauthorized copying of intellectual products can be interpreted as a mechanism to eliminate the source of economic inefficiency by reviving excludability in information market. In a pay-per-use world, fair use rarely works, for pay-per-use could be carried to an extreme in which all electronic access and use require permission and/or payment . However, if information is sold to each individual, it becomes private goods though it still has a characteristic of non-rivalry. Information (whether it is educational or not) with competitive edge tends to have a lot of windows (or outlets) for consecutive sales of information. As the number of users increases, its LRAC (long range average cost) declines, too. It indicates that copying of the competitive information at the early stage could hamper its marketability seriously, leading to less possibility of fair use, unless the information lies in public domain.

A combination of information type & previously mentioned four factors for fair use allows us to have somewhat clear and predictable interpretation in deciding whether copying behavior without permission falls in the fair use domain as follows:

1) Information which is essential and useful for economic and socio-cultural development should have a broader area of fair use. Here the problem again lies in the conceptual ambiguity.

News: In general, foreign news is in nature very volatile and not much marketable for domestic news market, though it sometimes has significant socioeconomic and political value. Therefore its transmission with good customary standards of "good faith" is likely to fall in the area of fair use. Especially in the sense that the scope of fair use is generally broader when the source of borrowed expression is a factual or historical work, transmission of news deserves to enjoy broader fair use scope.

Movie film/sound recordings: Basically unauthorized copying of copyrighted movie film/sound can not be defensive at all. The scope of fair use is narrower with respect to unpublished works. Here, the productivity of copying itself should be carefully examined in the fair use calculus, for subordination of the idea of productivity is essential in facilitating the creation of derivative works.

Therefore, copying information without any value of economic or socio-cultural development is not likely to be in the public domain.

2) Information with competitive edge in general has a strong potential in making a lot of profit than one without competitive edge. As described earlier, the LRAC of information decreases as users of it increase. This implies the importance of timing of copying when deciding the proper scope of fair use. The nature of copyright is not to allow copyright owners to enjoy excessive economic fruit for their creativity, but to make favorable conditions for wider dissemination of information without seriously eroding the incentives for artistic and intellectual innovation. Therefore the unauthorized copying of unpublished intellectual materials is likely to hurt the property right of copyright owners seriously due to its impact on potential market of copyrighted material, while copying of already sufficiently consumed copyrighted material is likely to have a broader scope of fair use if it serves public interest.

News: Unauthorized copying of "hot" news has broader domain of fair use, for copying of unpublished news is in nature inexistent. Due to its volatility, copying of already known (disseminated) news does not pose any threat on the potential market of the news. Therefore, news traditionally enjoys the broader scope of fair use.

Movie film/sound recordings: Copying of unpublished movie film or sound recordings without seeking permission is fatal in their potential market, leaving no room for fair use. For example, when the movie film ET (Extra Terrestrial by Spielberg) was firstly introduced into Seoul several years ago, its illegal copy version had been already prevalent in Korea, leading to disastrous failure in the market. Copying of intellectual material for personal use also deserves the broader area of fair use, in that it does not usually pose serious threat on potential market of the material .

So far, we have discussed about several factors that can be considered in assessing the proper scope of fair use. Both characteristics of information goods and its role in society are scrutinized. The factors were in fact thoroughly examined in courts, whenever conflicts between copyright owners and copiers have been raised. Various rights granted to copyright owners are mostly resolved in market.

The problem still unresolved here is that various criteria for fair use, mentioned so far, are not much helpful in determining the optimal level of copyrighted protection. The key is to prevent copyright owners from collecting monopoly profits in greater than optimal amounts, allowing judges to use the fair use doctrine for the balanced interest among participants. It is necessary to develop various ways to reduce the gap between copyright holders' monopoly influence and users' desire to access the information. Standardized contract, compulsory licensing system, blanket licenses can be examined in domestic level, and revision of international copyright system in international level.

Basic Directions for the Revision of International Copyright System

Based on the analysis of criteria in assessing the scope of fair use, several policy suggestions for the appropriate level of copyrighted material in the global marketplace are made as follows:

1) The scope of fair use for advancing social utility (such as education, library copying, or creation of derivative work) should be enlarged even in digital society. Specifically specific classroom exemption should be respected even in the information society. Until now, some of the fair use guidelines for educational copying limit copying to a certain number of pages. These guidelines represent the minimum amount of copying which is considered as legal for educational purpose. Educational uses of music, digital image, et. al is not an infringement of copyright if the minimum amount of copying is made by the non-profit educational institution. For the educational purpose of digitized material, international copyright system should guarantee that non-profit educational institution may digitized newly, lawfully acquired analog visual images to support the permitted educational uses . However this exemption can be considered only in the situation where digitized products are not readily

available in usable digital form for purchase or license at a fair price. Also so-called thumbnail images of lawfully acquired images for educational or librarian purposes should be allowed to advance maximized social utilization of intellectual material. In case of derivative works, if they have minimum amount of originality, they can be acknowledged as legal. In other words, derivative works elaborated in developing countries, based on the originally copyrighted material, should be understood as fair use, in the sense that they could stimulate further development of creative works.

2) "Implied permission" needs to be widely reflected and implemented into the international copyright system. Implied permission has indeed played a role of exception against copyright infringement claims. For example, if copyright owners publicly display their information on the web, they allow users to use their information without permission, i.e., implied permission.

3) Recently the WCT (the WIPO Copyright Treaty) and the WPPT (WIPO Performances and Phonograms Treaty) include various provisions necessary for the adaptation of the international copyright norms. Especially some legal issues about interactive transmission need to be carefully examined when revising the framework of international copyright system in digital society. As the number of interactive media increases, a need for the right of public transmission has raised. This is mainly because that traditional definition of broadcasting or public performance has been diluted, though the definitions and rights of broadcasting and public

performance have not changed for a long time in the international copyright system. The appropriate level of copyright protection for the material shown on interactive media needs to be reexamined.

4) Power dynamics among players in the market should be considered for deciding the appropriate level of copyright protection in international copyright system. For example, it is disclosed that performers in music industry in general do not enjoy economic benefits from the copyright law, for the law is designed to protect the right of information disseminators (such as TV or recording company), not for performers (such as musicians). This background lies in the EEC Rental Directive which was designed to prevent performers from being forced to agree to a buy-out of their rights. Nonetheless, excessive protection of neighboring rights of performers should be avoided for wide dissemination of information. Compulsory license and retransmission rule should be more actively utilized for the smoothing dissemination of information (which can be assumed as sufficiently consumed one in society) into developing countries. In sum, the application of the rules can be positively examined especially when the information serves for public interest.

5) Various international copyright systems such as the Berne Convention have changed over time to adjust themselves into new environment. As information society develops, copyright law will become more international than other areas of law. In this sense, international harmonization among countries is essential to avoid the conflict, and to fulfill the

economic & socio-cultural achievement in global marketplace. Fair use doctrine, if well defined and articulated, could serve to deter the excessive protection of authors' rights to serve somewhat contradictory goals of copyright, i.e., wide dissemination of useful information & incentive for creative works.

Highways in Developing Countires

The issue of information superhighway is currently mobilizing globalized attention. This attention is by no means solely confined to the Western developed countries; no less amount of concerns are identifiable in many of developing countries as well. Indeed it has become a world-scale topic.

Behind the evolving notion of information superhighway lies the sheer conviction that speedy adoption of digitalized information infrastructure and establishing a linkage with globalized information networks will provide a strategic imperative for promoting the nation's political democracy and socio-economic development. Developing countries are no exception to this globalized rush for the historical trend of "information revolution," allocating a large portion of financial resources to this end, regardless of their persistent lack of economic, industrial, financial and other social bases.

It is true, though, that the dream of developing countries to build up a modernized national information infrastructure as an essential technological basis for leap-frogging into affluent and democratic societies is sometimes confronted by skeptical questioning of its own validity in reality. Critical assessment of the informatization of developing countries displays in many instances not so much satisfactory consequences. The installation of advanced information infrastructure in the context of developing nations more often than not brings about not so much political and social benefits as system maladjustment. The socio-political potential of information technologies is least likely to be automatically realized in developing areas of the world.

If this is the case, what is called for is that a comprehensive and systematic evaluation of the conditions of applicability and possible consequences on the whole society must accompany the actual installation of advanced information facilities. Important is not the hasty involvement in the adoption of information technologies but systematic analysis of the conditions by which the potential benefit of informatization can be realized.

One of the most central issues related to the information superhighway project lies in the topic of the public's "universal access" to the information infrastructure. The issue of universal access and service centers around the policy concerns to extend the usage of information networks to the general public on a non-discriminatory and affordable basis. The idea contains the hope to ensure electronic democracy by enabling the public's equitable participation in the newly emerging information environment.

If we consider the agenda of universal access as a question of equitable participation of the general public in the nation's informatization infrastructures, the traditional notion of "universal access," originated from the experiences of Western societies, seems to contain some biases that are prone to restricting the scope of discussion about the informatization policies. More than anything else, the concept apparently carries the connotation of technological determinism in that top policy priority is placed on the provision of technological access. The concept of universal access carries an implicit theoretical assumption that the key to the successful realization of information society lies in the adequate provision for the widest public the "access" to information technologies.

The experiences of developing countries, however, teach us that the technological accessibility alone cannot easily open the way to the realization of a democratic and participatory society. In other words, the problem of information society does not solely exist in the matter of technological provision.

This chapter will suggest some lessons earned from the informatization processes of developing nations. It will focus on the question of how socio-political factors have caused major hindrance to the actualization of technological potential of advanced information infrastructures. More specifically, this chapter will propose a critical assessment of the informatization of Korean society, which has been deeply involved in diverse projects for introduction of advanced national information infrastructure since the inauguration of the Ministry of Telecommunication in 1994. By doing so, we hope this chapter can suggest some policy guidelines for many other developing countries eagerly pursuing the adoption of advanced information technologies. It is also hoped to propose a variety of practical and theoretical questions concerning the issue of digitalized information superhighway in the context of non-Western societies.

Disarticulation of Information Sectors

Amin (1982) and Evans (1979) mention that economic dependency causes the "disarticulation" of the periphery's structure of technology, social conditions, and the whole national economy. According to Amin (1982), the peripheral economy is, as a result of distortion, composed of sectors and economic entities that are not effectively integrated into an "autocentric" whole, but merely juxtaposed. Each sector of the national economy is to exist as an atom, independent of the others, preventing the economic activity of one branch from generating a "leading effect" on others. Disarticulation frequently takes the form of severe sectoral disparities, characterized by a fundamental absence of basic industries and a predominance of non-productive branches.

Serious disarticulation can be easily documented in the realm of national information infrastructure of developing nations. A certain sector of information infrastructure can be over-valued as compared with others, and the society can over-allocate resources to that sector at the expense of others, producing a structural gap within the development pattern of national information infrastructure. This is more or less a widespread problem confronted by many developing countries. Sussman reports that the actual employment of information technologies in developing countries is "geared mainly for prestige, with little regard given to long-term or social benefit."

This trend often leads to the disarticulation of information sectors such that, despite the overall underdevelopment of the sectors of information infrastructure having a greater public nature, developing nations are dedicated to installing the most advanced, expensive and computerized high technologies and international satellite link-ups, with the consequences of overdevelopment of elitist, advanced, and internationalized sectors as opposed to the retardation of less elitist, public, and grassroots sectors of information infrastructure.

In this regard, the Korean way of informatization also reveals a similar problem. As compared with the nation's deep and ardent commitment to the project of national information superhighway shown by the allocation of tremendous amount of financial resources to this end (Ministry of Telecommunication, Korea, 1996a), far less than a parallel amount of policy attention has been directed to more public sectors of the nation's information infrastructure. As an unavoidable consequence, even the metropolitan capital city Seoul has a very coarse public library system as compared with other capital cities.

This startling discrepancy between developmental levels of different information sectors gives rise to some important policy issues. Overemphasis placed on advanced and elitist information sectors at the expense of more basic, public and grassroots sectors can result in the reinforcement of existing gap between the information rich and the poor. Some critics may claim that greater policy emphasis should be laid on the construction of public libraries in order to provide the general public with more basic and essential information services, instead of allocating a vast amount of financial resources to the highly advanced and internationalized information superhighway project.

Similar patterns of disarticulation can be found in many other dimensions of the nation's overall information infrastructure. It is quite frequently happen in Korean society that a public organization's adoption of a digitalized information network tends to be utilized disproportionately more for bureaucratic and administrative purposes than for the its originally advocated public service functions. As an example of this kind of disarticulation, it is very common in Korea that newly introduced computers at public schools are exclusively monopolized by administrative staff members and not effectively utilized for the purpose of teaching.

The disarticulation of information sectors identifiable in the processes of informatization in developing societies proposes a variety of theoretical and practical questions. To begin with, disarticulation problem can lead us to question the validity of policy priority given to the advanced and digitalized information sector in the context of developing nations. It can be reminded that the substantial capital investment needed for the installation of sophisticated information networks requires the allocation of a large amount of financial resources for a developing nation, often resulting in the predicament of balance-of-payment shortage and augmenting foreign debt.

The second issue related to this disarticulation problem concerns about its effect of gap-widening between the information rich and the poor. The access to the advanced, computerized, and internationalized information networks are very likely to be limited to the information rich. And the pursuit of informatization of developing countries emphasizing the elitist information sector is also likely to result in the overequipment of most advanced and elitist technology at the sacrifice of more basic and public sectors of information infrastructure, thereby deepening the information gap.

Third, because digitalized information networks are ready to be incorporated into global information infrastructure such as Internet, the primary function they can serve is to work as the conduit for the unidirectional information dependence of developing nations on highly developed countries. This hypothesis can be easily confirmed by the tendency that, due to the underdevelopment of national information service systems, Internet users in a developing country are heading for international sources of information instead of national sources.

In sum, the problem of disarticulation raises the possibility that the top policy priority given to digitalized information superhighways by a developing country may not result in the fulfillment of the dream of socio-economic consequences in reality.

Networking from Above

The optimistic dream in regard to the coming age of informatization easily extends to the hope that digitalized information superhighway will provide a technological infrastructure for the promotion of participatory democracy. The hope usually stems from the expectation that advanced information technologies can make contribution to empowering of the grassroots sectors and serve as a backbone of democratic public sphere. According to this view, digitalized information technologies can help facilitate more informed and interactive public debates by enabling the mobilization of people's voices, especially those of the information poor. The era of information superhighway, this line of thinking envisages, will be characterized by more efficient public intervention in the political decision making processes.

However, the real world experiences make us very cautious about the suggestions raised by those who believe in this sort of technological determinism. One major hindrance to the full-scale realization of the technological potential for participatory democracy seems to lie in the traditional authoritarian political culture of Korean society. Critics like Yun argues that, contrary to the Western societies, technological introduction of on-line information networks alone cannot lead to the realization of participatory electronic democracy in Korean society where the long-standing authoritarian political tradition has suffocated the culture of free and open political discussions.

A close look at the actual ways in which Korean people use computerized networks frequently reveals the lack of the culture of rational public debate. People's actual pattern of telecommunication network usage is to a large extent limited to non-political and non-public purposes.

Discussion forums for public concerns are the spaces least likely to mobilize the public's participation. And even the communication taking place in them usually is not very likely to produce lively submission and exchange of opinions and ideas.

This might suggest that the public space generated by information networks are not so much successful in mobilizing people's public voices. The social culture of silence and underdevelopment of the cultural basis of rational debate seems to suppress the technological possibility of participatory democracy.

Another factor responsible for this general failure in the mobilization of the public's voice through digitalized information networks seems to be the government-initiated, centralized and authoritarian policy for informatization. The Korean way of informatization has been chiefly initiated and guided by the nation's central government. The nation's informatization process has been in a certain sense imposed on the civil society by the government, resulting in "networking from above".

The strategy of networking from above taken by Korean central government has made the national information infrastructure less responsive to the information need of civil society. Information networks in recent Korea tend to lack carefully designed services to encourage the citizen's suggestion of opinions about public matters. Public policy information serviced by public offices is also very limited in terms of both quantity and quality. Even the publicized information by a pubic office tend to be framed more for propaganda than for genuine information service for the public. Under these circumstances, it would be a rational choice made by the majority of network users to remain as passive consumers of entertainment than as active producers of political demands.

Communication Endogamy and Communication Closure

The original meaning of the term "communication" reminds us of the horizontal nature of human communication. The term, according to Cherry, originates from the Latin word "communico," meaning "to share." From this perspective, insofar as we are in a genuine mode of communication, we never simply send or receive messages, but always hold them in common. Communication by definition denotes inter-communication, a two-way process of interaction and mutual understanding.

This conception of communication also describes the principle of liberal democracy. The modern concept of democracy rose from the notion of open and free marketplace of ideas, within which a variety of opinions is publicly voiced and freely contended, finally culminating in the formation of the true and rational public will. The essence of modern democracy abides in the vitality of free and open discussion between contending views. The facilitation of free and full inter-communication between different social groups enables them to be transformed into the "democratically organized public".

Given that the original ideal of human communication lies in the horizontal exchange between multifarious and often competing social groups and meaning systems, genuine communication must occur across social boundaries and between multiple realities. This line of reasoning supports the idea that the sound basis of a society depends on the liveliness of "communication exogamy" as opposed to "communication endogamy." "Communication exogamy" refers to communication across particular social boundaries of any kind, while "communication endogamy" refers to communication within them. The former is typically two-way and transactional, while the other implies a one-way and oppositional.

When these two concepts are applied to Korean society, the predominance of communication endogamy over exogamy becomes obvious. Phenomenological examination of Korean society suggests the existence of a multitude of isolated and closed circuits of communication at every level of society. And each of these closed circuits being a communicatively self-sufficient and independent; not very effective social communication flows across these mutually isolated closed circuits. Endogamous communication seems to be the main rule.

The dominance of communication endogamy implies the functional breakdown of communication channels between social units. The possibility of open, free, and interactive flow of communication between autonomous social unites tends to be severely damaged. As a devastating consequence of the "communication closure" brought about by communication endogamy, a desirable social function of communication to unite and network the parts into a purposefully cooperative whole is to be severely undermined.

Communication endogamy, as a logical consequence, does seem to undermine the technological potential of digitalized information infrastructure in Korea. Under these circumstances, the introduction of modern computerized communication network services cannot effectively facilitate open flow of communication between diverse social sectors and governmental units, thereby inhibiting the possibility of mutual cooperation between them based on the exchange and sharing of information.

As an example, the pattern of computer network participation in Korea shows a contrasting discrepancy between the case of associations based on shared interest and that of forums designed for public discussions. Korean network users show only a lowest level of participation in the latter as opposed to their vitalized involvement in the former. In many cases, the linkages between autonomous computerized information networks display severe underdevelopment.

In this situation, the expected open and free flow of information between organizations and groups with the aid of computer networks tends to be cut off by their selfish sectionalism and other habitualized closure-oriented practices.

This tendency apparently suggests that the functions of modern computerized information superhighway are shaped and determined not solely by its inherent characteristics; but only in conjunction with the pre-existing structure of social communication. Thus, in order to achieve a full-scale actualization of information superhighway's technological potential, the general plan for national informatization should pay enough attention to non-technological factors at the same time.

Critical discussion about the consequences of Korean way of informatization suggest that the dream of information society cannot be realized by technological possibilities alone. Besides the technological side, the experiences recommend us to consider social, political, and other factors at the same time. The discussion gives us an obvious lesson that for the full-scale actualization of the technological potential imbedded in information highways, we should perhaps consider some socio-political factors more seriously. Frequently this non-technological factors are working as serious barriers hindering the free, open and multidirectional access to information in many developing nations.

Non-technological barriers can take a variety of forms within a society. For example, the information sectors of a country can reveal serious disarticulation with each other. In this case, the advanced information sector cannot be easily "networked" with more basic and public ones, thereby undermining the sound basis for the universal access to the information highways for information have-nots.

The connotation that information highways are not sufficient for the public unless supported and networked with "information local roads" or even "unpaved trails." In addition, special attention must be given to pre-existing social communication structure of a society. When communication endogamy prevails a society diverse social sectors, interests, voices, and visions cannot be properly networked and mediated. Political factors can add much variation to the shaping and usage of information superhighway.

The recognition of the central influence played by non-technological factors leads us to another lesson that the pursuit of informatization should be dynamically fused with a more general plan to reform undemocratic socio-political situation of a given society. The project of informatization should go hand in hand with a prospectus to reform a society's the overall authoritarian communication structure in order for the project of information superhighway to be more amenable to human needs and social necessities. Finally, if we can agree that simple provision of technological accessibility to information superhighway cannot effectively ensure proper utilization. The issue of information superhighway poses the important question of how we can establish a ground for free, open, interactive and democratic networking of diverse social sectors.

2

Global Information Society

Technical development and widespread use have, however, outpaced consideration for security, privacy, and the ethics of the production and dissemination of content. The prospects offered today by both the multimedia traffic and the millions of users accessing and transmitting digital information have also prompted the creation of large multinational conglomerates and agreements to exploit the resulting market potential. All of the above aspects need now to be addressed in order to make appropriate recommendations for their handling.

Nature and its evolution mechanism is an analogue process based on complex multilevel interactive matrixes. The nearest natural event that resembles a digital evolutionary step are large scale environmental phenomenons or disasters. Man is part of the analogue evolution and is in itself an analogue machine, consequently "Scientific and Technological" developments for the greater part of human existence tended to be of the same nature. The advent of electricity changed that tendency in a drastic way and opened up new scientific horizons in a very short historical period of time.

Digital evolution

The first large scale use of digital technology was not for processing or computing needs but for communications purposes in the form of telephone exchanges, even if at the time in a mechanical form using relays as digital switches. Thermoionic valves in turn replaced the relays for the development of computing technology and the transistor replaced these as science progressed in its search for faster and smaller means to exploit the digital potential. Although faster and smaller it is still the technology in use today.

Digital revolution

The fact that we are now witnessing a digital revolution is not in doubt, what is more difficult to pinpoint is whether the emergence of a single event or digital technology has acted as the catalyst that triggered it. Five elements are considered to have contributed to this revolution :

- The conversion of the telephone exchanges to all digital technology and traffic with the conversion of speech to a digital (PCM) stream at the exchange input.
- Fibre optics
- Packet switched networks
- The advent of the personal computer
- Large low cost memories both semiconductor and magnetic

This digital revolution is causing the complete reassessment of the way the telecom industry and the information content industry see their future developing. That both now consider the world as their oyster is clear but while the former is very slowly beginning to think that perhaps " The digital Traffic " on their pipelines rather than "Time" is THE future business and not discriminated by content, the latter considers this revolution as a world gone mad and their current perception is that once they make available their copyrighted content on the networks it will be left to the mercy of the users and abusers with no control on the revenues or their copyrights.

To complete this first phase of the digital revolution and usher in the information society era it is necessary for two things to happen, ONE is to replace the current phone sockets with a 2 Mbits digital interface box and TWO the price structure needs a drastic U turn. First it must in a short period of time be geared to the traffic on the pipeline in terms of digital quantity and not according to time elements related to distance and second it must be affordable to all. The cost of the information itself will be dictated by market forces as it has always done.

Freedom of information

An often quoted and equally often misquoted statement to mean many things and to suit specific occasions and arguments. Perhaps the most widely accepted version of "Freedom of Information" mean the freedom or the right of any individual, organization or institution to publish with a view to inform others any information they choose by any means they deem appropriate. The implied proviso is that they also assume the relative consequences of any such publication, like libel suits and even criminal prosecution.

Equally an even stronger belief bordering on a collective neurosis postulates that no government or other body, elected or not, must interfere with this "Freedom". The information industry at large has since it was recognized as such always strenuously defended this principle.

This digital information side of this industry is at present growing exponentially and the quantity and availability of digitized information is growing at the same rate, the financial interests and the lobbying power to ensure that this freedom is maintained keeps pace with the industry's growth.

Interference with the "Freedom of Information" principle means external and internal controls, legislation, selective exclusions and all of these applied within individual national boundaries to a dissemination media like digital information which has no geographical restrictions.

Socially unacceptable information will always be published and disseminated no matter what efforts are being made to prevent it and like any other unacceptable product the only way to eradicate it is for society to stop buying it and therefore cause the "manufacturers" to either go out of business or change the product line. Simple in theory; impossible in its expectation.

Privacy and confidentiality

Private information or information of a private nature as distinct and not to be confused with confidential information, copyrighted information and information security is more appropriately dealt in debates and congresses on human rights rather than information dissemination via communication networks as privacy is a right that every person is entitled to and nobody should take it upon itself to break such right. Unlike copyrights privacy has received little attention in debates within the context of networked information, even the more traditional channels of communications pay a limited lip service to this issue and then they touch only the periphery of it.

Any debate on privacy must have as a central argument the case of what is considered as private information and irrespective as to whom it applies to whether the holder of such information has the right to divulge it for whatever purpose. Invoking the cry of freedom of information to private data should not be permissible in the information society. Once available on the networks as digital information any information can no longer be considered private and it becomes de facto either freely available or confidential and subject to the applicable security rules and legislations.

Confidential information

Confidential information is often confused with private information. This type of data is collected/required for specific purposes and needs for personal , social and business requirements. Medical, credit, financial records or any records which contains personal records on individuals are already covered by some form of data privacy legislation or other in most countries. It is curious to notice how on forms requiring confidential details the option box giving the right to reuse that data is invariably presented in very small print hidden at the bottom of the form. And that when it is present at all. Confidential business information however does not enjoy such protection and it is up to the company concerned to ensure its security of storage and access.

Security

Securing information content digital or otherwise is an old and widespread concern and its practice involves all three principal aspects of information, storage, access and the transmission media (Networks). The security aspect is directly related to the information content and the nature of the providers and their user population (ie military, corporate, commercial). Security is also an integral aspect when dealing with private and confidential information. There are also varying degrees of security ; within the context of public networks like Internet any information requiring a high level of security should not in principle be on the network at all.

However there are some information elements within the communication transactions that should not be readily obtained by third parties (ie passwords and financial codes), if the information itself need to encrypted that it begs the question of what it is doing on a public network in the first place, or the converse why is the network so insecure and accessible by unscrupulous anonymous individuals as to warrant such drastic and expensive measures to protect one's intellectual property. Perhaps a more lasting solution is to ensure that all network users are clearly and uniquely identified at all time and at every step of their activity on the network and the use of illegal or system commands are monitored and allowed only by authorized personnel. Any unauthorized use of certain commands should ring loud bells in some control rooms. If not done already. Excessive use or need for security limits the use and increases the cost of the system and consequently has repercussions on the revenues potential. In the almost 30 years that the professional online dissemination services have been in operation there has never been the need to protect the use of the system beyond an access password. Perhaps their modus operandi should be taken as a reference model for the Internet.

The Information Society

Ten years ago computerized information was still an arcane art limited to those in the computer and database production profession and to those users called then information retrieval specialists whose task was to search the computerized records for the data pertinent to their business activities. Information was still more of an art than a business. This is not to say that the existence of such computerized information technologies and search capabilities was unknown to the rest of the professional communities it was just that it did not yet touch them directly, it was still something that somebody else did.

The moment the personal computer began its inexorable conquest of every working desk is when " Information " reached society at large and can be said to have acquired an awareness of its own. Information awareness created the need to communicate it, to exchange it, information in fact developed an irresistible urge to travel the rapidly expanding digital highways.

The personal computer became a repository of information and every PC user became a de facto information specialist, society now knows the consequential problems and benefits associated with storing retrieving and transmitting information .

Digital Information in the newly acquired societal awareness encompasses all aspect of daily life from speech to images and created a new term to define it " Multimedia ". The advent of the PC distorted the regular linear progression of the modus vivendi between science, information and society, there exist now a kind of symbiotic relation between the use that society at large makes of the technological development of computer science and information science. This new relationship appears to have speeded up the intellectual capacity in our everyday working life by increasing our ability to do more complex things in a shorter time and more efficiently.

The beneficiaries of the digital revolution

If this revolution was put on trial the defense would claim that everybody in the whole world is benefiting from it, while the prosecution would claim that in effect the defense is confusing between the part of society being exposed to it or having knowledge of its existence and the other part who actually benefits from it and that this division is applicable in varying proportion to all nations, developing and developed alike. The benefits of the digital revolution can additionally be classified as direct for those earning a living and making a profit from producing and delivering " Information " and indirect for those who, in a position to pay, use it in their daily professional and private lives. Then there is the rest of society who has a remote vision of this revolution in as much as it is limited to see only its results and its use in the availability of public information and some consumer products. There is no such thing as free digital information as there in no such thing as free communication, digital or otherwise. The most significant emerging parameter however is the spectacular growth in information traffic and the communications networks to carry it, this has lead to an equally spectacular growth on the part of communications carriers and owners of large " private " network of mergers, acquisitions and cooperative ventures to consolidate their relative positions in the global marketplace and to be thus better able to exploit the universally predicted Multimedia revolution.

In the same manner and for the same objectives the publishing industry and the online information services are slowly gravitating toward a small number of large conglomerates. The domination of the market place will then be monopolized by few and it is not difficult to predict that the divide between those who can afford to be in the information society and those who cannot will get wider and wider. Unless minority interests both in term of information content and social groups are openly debated, considered and protected. By suitable legislations if necessary.

Ethical considerations

In theory networked digital information knows no borders or boundaries. It travels free and it is available to everybody . In practice it is more controllable than any other media. Nations can create filtered entry and exit points, monitor its traffic and identify content sources and so can the network providers, corporations and institutions. The fact that it has not been widely done so far does not mean it cannot be done, the tools are all there. When we talk about applying ethical considerations to digital information we imply control, of the content, its access and of its dissemination .

This in turn impacts directly on the freedom of information argument and who controls the application of ethical rules, will this monitoring be done nationally or internationally , by the application of legislation or through semivoluntary rules by the three principal groups in this game, the network controller, the information dissemination services and content providers any of whom can veto information content they consider unethical.

And who controls the controllers That some ethical rules on certain classification of digital information content should be considered and tabled as agenda items for debate is not in question, their eventual approval and application may prove however to be a veritable legal and social minefield.

The world of digital information is slowly spiraling toward large concentration of power bases. On the one side the network providers who are de facto monopolies whether privately or publicly owned and on the other side the services and content providers who through mergers and acquisitions are rapidly becoming sectorial monopolies in their own right. With this scenario in front of us the ethical legal and societal aspects of digital information are in danger of being sacrificed on the alter of commercial profits and the catch phrase" Responsibility to the shareholders ".

An equally important aspect is the loss of valuable information that is not considered profitable especially in the scientific technical and cultural areas. The flow of information in the emerging Information Society was seen as the foundation to create a more level social playing field. It is instead fast becoming a divisive and dividing factor widening the gap between those who can and those who cannot. This congress should address these issues as a mater of urgency so that the emerging information society as envisioned by the world leaders is not held to ransom by monopolies unethical information content and practices and afforded only by the few.

The industrialized countries have an overwhelming lead in development over most developing nations. However, modern information and communication technologies offer a significant window of opportunity for developing countries to accelerate their development in all spheres of economic and social activity and to narrow the gap between countries. The world stands today on the threshold of a Global Information Society. This position has been arrived at through the truly remarkable advances that have been made in recent years in the development of ICT as well as the construction and development of national and global information infrastructure.

Through these developments it is now both technically and economically feasible to bring modern information and communications technologies to any part of the entire world. Equally as important, people around the world, including those in developing countries, are increasingly demanding access to the emerging global information network. Hence, communities in Mexico, for example, have installed personal computers and built microwave towers to communicate with the rest of the world, allowing school children to interact with other students all over the world and keeping farmers apprised of both local and world crop prices. Also, India launched a programme to link its biggest cities with a nationwide network that will facilitate the dissemination of government information and provide an infrastructure for commercial applications.

The present Global Information Infrastructure (GII) has evolved from a research and development programme in networking that was initiated and funded by United States government in the 1960s. This programme, which sought to establish a decentralized telecommunications system in which an assortment of variously located computers could communicate with each other even when one or more parts of the system had been seriously damaged, was primarily designed to satisfy the military requirements of the United States. From these origins, the Internet has since developed into a global network of computer networks with many different types of users.

Global Information Infrastructure (GII)

As described by the Vice President of the United States of America at the first World Telecommunication Development Conference held in Buenos Aries, Argentina in 1994, a major goal of the Global Information Society is to:

> ....build a global community in which the people of neighboring countries view each other not as potential enemies, but as potential partners, as members of the same family in the vast, increasingly interconnected human family.

The Internet today is a fast-growing, global network that enables people from all over the world to provide and access a variety of content, communicate with one another, purchase goods and services, and even co-ordinate complex, far flung worldwide activities at relatively low cost. The Net is estimated to be growing at a rate of 10-15% per month, with numbers rising from about 56 million Internet users worldwide in 1995 to about 200 million people in 1999. Also, its American origin notwithstanding, more than 50 per cent of current Net users at present are outside the United States and that percentage is rising; by 2000, less than 20 per cent of all Internet users are projected to be in the US.

At present, citizens and residents of industrialized countries enjoy good access to the Internet. For example, Finland and Iceland - first and second among countries with the most Internet hosts per capita - had 62 and 42 Internet hosts per 1,000 population, respectively, in 1997. At the other end of the scale, the information revolution has hardly arrived in Africa - the world's least developed region - where fewer than 15 countries had full Internet access in 1996. As a result of this situation, most developing countries have yet to assume a serious role in discussions on setting goals and standards for the GII. This should not deter them from seeking ways to ensure that their concerns and interests are included in the design, delivery, regulation and content of the world's information expansion. Clearly, a partnership between rich and poor countries is necessary in such an endeavour.

The potential benefits of the Internet for developing countries are well-known: namely that it presents exciting new opportunities to reinvigorate and accelerate the rate of economic and social development. However, the changes engendered by the Internet have been generally to the exclusion of the very poor people in developing countries that the Internet can particularly benefit. At present, the proliferation of the technology is restricted by the lack of appropriate infrastructure and the expense of computing technology. Hence, the dilemma for the average farmer in a developing country, say, would be to choose between spending about $3000 on the technology and approximately $20 - 50 per month on subscription fees or investing that money on farming tools, fertilizers or irrigation systems to produce a good harvest and an adequate income. Unfortunately, in nearly all cases in most developing countries, the question simply does not arise because the farmer lacks the necessary financial resources or access to them to enable him (or her) to use the Internet. Under these conditions, the race to effectively deploy the technology to increase productivity and promote social change and development may be over before it starts.

While it cannot be denied that top-level decision makers in some developing countries are not always convinced that investing in ICT should be accorded topmost priority, there is now at least a political will in many developing countries to support and encourage these processes. Much of this new spirit has been encouraged by industrialized donor countries and organisations such as the United States, Denmark, UNDP and the World Bank which have provided much financial and technical support to developing countries to strengthen and develop their national information infrastructure technologies. As a result, new legal frameworks and standards are being set up to promote the development and interconnection of national information infrastructures. In Ghana, for example, the basic policy instruments to encourage private investment and entrepreneurial activities to expand and enhance information technology has been put in place and the country has three licensed Internet Service Providers as well as five network services that provide mainly e-mail services.

Major challenges that confront developing countries in embracing modern ICT include the formulation and implementation of effective and practical strategies to enhance the capabilities of their populations to make the best possible use of information technology. Obviously, any country that wants to take full advantage of the opportunities provided by ICT will have to prepare its population to use the technology effectively. An obvious strategy to achieve this objective is to establish computer literacy courses. This may not be sufficient, however. Consequently, it will be necessary to ensure that these courses are complemented by teaching people - from primary school pupils, secondary school and university students as well as adult learners - skills to find information, critically evaluate it and also how to use it creatively to solve their problems.

A related objective is to ensure the effective application of information technologies to reduce, rather than widen and deepen social inequities or worsen inequality across the technological divide. Mechanisms to achieve this objective include, for example, public telecentres that have been promoted by the ITU as well as information service centres which are promoted by a coalition of private and public sector interests in the United States. These centres provide people with access to development-oriented applications and content as well as ICT-based facilities with associated training. Further, these centres can serve as the community libraries of the future and major instruments to achieve the goal of wide public access to the Internet.

Regardless of the sophistication of the technology or services being offered, a simple strategy to achieve these objectives could include the provision of assurances to potential users that they can allow the GII entry into their homes, workplaces and lives to access and share information safely and without forfeiting any of their rights. Governments, businesses and public-interest groups working together on information policy and content issues, must address these concerns. Equally as important, governments and the private sector must continuously seek to demonstrate in imaginative and practical ways the potential benefits of the GII to citizens, especially the more disadvantaged in society, for example, through tele-medicine or access to information on market prices for their crops. After all, it is only when people are exposed to, and see, tangible results of applications that they can begin to appreciate how the ICT can be used to improve their lives. This appreciation is the key to stimulating demand for the services and content of the GII, which in turn will provide the impetus to remove institutional and regulatory barriers to its full utilisation.

It should be noted that most young people, regardless of whether they live in rich or poor countries, will feel strongly motivated to learn and use ICT, from portable phones to the Internet. As a consequence all governments should place emphasis on educational programmes as a lever to increase the competence of the population at large.

Ethics and the development of the GIS

Decentralisation is an important characteristic of the Internet's culture and technology. Another important feature is that many Internet users view themselves as part of an "Internet community" that has its own culture, ethics and rules. We are all aware of "netiquette" as well as the existence of Internet jargon that has been developed by Internet users. As this community grows, many challenges concerning access and use as well as issues such as regulation, ethics and content on the Internet will confront policy makers.

There is a general consensus around the world that development of the GII and realisation of the goals of a Global Information Society will require concerted action and co-operation to develop a global information policy framework that will ensure, among other things, that:

1) the privacy of individuals and organisations using the GII is protected;
2) the security and reliability of the networks the information passes over are preserved;
3) the intellectual property rights of those who create the information, education, and entertainment content are protected;
4) that the content of information (particularly that of an intolerant, racist or pornographic nature) circulating on the Internet and access to it, especially by children, is regulated.

Deliberations and action on all these issues must involve all countries represented by their governments, private sectors, labour, academia and the general public. Wide consultation involving all the major stakeholders should foster the formulation of a constructive regulatory framework that will be attractive to all and safeguard the interests of individual countries or groups of countries.

In these deliberations, the stakeholders must seek to avoid or iron out potential discrepancies. For example, an impending EU law that aims to safeguard the privacy rights of European citizens by setting common rules for the export and use of many kinds of personal data has an unintended consequence: a chance of trade conflict with the US. More generally, if exercised, the data protection directive could play havoc with global trade flows by cutting off companies' international communications networks.

Another concern involves the potential of ICT to have a negative effect on the social behaviour of users. For example, the range of services that can be accessed on the Internet is so comprehensive that it can, as stated by UNESCO, "unduly privilege the 'man-machine' relationship" to the detriment, on the one hand, of social intercourse and, on the other, the development of self-reliance.

At present, however, many of the risks associated with some of these phenomena are poorly understood and more detailed study and research is needed to enable policy-makers adequately consider the necessary actions, if any, that will be required to address the problems.

There is also considerable concern in many quarters about the maintenance of linguistic and cultural diversity. Given its origins in the United States as well as the dominance of the English language as a medium of international communication, 90% of the databases on the Internet at present are in English. Consequently, non-English speakers do not have effective access to the content available on the Internet.

However, there are few technical constraints on the development of databases in other languages that can serve the interests of a variety of local communities. Nonetheless, technology-induced globalisation is seen by many as a threat to local customs, values and beliefs. This is therefore an area in which further research.

Promotion of the growth and development of the Global Information Infrastructure and its use presents several challenges to all countries, perhaps most especially for developing countries.

Developing countries will, in particular, have to develop cheap, simple and robust technologies for coping with increasing numbers of users and traffic. In pursuit of this objective, research and development is required on the development of means for promoting equal access to cyberspace.

In addition, and as part of the overall strategy to achieve this objective, research will have to be conducted to identify and develop innovations to promote the use of ICT by different population sub-groups as well as to study its effects on society and development. An important topic that must also be researched is how ethical principles related to globalisation can be implemented.

3

Information Transition

The source of most of this change is new technologies and the Internet. In the past decade we have seen every aspect of the lives of individuals and organizations go through many evolutions and uncertainties. Large, medium and small corporations alike have discovered the need to adapt to the new technologies, or sink in the emerging global knowledge economy. There is no facet of life in the industrialized world that has not undergone some form of shift.

The resultant new information economy has brought with it different approaches to work. There has been a surge in tele-workers, entrepreneurs and home run businesses. Corporations have downsized and knowledge workers migrate from company to company, open to the highest bidder and the organization with the best deal. The highly proficient, intelligent and innovative knowledge worker is in demand. Knowledge itself seems to have become a commodity in the marketplace of ideas. The pace of change has been so dizzying to some they have difficulty in meeting the challenges these shifts have brought. We now live in an information intense driven society.

Nowhere has this been more evident than with government, who are constantly having to cope with the persistently emerging new technologies and demands from citizens. In today's wired world, the interactive citizen is one of the fundamental cornerstones of change. The Internet has put new power into the hands of the citizen. Governments can no longer simply be dispensers of information, even in sophisticated forms being developed by many governments. But governments have not been passive observers and are rising to many of the challenges. New technologies are being used not only to deliver services to the public but also to enhance government administration and facilitate businesses.

This section looks at the means by which some governments are moving to electronic governance and what role information will play in the future. In this context, governance can be seen as both a means of using new technologies to deliver services to the citizen, and ways in which to change and improve the efficient methods of administration within governments themselves

Impact of the internet

At this stage of development few governments have effectively been able to involve their citizenry electronically in the democratic process. Many governments have been effective dispensers of information, which often passes as a means of enhancing the democratic process. There are many government initiatives seeking to help citizens to get online, seek feedback on government reports online, and develop listservs and discussion groups to elicit the views of the citizens. There are also many groups actively participating in online activities in the hope of influencing government policies. But for the most part, governments are far behind the activities of citizens online around the world. Those actively engaged in online activities involving social or political change see the Internet as a medium to foster, enhance and change the way people have traditionally engaged in the democratic process.

The story of the Internet and electronic democracy is a cautionary tale. Much of the enthusiasm and hope for new forms of democracy and citizen input into public issues, sound very like the gushing optimism expressed about the potential of television in its nascent years. It is not yet known if the potentials offered by the Internet will be met. Will the Internet become like television, an arid desert with only a small oasis of excellence? This is an important question because the potential is there for the Internet to become dominated by a few large, corporate interests, or subsumed by government regulation that could inhibit the freedoms offered by this new technology. There is also the danger in a recent trend indicating that people are increasingly spending more time in isolation sitting in front of their computer terminals.

A recent survey of 4,113 adults conducted by Stanford University's Institute for the Quantitative Study of Social Sciences found that "55 percent of Americans have access to the Internet at work or at home, and approximately 20 percent of regular Internet users spend more than 5 hours a week online. Of those 20 percent, 13 percent spend less time with family and friends, 8 percent attend fewer social events, and 25 percent spend more time working at home in addition to spending a full day at the office.

The findings of the study also support the assertion that Americans are abandoning traditional forms of mass media, such as newspapers and television, in favor of the Internet." There is wide potential of change here for the way people will interact as a society as the Internet continues to grow.

Suffice to say at the moment the Internet is creating major change both positive and negative. One of these changes is in the ways citizens are engaging in the democratic process and beginning to slowly altering the face of democracy. The next section looks at some of the initiatives and the reshaping of the face of democracy which online citizen participation is bringing.

Information as a democratic tool

This could well be the anthem for all those netizens who want to continue to recognize their particular identities on a medium that is increasingly being dominated by the corporate world. "We are the Internet" could well be the clarion call stating loudly and clearly that this medium is for all the people, that this is the medium, which will bring new forms of expression of the democratic will of the people.

However, "we are the Internet" is taking on a more prosaic meaning in that the growing connectivity with many forms of media is making all users of the Internet increasingly one with technology.

Within the next decade, or sooner, we will probably not even use the word the Internet, or the Net, because the actual convergences of technologies is creating a new phenomenon. Now an individual can be connected to the online world through a variety of technologies. In experimental stage in the labs now are glasses you will wear that will bring the online world to your lenses. You wont need to boot up and go through all the messy program commands as these glasses will be linked to a micro cellular device which will be voice activated. You will just say what you want, get your email, send a message, take a virtual tour of the office, meet others in virtual meeting spaces, go there anonymously with created identities, book a holiday, look for new online or whatever any of the things you want to do. You will be in cyberspace, disconnected from the physical offline world except for the glasses you are wearing.

Experiments are currently ongoing to have automated automobiles on the highways so all you have to do is program your destination (probably by voice) and off you go. The car, as it travels, will not necessarily go to the route you (once known as the driver) will tell it, as it is will be connected to a GPS (GeoPositioning Satellite) which will alert your autocar to any potential traffic jams or road problems ahead. Thus, your car (or, that is to say, the machine the technological masters are letting you occupy) will be diverted as needed to the most desirable and quickest5 route.

This mapping of cars is not a fantasy or possible scenario for the future but a reality, as mapping programs already exist to get you to your destination by the quickest route. In much of the industrialised world most countries are already mapped electronically, thanks to satellite technology, and available on the Internet. Other ideas for the Internet include the wired home in which everything from your electricity to your heat to your refrigerator would be connected to the Internet and connected to whatever company is providing you with the service. Thus, the electricity corporation can adjust uses of electricity and your refrigerator can alert you when you are low on milk or, more probable still, send a message to your grocery supplier to send more supplies to you. This is all very efficient, and perhaps even a time server for the consumer, but do we want our lives to be governed by disparate pieces of technology? For the sake of efficiency and time do we really all want to be wired to a seamless technological mosaic? But this is just one small example of the technological world we are building.

That is not to say there are not intrinsic values to the Internet and the new technologies and that many have benefited. The Internet has been a tool of enrichment for large numbers of our populations. It has allowed diversity, the rise of the entrepreneur, the mushrooming of home businesses, the bringing together of family and friends through instant communications, the Internet has been a voice for many who for too long did not have the means to express themselves because prior mediums of the expression of communication have been controlled by the few. The Internet has been many things to many people. New, advanced medical technologies and scientific breakthroughs have lengthened our average life span and brought us better health and lifestyles.

On the Internet, there are pockets of dissent and discourse. there are many who use the new technologies for learning, to facilitate their businesses, to get a service, whether from government or business, play games with each other over long distances, keep in contact through email and a thousand and other good usages that can benefit the individual. We know the benefits, we know of the attempts of many professionals who seek to use the Internet to both gain knowledge and dispense and share knowledge. Perhaps, the most important feature of the Internet is that it has allowed individuals to communicate in ways not available before. This is an important new channel through which communication, ideas and knowledge can flow. The Smithsonian Institute in the United States, the British Library along with a wider consortium of universities and libraries are joining together to put online the Magna Carta, the Lindisfrane gospels and the entire contents of the Smithsonian online.

Their purpose is to take the massive volumes of knowledge available in off line libraries and to make available online for the whole` world to benefit. The intent is simple: what an individual can get by going to a library should be available to the world through the Internet. But as with all things in life there are positive benefits and negative impacts. The questions now we must ask ourselves collectively are: how do we manage to grow the benefits while neutralizing many of the negative elements? And there are many negatives surfacing as technological advances far outstrips society's ability to determine the direction we will go as a result of the developments.

Technology is the modern spider that has increasingly built a web around our lives. The collective question for us as a society is: are we the fly now captured in this complex, intricate web or are we still the masters of our destiny? Where is the debate, discussions about the social, cultural and political impacts of technologies on our lives and what these technological changes are doing to our humanity? Has society become the fly willingly ensnared in this new web (and not simply the Web on the Internet) actually created by a few and used to drive the new economy and the engine of consumerism? Has electronic commerce and the burgeoning global information economy so subsumed the agendas of world governments that we can no longer objectively look at where we should be going? It can be persuasively argued that throughout history all new technologies have changed the way the world lives and operates as a society.

Transportation brought the world together and television resulted in the global village that brought all of us on the planet closer together as a people (though not necessarily in a harmonious way). Now tourism is the world's second largest industry with millions of people on the move all around the world, experiencing and sharing in other cultures.

Of course, these millions are mostly from the rich nations. It appears we see nothing wrong in going to exotic and culturally challenging parts of the world, in the quest for something new and exciting and the next best thing to experience, and then pay scant attention to the many more millions of poor. Ironically, many will argue that tourism brings needed dollars and helps these economies. But even this does not ring with the hallowed sound of truth as studies show that those who benefit most are the western multinational recreational chains and others who sell their wares globally to all and sundry. Usually, the locals benefit only to the extent they receive minimum wages.

The point here is not a quick analysis of the rich vs. the poor but rather that we as a people who experience the offline world as we do, and are often blinded to the consequences, might be just as blinded to what technology is doing to us. The message might also be that most people don't really care and are happy to carry on enjoying the new wealth and comfort that technologies are bringing.

Whatever the opinions or views of individuals and governments in society it is evident that we need a far deeper debate and discourse over the impacts of technologies. There are concerns over ensuring all citizens have universal access to the Internet (and are free to use it or not use it as they wish), there are serious, abiding anxieties about the digital divide that is occurring throughout the world. Privacy laws, to protect people's information and endow on their certain rights over their own personal information, are spreading. But the implementation of such laws is but one small step. Articulation of these issues is just the start. We need deeper discourse. Ironically, it is this medium that affords the opportunity to bring such discourse forward.

This is why online e-Democracy is so important as this activity represents the power of this technology and how it can be used to embrace democracy and involve people in the social, economic, cultural and political issues of the day. This is a tool that can give people, the individual citizen, the power to influence public policy. Governments are slowly coming to realize that there is an undercurrent of democratic change going on in the world. The face of democracy is beginning to change and a few thousand at the moment are doing it. But this is a change that has the potential for growth.

Technology is a cold and neutral medium. It is people, individuals that bring passion, life and meaning to this medium. It somehow seems that this point is missed as society collectively races to embrace technology. We are the inheritors of our past that we did not bring about but the creators of our collective futures. At this point in our history we have a collective responsibility as to how our society will shape itself. We have the capacity to create change in our societies through speaking out.

Many changes do occur in society when people speak out and spark debate. It is now time for such a discourse over the future of technology. We need to develop a philosophical base about all these new technologies so society drives technology and not technology drives us.

This next section looks at the distinctions between electronic governance and electronic democracy and how the latter is having a wide impact on civil society. The move towards online activism, and the use of the Internet as an information and communications tool to forward common social goals, is important to understand. The mechanisms evolving in the developed world to influence government policy can also be used as tools to help those in the developing world.

Electronic democracy

Many governments are moving to electronic governance. In this context governance can be seen as both a means to using new technologies to deliver services to the citizen and ways in which to change and improve the efficient methods of administration within governments themselves. Another element looked at in this section is the means as whereby governments will increasingly be able to involve citizens in the democratic process of government.

At this stage of development few governments have effectively been able to involve their citizenry electronically in the democratic process. For the most part, governments are far behind the activities of citizens online around the world, who see the Internet as a medium to foster, enhance and change the way people have traditionally engaged in the democratic process. There are some efforts on different government fronts.

In the United States and Great Britain governments are looking at setting up online voting. The British Electoral Commission recently announced that they would be looking into the feasibility of online voting. A similar announcement was made in California in January 2000. February 28, 2000 saw the meeting of the first Internet Voting Technology Alliance in Washington, D.C. Initial p ticipants included: Safevote, of San Rafael, Calif.; VoteHere, of Kirkland, Wash.; Modulo Security Solutions, of Rio de Janeiro; International Foundation for Election Systems, of Washington, D.C., and e-Elections, of Oakland, Calif.

The group met to get public funding for their activities. The group's goal will be, amongst other things, to develop the proper tools and protocols to ensure online voting is safe and secure for the citizen and is not subject to corruption or manipulation. But this is a tool for voting under the current system of democracy as we know it. People were able to participate online in this opening assembly at Governments, for the most part, are far behind the public in developing tools for electronic democracy. There are some good initiatives, such as the web sites of the British Prime Minister, which seek to garner public comment, opinion and discussion.

There was also an online consultation run by the British parliamentary Select Committee on Public Administration. It was run from mid-November 1999 for one month, in connection with their inquiry into e-democracy and e-government. The online discussion centred on "innovations in citizen participation in government". The Committee sent out electronic notices, which were picked up around the world, asking people to send in their experiences in e-democracy and e-governance.

These are true, but limited, steps towards electronic democracy. However, on the whole, governments tend simply to provide information on their web sites and use the Internet, and other technologies, to deliver services electronically. The prime example of this is the US White House site which is primarily an information tool and conduit to executive agency web sites. It was only in January 2000 that President Clinton announced that government had to be interactive with the citizen.

The dispensing of information, without substantial input from the citizen, is not a real interactive transaction. Yet, the Internet in and of itself is an interactive medium. Individuals on the Internet understand this and, for growing legions of people, it is becoming a force that is changing the nature of democracy as we know it today.

But this is just part of the wider picture of developments in electronic democracy. In fact, individuals and groups are coming together online around the world to influence policy. Politicians are also using the web. In the United States every Presidential candidate has a web site. There are also alternative web sites by interested citizens or groups who want to have their say about the candidates. There are also other groups who are offering sites which will present in-depth analysis of the issues in the upcoming presidential and congressional elections as well as elections at the local and state level. Those wanting to check out the activities of the US Democratic party or the Republican Party can go to either: http://www.democrats.org or http://www.rnc.org. If you want in-depth details on the 2000 Elections in the USA you can go to: http://www.Politcaljunkie.com There are also many independent sites that either oppose the mainstream candidates, satirize the candidates, or offer alternative in-depth information and analysis of the issues. But the phenomenon of engagement in politics online is not restricted to the United States.

There are thousands of other individuals who are active online and attempting either to get more information from their government or to influence policy. The online world of democratic activism is growing around the world. This section looks at the emerging trends in electronic democracy, how citizens active online are changing the nature of democracy as we have understood it, and how governments are going to have to tap into this emerging trend. This section shows the distinction between online democracy, and what its participants are achieving, and electronic governance.

In the wired world, the online citizen is increasingly playing more and more of a role in the democratic process. There are now hundreds of groups involved, from the community and local level to the national and international stage, in some way working to have an influence on government policies and programs, and on societal issues of our age.

Because of these changes, the process of government will soon no longer be controlled from the top and micro-managed by a few when it comes to public policy. In the changing wired world, citizens are voicing their say. Governments may not necessarily be listening, but the thousands upon thousands of people engaging in discourse on the thousand and one issues of the day are certainly listening to each other. This is resulting in powerful currents of change which are only beginning to manifest themselves. Electronic democracy is not about citizens voting on a multitude of referendums as laid out by governments. Electronic democracy is citizens engaging in the political process in means chosen by individuals.

E-Commerce currently dominates the mass media as the main phenomenon of the Internet. But the real story lies in the changes being brought by the thousands of groups and people online around the world, who are engaged in some sort of civic activism, political engagement, or just plain discourse and debate, on the issues that are important to them.

The most evident manifestation of this was in Seattle in December 1999,subsequent events at the IMF and World Bank meetings in Washington, D.C. in March, 2000 and the meetings in Prague in September, 2000. The massive protests in Seattle, Washington, D.C. and Prague over the rise of corporate elitism and globalisation on the agendas of governments, demonstrated the power of the Internet in bringing people out to express their demands to be part of the process. These people were determined to have their say. Not only did they express their beliefs and ideas but governments were forced to listen.

There is some growing awareness in government that their old dynamics of secrecy, closed meetings, and invitations to the special few to be part of the process, are starting to fade. In Seattle we saw the first shot fired across the bow of the old world order of democracy as we have known it. What we are witnessing is an emergence from the traditional forms of representative democracy to a new form that has yet to be given a name. For the moment, we can call it cyberism, as an expression of a particular form of politics. But that is still an expression born out of the old paradigm.

The new democracy we see surfacing is more the expression of individual voices that congeal into a collective whole over ideas that the society of peoples online develop into a consensus. And while a consensus might be formed on major issues, people are still in a position to express their individual thoughts and ideas (even if they range from the erudite to the opinionated). In this emerging world we see the evolution of a true populist democracy (albeit a small one at this point in time).

Although people's ideas do not necessarily have to be acted upon individually, the means exist for individuals to communicate freely to an audience. That audience can be large or small, but it represents a freedom for the individual that has not existed up to this point in time. The mass media still hold the reigns of mass communication. It is still important to get that letter to the editor published so you can reach a wide readership. But with this new medium of the Internet you can write something and it will reach the level of interest in the audience out there.

In Seattle, Washington, D.C. and Prague, the initial protests were organized off line and online. And it was the Internet that gave this movement the international momentum to make it the effective demonstration, and the somewhat collective voice of outsiders, that it became. It was the clarion call for democracy from voices across the world. It has become the symbol not only for the voices able to speak from the Internet, but of the fact that the citizenry has found the ideal tool by which they can bypass all the normal channels of government. This is not a small development at this stage in our history.

Many people talk about the "Individual" being in control, or having great power because of the ability to tap into the world through the keyboard, but it is not certain if the real power is understood. It has mostly been identified as the power of the consumer to buy the product he wants, or read the online newspaper of choice. In fact, what has actually happened is we have collectively opened a Pandora's box. And it really is too early to state exactly all the changes that will occur. It can be said with certainty that there is a powerful current of knowledge and ideas now circulating the world.

What once took months or years to turn into an issue now can occur in less than a day. This is the true power of the citizen. This is the story of the evolution of a truly populist democracy, an emerging democracy in which issues are being transformed from the hands of the few elite to thousands (and one day will be millions). It is like throwing one seed into the garden and from it a flower grows. Throw the seed of an important idea or issue out onto the Internet and it flowers thousands of times over. This is a key development in our evolution at this point in our history.

Central to this development is the degree to which people can communicate, form opinions, make judgments from available data, and then act upon them. The Internet is a medium that allows ideas to flow among thousands of channels. People are empowered not because one can get onto the Internet and get a product, read a newspaper or research out some knowledge. That thinking is from an old paradigm succinctly expressed in the saying: knowledge is power. The new paradigm is the ability to talk back (true interactivity), dialogue and go to whatever source an individual wants to choose. This is not to say there are thousands upon thousands of people out there engaged in political activism. There aren't.

There are legions of people who are out there ruminating and thinking, or engaging in conversation (or whatever activity one chooses). Many of these people are not restrained by the dictates of mass media which tell us what we must read, what is the story of the day, or what we must listen to on the radio or watch on TV. None of these media afford the independence of operation that the Internet allows. This is another reason why the Internet is developing into such a strong, world political force, not captured by boundaries, time, space or distance.

It is true that many in the world still very much reflect their religious beliefs, cultures, ethnic or political bias. Beyond this lies the opportunity to break away from the intellectual and emotional chains of the past and be free as an individual. And this is occurring on the Internet. However, even with these changes, there are still opportunities for governments themselves to benefit from the changes. There are also efforts by many governments, worried about the potential freedoms a medium such as the Internet brings, to curtail both access and content on the Internet.

Because the Internet as a medium is becoming the tool through which the nature of democracy itself is changing and taking new shapes and forms, it is important that governments understand this phenomenon. Increasingly, public officials and elected politicians are going to be faced with not only an informed citizenry but a citizenry that wants to be engaged in the decision making process in some form or another. An analysis of the numerous groups springing up on the Internet on a multitude of issues illustrates that there are voices out there that governments are going to have to tap into.

The Internet has brought about a decentralization of power. In the wired world, individuals can now make their own choices as to which authorities and information sources they will accept.

This is leading to a greater democratization of knowledge, empowerment of the individual, and the potential for more informed interactions between the citizenry and organizations, including government. Moreover, since individuals now have ready access to a variety of information resources, organizations have to adopt new proactive measures to compile and disseminate information in a competitive information environment.

A citizenry that is able to seek and obtain information and knowledge from any place in the world through the Internet will, in all likelihood, also expect more from government. One of the means that people can collectively work together to bring about change is through the strategic gathering, absorbing and using of information. Online groups and online activists, researchers and others involved as information professionals, instinctively understand this. It is the understanding of the nature of information and how it influences us as individuals that is going to bring the next big shift in society.

As the Internet takes hold in our daily lives, and begins to take a new and ubiquitous shape and form, the need for governments to develop information policies to suit the changing nature of these technologies is becoming more evident. In much of the developed world, the Internet is a communications force that is growing. According to NUA plc, a company in Ireland, that tracks the growth of the Internet and the implication of our growing information technology infrastructure, as of the end of the year 2000, 60% of the population in the United States and Canada will have some form of online access to the Internet. This can be in the office, the home, an educational institute or some public space, such as libraries, community halls, Internet cafes and other public venues.

In the United Kingdom, over 50% of the population now enjoy some kind of Internet access. There, much of the growth of the Internet has been stimulated because many companies offer Internet access free. The citizen pays only for local calls. In Europe, the whole question of measured rates is a serious issue, as many contend, this does impede not only access to the Internet, but, even if there is access, then the individual has to be careful about how long one is online. This is because the cost factor can act as an inhibitor to accessing the Internet and the amount of time spent online. However, despite these problems, there are now over 200 million people online around the world.

We are now awash with information in our new cyber environments. There are currently billions of pages out on the world wide web. There is so much information that no single search engine can go out and suck up all the information an individual might be seeking.

In fact, there is such a proliferation of information that many search engine companies now do not give total access to everything that is on the web. What some of the search engine companies are now doing is giving priority to companies who pay to have their company or organization show first on a search, when a given topic or key word is entered into their search engine. This is now giving an edge to those who can afford to pay the necessary fee to be at the top of the list.

The world wide web is now so big that some web sites are not even getting joined to the network of networks because there might be a connection problem in their local area. Also, government and private organizations are now building web sites that can only be accessed through their own Intranets, or by having a specific address for a web site with a password to enter.

The world is at the fingertips of the citizen, but the new challenge is actually finding what is out there. The freewheeling, widely democratic, open, ubiquitous, and accessible Internet is still there, but the shadows of secrecy are beginning to move in. The danger exists that corporate dominance, with the economic rules of the market force at play, could inherently impede the free nature of the Internet over time. When entering cyberspace, the challenges for the citizen who wants an open and accountable society, both from government and the private sector world, are now many. The success of our new information technology environments is going to depend on how much say and control citizens will have on information in the decade to come.

Information is shaping our world. We now live in the Digital Age, in which information, in a global knowledge economy, has become the supreme commodity. Information is not only a piece of barter for the business world to use for competitive and commercial value. Information is now a precious commodity for the citizen.

In our new Internet environments, citizens are increasingly demanding more privacy rights to protect their personal information. However, there is also a contradiction here, as at the moment, citizens are sharing and using personal and aggregate information more than ever before. But in a cyberspace environment, the citizen is becoming increasingly sophisticated in understanding the impact that information can have on one's life. The individual wants to ensure that one's own personal information is not abused.

The individual wants the ability to control his/her personal information environment in cyberspace. At the same time, the individual wants unfettered access to all manner of information. But the sheer amount of information available, the ability to communicate information, and the value that individuals put on information, is bringing a new understanding of the nature of information itself. This understanding is also what is driving the new forces for change in the growing democracy online movement around the world.

Thus, on the side of freedom of information, the public is starting to demand more information for all facets of their lives. We see more data on labels of commercial products; shareholders demand more information about the activities of the companies in which they are investing (not just the usual "hyped" good news about the company's activities in the past year). Citizens are demanding and seeking more information about many activities in society. The Information Age appears to be bringing more demands for accountability. In the years to come, the public will come to expect more and more accountability, in the form of enlightening information, from private sector organizations. The Internet is an open network, which has created open environments.

With this openness has come a demand for certain rights, to ensure the inherent democratic nature of the Internet is maintained. This idea is now spreading into society as a whole, resulting in demands for more and more accountability from all our public and private sector organizations.

Thus, it appears that the next wave of information rights will spread out to the private sector. As the average citizen becomes armed with more knowledge (or at least has the capacity to be armed with knowledge), then it will be private sector organizations, along with governments, who are going to have to become more forthcoming about the information held in their organizations.

The private sector here means not just large corporations or businesses, but rather all organizations, including non-profits. Just as privacy moved into the domain of the private sector thirty years ago, when Sweden passed the first data protection law in the world, so will freedom of information become a part of the private sector domain. The shape and form it takes will be different, but the providing of more information to society will occur.

We currently live in an age of individuals' rights, because in our current climate of the citizen as consumer, the individual is paramount. This will change, as the recognition dawns that it is also aggregate rights that strengthen the citizenry as a whole. As this idea flourishes, then privacy will now hold the same sway, and demands for information on a more sophisticated level will grow. Privacy will become a part of civil society's infrastructure. As the knowledge economy grows, and the knowledge professional comes to be seen as a powerful force in our society, so will the demands for wider swathes of information grow. It might seem at the moment that we already live in a world with too much information. This change of demand for information will be for "organized" information that informs, not overwhelms, the citizen.

Information is now an issue in a new form. Governments are also going to be subject to pressures from emerging information forces in society. For example, the secrecy of governments, at the moment, is defined to the degree that information is shared with the public. The lack of efficacy of a freedom of information law is shown by the narrowness with which government exempts information from the public. Canada's information law is currently under review, because of the criticisms that the statute too much favours the public sector, and too much information is withheld on specious grounds.

Another reason for a review of the Canadian Access to Information Act is that it was developed in the late seventies, and passed by Parliament in 1982, before the emergence of new information technologies. But the challenge of governments now is not just to pass or amend freedom of information laws.In our new environments, we have to look at information as the force it has become in society. Changing environments bring different attitudes. For example, as governments go online with electronic service delivery, more content is going to become available to the public. But it is not going to be enough to put information up on a web site. Any information is going to have to be organized.

In many cases, there is too much information on a web site, which makes the site virtually unusable by the citizen. Thus, information management is rising as a discipline within government. This is vital, so that policies can be evolved which ensure citizens are getting the information they need and want (not what someone 'thinks' the public want), while at the same time protecting individual privacy. Once governments put content online, a policy issue will immediately emerge. The private sector learned this in the early days of the web. The growth of online marketing and ecommerce brought with it major privacy and copyright issues. For the citizen, who is going online for government information, if a request is rejected, the issue will become: why can't I have access?

In an information-intensive society, citizens want more from both governments and the private sector alike. The above is simply an overview of the emerging issues and problems. Solutions need to be sought, as these new technologies become even more persuasive forces in our society.

There are numerous ways that governments at the local, regional and national level can facilitate these new forms of democracy that are emerging. One is to take the example of Canada. The Canadian government, through their Community Access Program (CAP) has a goal to establish over 10,000 public access sites in rural and urban communities across Canada. Launched in 1994, CAP has already established over 4,200 sites in approximately 3,000 rural and remote communities and is a key component of the government's "Connecting Canadians" strategy - aimed at making Canada the world's most connected nation."

4
Information Age Reforms

India has consisted of five main components: increased efficiency, decentralisation, increased accountability, improved resource management, and marketisation. 'Information age reform' means delivering these ongoing reform components with a more overt role for information and with greater use of information technology. A review of global experience suggests that information age reform has great potential to improve public administration and other components of the public sector.

However, the Indian reality – like that for many developing countries – has been more problematic, with many failures of such reform; failures that can be described as total, partial or failures of sustainability and replication. The explanation for such failure lies partly in the approach to reform adopted by senior public officials. A 'four Is' model of approaches is described: the pre-information age approach of 'ignore', and the information age approaches of 'isolate', 'idolise' and 'integrate'. Analysis of Indian cases suggests it is the last approach that is most likely to deliver reform objectives; yet it remains the least commonly-adopted. Changes are therefore required in current strategies for public administration training and the management of change. Such findings will hold true for many other developing countries.

Public sector reform is, if generally defined, change within public sector organisations that seeks to improve their performance. As such, reform can be seen as an ongoing process in India since the inception several centuries ago of institutions that we now label 'public sector'. However, reform is typically defined more narrowly. It is often associated with the ideology of the 'New Right' towards the public sector; an ideology that grew up especially from the 1970s and which sought particular types of change in the way the public sector was run. This ideology has, albeit slowly and by 'fits and starts', increasingly begun to shape the agenda for change in the Indian public sector.

What constitutes the public sector reform agenda in India? There has been no consistent menu of elements but typical components – driven by the global agenda of new public management – include those listed below.

— *Increased efficiency*: improving the input:output ratio within the public sector. The rationale of such reforms is to address the large size of public sector expenditure and/or the inefficiency of many of its processes.

— *Decentralisation*: the transfer of decision making to lower, more localised levels of the public sector. The rationale of such reforms is to reduce the costs of centralised decision making, and to create more flexible and responsive decision making.

— *Increased accountability*: making public sector staff more accountable for their decisions and actions. The rationale of such reforms is to increase the pressure on staff to perform well, to make them more responsive to recipient groups, and to reduce inefficient or corrupt practices.

— *Improved resource management*: increasing the effective use of human, financial and other resources. The rationale of such reforms is clear from their definition. It often includes a refocusing of the way the performance of these resources is planned, measured and managed.

— *Marketisation*: increasing the use of market forces to cover relationships within the public sector, relationships between citizens ('consumers') and the public sector, and relationships and boundaries between public and private sector. The rationale of such reforms is that market relations will drive costs down and increase efficiency and/or effectiveness of service delivery.

There has been much criticism of the components listed: of what they seek to achieve in theory, and of what they do and do not achieve in practice.

Indian Realities of Information Age Reform

Almost simultaneous with the development of a reform agenda, there has been a growing sense in India of a real or impending 'information age'. The roots of ideas about a new 'information age' – treated here as synonymous with emergence of an 'information economy', 'information society' or 'post-industrial society' – are invariably traced back to the work of writers such as

Daniel Bell, Fritz Machlup, Yuji Masuda and Alvin Toffler. Through analysis of extant trends, they described a vision of a new world paradigm that was already coming into existence and that would increasingly develop. General features of this new paradigm include a domination of services over other economic sectors, niche instead of mass markets, and the emergence of a 'post-bureaucratic' form of organisation.

The early, and optimistic, writings about the information age have been much criticised. Critics argue:

— That things have not changed as much as predicted. Peasant farmers – who, with their families, form a major proportion of the world's population – continue to live and work much as they have ever done. They have yet to appreciate the pleasures of surfing the Net or teleworking. Even in the high citadels of the new world, shifts in working patterns and social life may be tangible and important, but they are not yet revolutionary. A modified criticism is therefore that change has been, and will be, a very uneven process that creates inequalities.

— That, when things do change, there will be problems as well as benefits. The information age may be marked by higher living standards but also by unemployment, insecurity, electronic surveillance and alienation.

— That the technology focus of information age writing distracts us from the human, social and political factors which explain – and therefore ultimately determine – what happens in our world.

There is a great deal of validity in these criticisms, but what they do not deny is that – albeit slowly and unevenly, for better or worse – there are identifiable information age trends. Thus, while the concept of an information age retains a large measure of hyperbole, it does serve to highlight important trends that are shaping the world in which we live.

It is certain that they have begun to shape the economic and political context in India. Whilst many see the 1970s as something of a 'lost decade' for India in computing terms, the country more than made up in the 1980s. The 1984—87 period in office of 'Rajiv and his computer boys' marked a defining moment during which India's image and activity as a global software player really began to take off, and during which a clear link was made between computing and reform of Indian public administration.

Although information technology (IT) has never since been so heavily-championed at such a high level in government, the catalytic actions of the mid-1980s set loose two specific, related and seemingly unstoppable information age trends in India:

— The increasing importance of information, including the increasing visibility and value of information systems.

— The increasing use of information technology.

Defining IT and IS

Information technology can be defined as computing and telecommunications technologies that provide automatic means of handling information. IT is therefore taken here to represent equipment: both the tangible hardware and the intangible software. A computer linked to other computers on a local area network represents one example of IT.

Information systems (IS) can be defined as systems of human and technical components that accept, store, process, output and transmit information. They may be based on any combination of human endeavours, paper-based methods and IT. A financial information system of staff and computers that gathers data and processes it into reports used for managerial decision making represents one example of an IS. Thus:

— IT on its own does not do anything useful; in order to do anything, it must become part of an information system.

— Information systems do not necessarily involve computers and telecommunications equipment.

— Even when they do, information systems are much more than just IT because they involve people and their actions.

For the public sector in India, this means that one can therefore see a trend of 'information age reform' that combines the existing reform agenda with the promise of the information age. Indeed, from humble beginnings in the Indian Statistical Institute in 1956, government expenditure on IT has grown to average more than US$350m per annum by the late 1990s.

Information age reform is therefore a growing reality for India which means two things that are different from traditional reform:

— A much greater role for information and information systems in the processes of change in the public sector.

— A much greater role for information technology in the processes of change in the public sector.

There is great potential for these trends of information age reform to bring significant benefits to India because government has been, and still remains, the single largest collector, user, holder and producer of information. Information is a central resource for all staff levels and for all activities: 'In pursuing the democratic/political processes, in managing resources, executing functions, measuring performance and in service delivery, information is the basic ingredient'.

The work of government is thus very information-intensive, and four main types of formal information are identifiable:

— *Information to support internal management.* This includes information about staff for personnel management, and information about budgets and accounts for financial management. Like the other three types of information, it can be used for everything from day-to-day operational implementation up to long-term policy analysis and planning.

Information to support public administration and regulation. This includes information that records the details of the main 'entities' in India: people, business enterprises, buildings, land plots, imports/exports, etc. It is used for a variety of purposes such as legal, judicial and fiscal.

— *Information to support public services.* Examples include education, health (e.g. patient records), transport (e.g. passenger reservation information) and public utilities (e.g. customer billing information).

— *Information made publicly available.* This includes:

  — Information government wishes to disseminate such as press releases, consultation papers, details of policies, laws and regulations, and details of benefits and entitlements.

  — Information government collects that it may make available, such as demographic or economic statistics.

  — Information government is required to supply such as audited accounts, internal policy documents and correspondence, and responses to requests from politicians or journalists or citizens.

Given this information-intensity, changes in information systems must be an essential part of all reform initiatives in India, and changes in information technology will also have a great potential.

In theory, everything that IT can do could be done by some other means. In practice, its ability to increase the speed and/or reduce the cost of information tasks mean it can do things that would not otherwise be contemplated. IT therefore can bring change and has three basic change potentials within reform:

— *Supplant*: automate existing human-executed processes which involve accepting, storing, processing, outputting or transmitting information. For example, the automation of existing clerical functions.

— *Support*: assist existing human-executed processes. For example, assisting existing processes of government decision making, communication, and decision implementation.

— *Innovate*: create new IT-executed processes or support new human-executed processes. For example, creating new methods of public service delivery.

IT can bring five main benefits to the reform process. In practice, these are not neatly differentiated but they can be summarised as:

— *Cheaper*: producing the same outputs at lower total cost.

— *More*: producing more outputs at the same total cost.

— *Quicker*: producing the same outputs at the same total cost in less time.

— *Better*: producing the same outputs at the same total cost in the same time, but to a higher quality standard.

— *For the first time*: producing new outputs.

The first three represent efficiency gains for the public sector; the last two represent effectiveness gains. Of course, these are the direct and objective benefits. IT can bring many others such as better staff motivation, greater political control, or an improved public image for the organisation (with Indian Railways being a case in point for all three of these indirect benefits).

IT is therefore seen to have a great potential to contribute to reform, with this potential being illustrated by the following examples from around the world:

— *Increased efficiency*: IT's role in increasing efficiency has been described above, mainly relating to its 'supplant' role. In the US, the Lawrence Livermore National Laboratory developed a World Wide Web-based system to reduce the cost and increase the speed of parts procurement.

— *Decentralisation*: IT can provide support for more efficient and effective decision making at decentralised locations and create new information flows that incorporate those locations. In Ireland, the Department of Social Welfare created more than a dozen computerised applications in order to support the decentralisation of responsibilities from Dublin to outlying offices.

— *Increased accountability*. IT can create new accountability information and can deliver accountability information to new recipients, providing for more efficient or effective accountability. In the US, 'collusion detection software' was developed and applied to root out impropriety in bids and contract awards for supply of public school milk.

— *Improved resource management*: IT can create new performance information and deliver it to decision makers, providing more effective managerial control over government resources. In Malaysia, government development authorities collaborated to develop a computerised system to facilitate land resource management.

— *Marketisation*. IT can supply the new information necessary for the establishment of market relations, and can also form the conduit for delivery of new forms of public service. 'In Spain and Portugal, smart cards are issued to people to claim unemployment benefit at kiosks, and to check on job vacancies and training opportunities.'

Globally, then, new information systems and new information technology are both supporting and driving forward the process of public sector reform. But what of India? Has the country unleashed the power of information age reform, or does the potential still lie mainly dormant?

Objective reporting of information age reform cases in India (and elsewhere) is rare. Many reports are written from a 'rose-tinted' viewpoint by those with a vested interested in the reform initiative. Their glowing and uncritical claims of success frequently bear little relation to reality. Nonetheless, reliable cases can be found and one can place these into three categories.

Computerisation of the Indian Railways' Passenger Reservation System may be branded a success. Not only did it significantly increase the efficiency of the reservation process, but it also reduced corruption (though did not eliminate it), increased rail staff morale, and improved the quality of customer service. Beyond these reform components, it also gave Indian Railways a more modern image, and it helped to build information age capabilities within the country. Sadly, this case remains almost a lone beacon in India which 'seems to stand out as a solitary example of success.'

A few ongoing information age reform projects have yet to fall clearly into the categories of either success or failure. Perhaps the best-known of these is CRISP, the Computerised Rural Information Systems Project. When initially analysed, after some five years of operation, this appeared to have made little impact and to be heading for failure. Subsequent analysis, however, revealed 'sparks of life' within the project, with some computers being used to support analytical management decision making, thereby enabling decentralisation and improved delivery of assistance.

By far the largest category of reports – both from the formal literature and from the dozens of Indian public servants trained each year by the author – is that of failure. There are no cast-iron statistics on this and there are unlikely ever to be. Nonetheless, based on the available evidence, one can state with some degree of certainty that the majority of information age reform initiatives in India end in failure.

This may be the *total failure* of an initiative never implemented or in which a new system is implemented but immediately abandoned; the *partial failure* of an initiative in which major goals are unattained or in which there are significant undesirable outcomes; the *sustainability failure* of an initiative that succeeds initially but then fails after a year or so; or the *replication failure* of an initiative that succeeds in one place but cannot be repeated elsewhere.

Formally-reported examples include the following:

— The Director of Adult Education in the National Literacy Mission Authority was smitten by the potential of IT to improve the management of literacy programmes. Having seen a software firm's demonstration, and despite glaring technical and data constraints that were obvious to any neutral observer, he commissioned a complex executive information system (EIS) that soon fell squarely into the 'total failure' category.

— Part of the Income Tax Department's tax system was computerised. The project ran into difficulties due to political antagonisms between various groups;

notably between regional tax commissioners and the central tax board, and between management and unions. As a result, only parts of the information system and only a sub-set of intended process reforms became operational and even these were resisted by staff. There was therefore only very limited achievement of reform objectives.

— A computerised decision support system (DSS) was created for the Narmada Irrigation Project Authority. The system was initially used to increase efficiency by helping engineers save time in their cost estimations of canal engineering work. However, the system was never properly used for its main intended purpose: the production of improved canal design. Upon retirement of the Chief Engineer who had championed use of the DSS, even the estimation use was discontinued.

— A computerised management information system was developed in Surendranagar district, Gujarat state, to demonstrate the feasibility of providing computer support to planning and monitoring tasks at the district level, thereby enabling decentralisation. Although the system proved useful, it was never adopted elsewhere because other district officers had a 'not invented here' mentality that rejected innovations made by anyone other than themselves.

One is naturally drawn to analyse why failure should be so prevalent in India. There are almost as many explanations for failure as there are information systems. However, one key factor that emerges again and again from case study analysis is the attitude and actions of senior public officials, both politicians and managers. Based on discussions with such officials and their subordinates, and a review of relevant cases, we can create a 'four Is' model of different approaches to information age reform that appear over time, as described below.

The 'Ignore' Approach: In this case, public officials are ignorant about IT and information systems. They therefore do not include consideration of either in their plans for reform. IT expenditure is minimal or non-existent. This approach does not constitute information age reform and will therefore not form a major focus of this chapter. Nevertheless, this approach is still found in many – perhaps even most – Indian public sector organisations. This is sometimes even so when computers are present for, in some cases, those computers remain unused and merely act as costly 'executive paperweights'.

The 'Isolate' Approach : In this approach, public officials remain computer-illiterate and lack an understanding of information's role. They nevertheless are aware of IT and its potential. Investment in IT is therefore included in reform plans but is seen as the separate responsibility of 'computer experts'. It is mainly associated with automation and some (often spurious or concocted) idea that efficiency gains will result. For other reform agendas, it is added as an afterthought and is not linked in any systematic way to the process of reform. This, nonetheless, represents the first step on the path of information age reform.

Both the early years of the CRISP project and the Indian Income Tax project cited above are examples of the isolate approach. In these cases, the introduction of computers was seen as the responsibility of technical staff rather than being something in which mainstream managers should become involved. As a result, huge investments made very little, if any, contribution to reform agendas in these Indian public sector organisations.

This approach should not be seen as some historical aberration for it can still be found. The recent Asian Development Bank-supported project for restructuring of Gujarat's financial sector provides an example:

'Yet when it comes to computerisation, the cart has been put before the horse. There is a separate allocation for computerisation ... The type of hardware and its allocation to various tax collection agencies has already been decided. It was envisaged that the process of computerisation would be completed even before the thinking on financial sector reform made any headway.'

The 'Idolise' Approach: In this approach, public officials have become semi-literate. They use computers and are over-aware of IT's potential. They believe that IT can transform the business of government (or at least transform their own career/political prospects if they are seen to initiate a high-profile IT project). They are dimly aware that information is something important. The public sector becomes awash with IT-driven reform projects which place technology at the heart of the change process.

This approach has recently leapt to prominence thanks to N. Chandrababu Naidu, Chief Minister of Andhra Pradesh state. In 1997, he launched a high-profile project – the LEAP21 (Leadership and Excellence in Andhra Pradesh in the twenty-first century) initiative – that exactly fits the idolise description. This initiative aims to use IT as a main lever in the creation of better government in Andhra Pradesh and, more generally, 'focuses ... on using Information Technology as a strategic tool for improving the quality of life for the people of Andhra Pradesh.'

The jury currently remains out on LEAP21. Chief Minister Naidu's intention of using state promotional interventions to support the development of the IT industry and IT technological capabilities is based on sound historical precedent. However, his hopes of driving public sector reform with IT are not. There is a long history of failure to deliver reform objectives via technology-driven projects, of which the literacy EIS case cited above is but one example.

Even where technology-centred projects initially appear to succeed in delivering reform objectives, Bhatnagar warns that they may not be sustainable or replicable since they so often depend on a single 'idolising' figurehead. When that senior official transfers to a new post, the project often collapses; when other organisations try to copy, failure ensues because the originator's drive or skills are lacking; and copying rarely takes place because 'a replication will never attract the same attention as a first time use'. In all situations, the cause is the lack of the original IT-focused champion.

Examples of these sustainability and replication failures from India include the canal design and district administration cases cited above, and another DSS used to support improved planning of resource usage in two zonal railways which was never used in other zones. With LEAP21 so focused on Naidu himself, prospects are limited for the sustainability and replication of any successes it may fortuitously achieve.

The 'Integrate' Approach: In this approach, public officials have become information-literate. They recognise information as a key organisational resource that is central to all government functions. IT is relegated to a secondary role: it is seen as a valuable means to achieve certain reform ends, not as an end in itself. The reengineering of information systems and the introduction of IT are now fully integrated into the process of organisational change, driven by reform objectives.

The integrated approach therefore places information in the driving seat, relegating technology to an important but enabling role. In very simple terms, we can see four main steps in initiation of this approach:

— Acceptance by key stakeholders of the need for reform.

— Identification and communication of an agenda for reform.

— Identification of the new and/or reengineered information systems requirements of this reform agenda.

— Identification of the role, if any, that information technology has to play in meeting these requirements.

The successful computerisation of passenger reservations on Indian Railways can be seen to have followed this route. The need for reform of reservations was understood since at least the mid-1970s, with an agenda of modernisation widely discussed and the need for reengineering of systems to escape the old 'one-train-per-clerk' situation widely accepted. Information technology was then identified as the servant of this pre-existing reform agenda, not as the master of reform. Despite undeniable hiccups, this project was kept on track thanks to a vision of efficiency, accountability and customer service objectives that was shared by key stakeholders, not held by just one champion. As a result, technology solutions were shaped to fit reform objectives rather than vice versa, as is so often the case in examples of the idolise approach.

However, other examples of the integrated approach hardly exist in India. Approaches and chronologies remain unevenly distributed in India, but Bhatnagar sees much of the public sector still struggling to move away from the ignore stage. If anything, it seems likely to move on to 'idolise', as exemplified by the LEAP21 initiative, rather than 'integrate'.

Information age reform is seen as a relatively new activity in the Indian public sector that recognises a significant – at times even central – role for information systems and information technology. Information systems change has always been an essential part of all organisational change in government (though this may not have been well recognised at times). But what is palpably new in information age reform is the presence of information technology, which has been seen to have great potential to contribute to the reform process. Public officials are central to information age reform and they can take different approaches in trying to realise the potential of information and IT

Despite the potential of information age reform, there remain substantial problems a) for the Indian public sector to enter the information age reform era at all; and b) for it to move on within that era to an integrated approach that will use IT to effectively enable delivery of reform objectives.

There is no magic recipe for ensuring widespread use of the integrated approach but education and training must surely form a substantial part of the package. Yet any review of current public administration training programmes in India will show that most can be described as 'ignore going on idolise' in their approach. There is little attempt to build the hybrid managers – spanning managerial, IT and IS skills – that information age government requires (Mundy, forthcoming). These skill sets remain unintegrated within current training and often ignored. Some potential public employees and in-service trainees may gain computing skills on their training programmes, but they do not gain information or information systems knowledge and skills. Any view of IT beyond the hands-on is typically simplistically-positive.

Not only does this hamper integrated approaches today, it also hints at a dangerously self-reinforcing spiral. If the present generation of Indian public managers cannot value or manage information, that sets the 'information-blind' agenda for current training and debate, thus ensuring that the next generation, too, will be unable to value or manage information. A similar spiral runs the risk of developing a 'blinded by computers' agenda of IT idolatry.

Indian public managers will also need to adopt a more strategic approach to change that drives technology needs from information needs, and information needs from reform objectives. Strategic information systems planning of this type is very much in vogue in the private sector, though the application of such techniques in practice and in the public sector remains questionable (Ballantine and Cunningham, forthcoming). Perhaps more realistic is a 'core-periphery' approach that balances strategic and tactical, central and local needs.

Finally, encouraging an integrated approach will require cultural and structural changes in the Indian public sector to ensure that technology is the servant of reform. Such changes are never quick and so the move to an integrated approach can only be seen as a long-term process. In the interim, such information age reform initiatives as do take place in India are likely to remain dominated by isolate and, increasingly, idolise approaches. The true potential of information technology will therefore remain untapped in most cases, with initiatives undershooting in their delivery of reform objectives.

The importance of encouraging private sector contributions of public domain information cannot be underestimated. The trend over the past decade has been the increasing privatisation of research. Government fiscal pressure has resulted in the proportion of public funding for science and technology research and development to fall throughout the world. This has been replaced by more private sector involvement, resulting in greater reliance on patenting. For example, the Human Development Report 1999 cites that the portion of public sector patents in biotechnology sold under exclusive licence to the private sector rose from just 6% in 1981 to more than 40% by 1990.

The 1990s have also seen a boom in the number and value of mergers and acquisitions (especially in the biotechnology, telecommunications and computing industries), due to the increasing privatisation of research and rising costs for risky innovations. One of the recurring themes in the previous discussion is the delicate balance between the effect of incentives on knowledge creation and expanding and accessing public domain information. Without the appropriate incentives, whether financial or in some other form, the risk is that the knowledge creation process will be stymied. This needs to be borne in mind in any discussion on how the private sector can be encouraged to contribute to the information commons.

The measures to achieve private sector participation must be focussed on the returns, but in a way which recognises that returns on investment can take many forms. For example, in respect of any programme which is aimed at generating information which is a global public good, or facilitating universal access (whether in the national or international context), it may be worthwhile exploring measures such as:

— 'Tax incentives for participating in a partnering programme identified under the Action Plan of the country's National Information Policy.

— 'Subsidies or other assistance for properly targeted R&D, with formal agreements on how the knowledge may subsequently be commercialised and what must be put into the public domain.

— 'Knowledge transfer and skill building, by leasing private sector specialist personnel to a development project, so that the returns are the benefit of the expertise built up during the secondment period.

In order to achieve the right balance between the competing interests in each of the above suggestions, it is necessary to resolve the following issue in respect of each project or public funding proposal; at what point in the development cycle is it possible to redistribute the knowledge gained from these processes to those who need it most, without seriously undermining the incentive system which is fundamental to stimulating large-scale investment in research programmes and to producing technological breakthroughs?

Any strategy to encourage private sector contribution should include lobbying on the significance of the public bargain implicit in the fair use doctrine. Much information of value which is generated in the private sector is subject to copyright, therefore it is extremely important to retain the fair use exception in copyright law as this is a significant source of public domain information.

The processes inherent in the knowledge society, particularly the empowerment of citizens, results in a more vocal and demanding environment not just for public authorities but also for the private sector. This is most apparent in the area of consumer protection, health, the environment, safety and basic rights.

As citizens become more computer literate and knowledgeable, their expectations will rise in respect of the information demands placed on business and industry. It is expected that, in response to consumer demands, the private sector will contribute to the growth of public domain information through the dissemination of information: about its policies, procedures or processes; what it has to offer in terms of marketing its goods and services; consumer rights and protections (for example, complaints procedures and other mandatory disclosure requirements); contractual terms and conditions; and, other forms of information deemed relevant to the relationship between a company and its consumers, not just by the company but by its citizens.

One development on the issue of private sector contributions to the information commons, but which is not without significant difficulties, is the mechanism of contingent lending. For example, the World Bank and other development institutions are investigating a new financing mechanism for AIDs research, known as a contingent loan. These types of loans recognise the scale of the contribution that private sector developers can make (in terms of having the requisite resources), but also the need to work within existing incentives paradigms.

The advantages of such a mechanism are described by the World Bank as follows, "The use of contingent lending might reduce uncertainty about projections of the price and quantity of future vaccine sales in developing countries, while leaving key product R&D in the hands of the private pharmaceutical firms (which are the entities with the resources and expertise to undertake this type of research). Under a contingent loan scheme, the international community would make binding commitments to lend to developing countries sufficient funds to buy large amounts of an AIDs vaccine, once such a vaccine has been invented and demonstrated safe and effective. By assuring the pharmaceutical firms of a future market, the scheme would reduce the risks to which those firms are exposed, giving them a stronger incentive to conduct the necessary research."

Another suggestion in the Human Development Report 1999 is the establishment of a representative group of independent scientists to identify critically important technological challenges which, if solved, would substantially improve the human development of the world's poorest people and address other global challenges to human security. The suggestion is that every five years the group could offer financial incentives and public recognition to researchers, public and private alike, for innovations that would be used in the global public interest. The Report suggests that funding of such initiatives could be by a levy on patents registered under the World Intellectual Property Organisation. As an alternative, it suggests that funding could be reallocated from research subsidies, grants and tax breaks which are currently provided to industry.

The dilemma is that in respect of the many significant and promising technological advances for human development, public institutions cannot afford and do not have the resources to carry out the research and development, whereas the private sector can only do so if the incentive structure is effective. The future may be in collaborative efforts, "Innovative policies are needed to ensure that much needed solutions for human development are pursued. Incentives are needed to turn research towards the pressing needs of the world, not just of those who pay."

Potential of digital technologies

Despite the great advances that have been made (such as through the advent of telecommunications), and despite the potential of digital technologies to bring about harmonisation effects and to facilitate collaboration, serious global imbalances persist. At a community level, addressing the digital divide is imperative for reasons of economic inclusion and social cohesiveness. In global terms, the polarisation effect of ICT and its exclusivity has been described as creating parallels worlds, "Those with income, education and - literally - connections have cheap and instantaneous access to information. The rest are left with uncertain, slow and costly access. When people in these two worlds live and compete side-by-side, the advantage of being connected will overpower the marginal and impoverished, cutting off their voices and concerns from the global conversation".

The previous discussions (for example on citizen access to and participation in the knowledge society, on the pre-requisites of e-literacy, and on knowledge as a global public good) are all applicable to developing countries and disadvantaged communities. The purpose of this section is to focus more sharply on the special needs and problems of these stakeholders and to identify potential measures to improve their access to public domain information.

The gap between the information rich and information poor has ominous implications in terms of its marginalising effect and the emergence of an "information underclass". What special measures are required to ensure that the deployment of ICT will meet the basic economic, social, political and cultural needs of all citizens, regardless of their ability to pay or where they live? More particularly, if universal access to public domain information is a foundation stone in building a global knowledge society, what special measures are required to ensure the development of and access to this information?

In terms of high level policies, the dilemma for developing countries and for very poor and disadvantaged communities is that they lack the basic utilities and fundamentals of human existence. It is difficult for the citizens of such countries and communities to appreciate the relevance of accessing public domain information if they still lack clean water, sanitation and vaccines. As well as lacking health and educational resources, there is a lack of suitable infrastructure (in the form of power supplies, telecommunications, and the appropriate operating environment and climatic conditions for computers and their networks).

The World Bank has identified three critical steps that developing countries must take to narrow knowledge gaps. These are:

— "Acquiring knowledge, which involves tapping and adapting knowledge available elsewhere in the world —for example, through an open trading regime, foreign investment, and licensing agreements - as well as creating knowledge locally through research and development, and building on indigenous knowledge.

— Absorbing knowledge, which involves, for example, ensuring universal basic education, with special emphasis on extending education to girls and other traditionally disadvantaged groups; creating opportunities for lifelong learning; and supporting tertiary education, especially in science and engineering.

— Communicating knowledge, which involves taking advantage of new information and communications technology - through increased competition, private sector provision, and appropriate regulation - and ensuring that the poor have access."

For those countries that are in a position to develop a National Information Policy, with specific action plans, there are a number of relevant themes and models which could feature in their information strategy. The following list illustrates the range of measures which could be considered to benefit both developing countries and disadvantaged communities:

ICT and Education

Continued investment in education and in building human capacity is fundamental. As well as addressing basic educational needs and literacy, the measures should focus on issues wider than just classroom use and connections. Teacher training in ICT is essential, particularly in schools serving low income communities because these students are less likely to have access to home computers or to have the resources for technological support. As well as training, there is a need for ongoing ICT support and mentoring.

Distance learning initiatives

There are many example of distance education, whether in the form of open universities or virtual classrooms. The African Virtual University is one such example. There has been much written about the pre-requisites for successful distance learning, including the need for connectivity and interoperability, equipment, properly tailored course content, and technical support to help students use and get the best out of their network.

Community Access Programmes

Examples include the advent of telecentres in developing countries, and specific programmes in industrialised countries with targets to establish public access sites in remote and disadvantaged urban communities.

Networked information

For example, HealthNet supports healthcare workers in more than 30 developing countries by providing summaries of latest medical research, e-mail connectivity and access to medical libraries. It also supports a moderated, free e-mail list (ProMed) for the reporting of and requesting assistance on outbreaks of emerging infectious diseases. HealthNet uses radio and telephone-based computer networks and a low-earth-orbit satellite. It provides slower but cheaper access than the Internet and is accessible in areas with no telecommunications infrastructure.

Compromises in technology

The optimum capacity and speed in ICT should not be a pre-requisite to connectivity. For example, access need not be real time, particularly if a developing country or project sponsors can negotiate lower rates for using satellite down time. Other examples include the use of reconditioned second-hand computers. There are projects which use free-standing, solar powered computers which are updated daily with information relayed through radio handsets and cell phones from a regional centre with direct Internet access. The village computer acts as a bulletin board for the availability of information on medicines, credit, market prices, transport services, warnings of pest, weather and water risks, and provides educational material.

Leapfrogging

Developing countries do not have to experience all the various stages of ICT development as has been the case with most industrialised countries. Developing countries can take advantage of the time lag in technology developments to leapfrog technology. Examples are moving straight from under developed networks to fully digitised networks, bypassing the traditional analogue technology that is in use in most industrial countries. Developing countries can take advantage of new wireless technologies that require less fixed investment than traditional wire-based telecommunications and which can be more cost effective in countries with sparse populations, difficult terrain and harsh climatic conditions as they require less maintenance. Therefore, rather than relying on fixed telephone lines, under leapfrog technology the user may be able to obtain a cellular phone instead.

Leverage

The use of collective bargaining power based on a regional approach or shared interests, where countries or communities form a united negotiating block, can result in connectivity arrangements and discounting which would not otherwise be available through bilateral negotiations with service providers.

Advocacy

Developing countries must seize opportunities to make their presence felt and have their needs taken into account in negotiations on any review of the TRIPS Agreement, and in the international debates over governance of the Internet (including over the allocation of domain names, proposals to tax electronic commerce and privacy developments).

Community focus

An important principle is the need to focus on group or community access, rather than individual or household ownership of ICT. The structures for enabling access (including the location and management of terminals and telecentres) must reflect the structures within the local community and the ways in which people prefer to congregate. The pilot Technology Access Community Centres (TACC) established in Egypt act as hubs for skills training and capacity building. Depending on the community, and any cultural constraints, access to ICT needs to be provided in places where people feel comfortable congregating. In respect of disadvantaged communities, such as low income neighbourhoods, public access sites can be situated in a variety of locations, ranging from the local tavern to state housing complexes.

Local content

Displaying local news, culture and other information relevant to the local community not only builds human capacity but demonstrates the relevance of ICT to the daily lives of those whom it can benefit most. In Canada, funding is provided under the Youth Employment Strategy to give young people experience in creating web sites featuring Canada's information resources. This is a type of "brokerage" arrangement where firms and other organisations are awarded contracts to hire young people to digitise their texts. There are other similar initiatives in respect of aboriginal and indigenous schemes to encourage the creation of content and the design of web sites.

Local leadership

The successful implementation of ICT relies on finding leadership and support from within the community, rather than this being imposed from the outside or top down from government. The Benton Report observes that efforts to encourage the spread of ICT in low income communities stand little chance of achieving lasting success unless they are firmly rooted in the community's own sense of their goals and needs. This emphasises the importance of nurturing individuals and indigenous community organisations that are already playing a helping role in the community, rather than trying to impose technology from the outside. This recognition involves identifying and working with recognised community leaders on ICT projects.

Telecommunications competition

Opening up a country's market to competing telecommunications and Internet service providers has resulted in significant increases in connectivity.

There will be other needs which must be protected in a competitive market, to ensure the benefits can reach all customers, such as those in rural or remote areas and not just those users who are located in the more lucrative urban areas. The radical changes in telecommunications markets, with the introduction of competition and new technologies, means that there is currently huge debate over the future of universal service and as to what form of regulation can best achieve this objective.

There are a number of ways that governments can provide incentives to encourage either the use or ownership of certain types of technologies. Examples include: eliminating tariffs and taxes on personal computers to encourage ownership; tax incentives to those businesses who supply equipment and ICT training to their employees; allowing employees to be able to borrow computers from their employers as a tax free benefit; significant discounting of course fees to encourage adults to enrol in training programmes to improve their basic computer literacy; start-up funding for individuals and small businesses to enable them to access ICT training; requiring a fixed number of free places for people who are unemployed, on benefits, on a low income, have disabilities, or are single parents, to enable them to attend introductory ICT courses; and specific opportunities for low income people to lease computers and software and to be provided with connectivity and advanced online and offline learner support.

It is important to take advantage of opportunities for developing countries (and communities) to consult and co-operate where they face similar challenges. In respect of resource intensive activities, it may be possible to achieve economies of scale, such as for ICT training of teachers, the development of support personnel, etc. A key issue for collaboration is the interoperability of networks and systems.Most recommendations on addressing the digital divide emphasise the importance of exploring partnerships among governments, industry, service providers, communities and interest groups. This is particularly important for the funding of research. There are other implications, such as illustrated by the numerous partnering arrangements set out in the Information Strategies of Australia, Canada and the United Kingdom.

An example is VolNet, which is a joint undertaking by the Canadian Federal Government and private and voluntary sectors. Under the administration of Industry Canada and the guidance of a National Advisory Committee (comprising private and voluntary sector representatives and Federal Officials), VolNet is seen as a model for providing structured support to the community and voluntary sector. It comprises a network of VolNet delivery agencies to provide services to eligible charitable and not-for-profit organisations. Through the partnership arrangements inherent in VolNet, it has been made possible to offer Internet connectivity (including equipment, skills development and support) to thousands of voluntary organisations.

Universal access, through formal training and support (such as in schools and libraries) is proving insufficient to overcome the ambivalence of many community groups to the uptake and relevance of ICT. As a consequence, the dissemination of technology must be through traditional and socially recognised learning channels. Many groups tend not to take advantage of formal avenues of training (such as provided by classrooms and libraries), but learn best from their peers (including friends and family). An adjunct to this requirement is the need to adapt public domain information to a form and manner that can be used by those whom it is intended to benefit.

Building trust is a priority because enabling access to information is of little long term benefit if people do not trust its source. This makes it essential to understand and listen to the needs and concerns of those who are the target of ICT assistance. It is essential to involve the beneficiaries of ICT projects in their design and implementation. When obtaining data on information and access needs, it is also important to ensure quantitative techniques are complemented by qualitative methods.

Producing local knowledge, and adapting existing public domain information to local conditions, is essential. This emphasises the need to inject public funding into local research. The World Bank sees adaptation as crucial, because for knowledge to be effective, it needs to be locally created or recreated, domestically "owned", and internalised. The World Bank Report notes that good principles must always be adapted to new circumstances, with domestic stakeholders (governments, businesses and citizens) taking the lead. Effective adaptation requires that governments and donors elicit and really listen to feedback from those whom the project is supposed to benefit.

There is a need for strong activism at the local and regional levels to ensure local communities have a voice in making their needs known to government, to service providers, and to other agencies, who have control over ICT and funding resources. Technology activists are necessary to lobby for local ICT training and educative initiatives to foster small business and regional and community development. As the Benton Report comments, "In the absence of strong grass roots pressure, telecommunications providers appear unlikely to deploy new technologies to low income communities voluntarily any time soon."

International agencies have a vital role to play in the provision of information as a global public good, particularly for the benefit of developing countries. This role can include the sponsorship of research where there are large social returns or benefits (which exceed private returns), but there have been insufficient incentives for any one company or country to invest in the research. The World Bank Report notes that many types of knowledge fall into the category of a national public good, but no single country will invest enough in the creation of such goods because the benefits would accrue to all countries without the creating country receiving full compensation.

However, the Report notes that international institutions, acting on behalf of everyone, can fill this gap. It cites the example of the Consultative Group for International Agriculture Research. The other role for international agencies is that of the intermediary. As the World Bank Report points out, the most important knowledge for development comes from developing countries and that it is this local knowledge creation, particularly its transfer between countries, which has the potential to unleash powerful development forces. It notes that each change in policy, and each development in a project, produces information that could be of benefit to another country.

However, amassing that knowledge, assessing it and then sharing it with other countries is a task beyond the capacity (and self interest) of any single country. This provides a vital role for international agencies to support developing countries (and in some circumstances, at the community level) to innovate, adapt and evaluate projects, to assess policy changes and outcomes, and to build local capacity for policy analysis and evaluation.

Funding initiatives

A number of the measures discussed above include funding initiatives:

— 'There is the concept of contingent loans to fund the development of certain types of knowledge as a global public good.

— There is the proposal for a levy on patent applications filed with WIPO.

— The partnering arrangements, discussed in the context of private sector contribution to the information commons and R & D research projects, involve a mix of funding initiatives, such as allowing a certain level of commercialisation provided a significant amount of the research output is placed into the public domain.

Public funding initiatives can take many different forms. Some of the ideas which have been floated in the United States and elsewhere are as follows:

— Establishing a fund to make loans (among other objectives) to stimulate new technology development. An example is the Telecommunications Development Fund (USA) which apparently operates as a non-profit corporation and is capitalised with interest earned on money raised from spectrum auctions. One of the intentions of the Fund was to support universal service and to promote the delivery of telecommunications services to under served rural and urban areas.

— Assistance Programmes which can award grants for projects aimed at helping non-profit hospitals, tribal and local governments, libraries, schools, and community centres to use information technologies. These Programmes may include a concept of matching funds so that for every dollar obtained by grant, the applicant must raise either a percentage or an equivalent amount.

— Penalties awarded by telecommunications regulators (such as US State Regulatory Commissions) can be applied as a source of funding for technology initiatives which are in the public interest (for example, telecommunications education trust funds which finance research and education programmes aimed at minority and low income communities).

— Another funding initiative, similar in concept to the idea of a patent levy, is the concept of a "Bit tax". This proposal would impose a very small tax on the amount of data sent through the Internet, so that the cost for most users would be negligible, whereas the cumulative amount raised would be significant. This fund could be applied to the development of and facilitating access to information which is a global public good. The feasibility of such a proposal, let alone its logistics, is dubious, particularly given the inability to control cross-border Internet transactions. If these were amenable to taxation, it is likely that (despite the current debate over the pros and cons of e-commerce taxation) the means would already have been found to implement a "Bit tax", but for domestic objectives rather than those of global public good. However, there are other taxation proposals which merit further consideration.

The impact of globalisation is such that proposals to impose a global tax are not nearly as far fetched as they might have seemed a decade ago. There has been growing interest in such mechanisms, with an early proposal by economist James Tobin (in 1978) for a tax on foreign exchange transactions to be applied uniformly by all major countries, to deter speculation on currency fluctuation (known as a "Tobin Tax"). This initiative grew out of a shared concern among governments at the perceived irrational activities in global financial markets which can have a significant adverse impact on national economies . Another development along similar lines was the proposal tabled at the International Monetary Fund (IMF) in May 1998 to create a World Taxing Organisation, with the power to levy a global tax on international financial transactions and to orient the taxing policy of countries. Proposals such as the Tobin Tax provide an interesting analogy when considering the funding and incentive problems of addressing the digital divide and the global information commons.

The purpose of a global "digital tax" would be to facilitate the development of, and access to, information which is a global public good; for example, it could provide funding for research (or for the purchase of intellectual property rights) where there are significant social returns or benefits but insufficient incentives for any one company or country to invest in the research or to acquire the rights to that knowledge. As well as knowledge creation, the tax could also fund specific measures within developing countries to address the digital divide. There may be a role for an international agency (such as ECOSOC or one of the other agencies within the United Nations) to oversee these developments. The taxes collected by each country would need to be remitted to the supervising agency, and decisions made on the distribution of these funds. This would require the establishment of governance and accountability structures.

The intangible nature of the knowledge economy, and the difficulty in controlling cross-border transactions and communications, raises issues as to what revenue-generating activities (ICT or otherwise), or organisations, could be the subject of the tax. If spectrum is viewed as a global good, then there may be an opportunity to raise funds by imposing a levy or tax on a percentage of the money raised through spectrum auctions. Obviously, any taxation proposal requires a significant administrative infrastructure for collection and enforcement.

However, the real barrier is not the technicalities of a "digital tax", but the development of international political consensus. This would require a lobbying campaign to develop awareness of the deepening crisis in global knowledge creation; as stated previously, research priorities are determined by the financial returns, rather than by global need and human welfare and security. There is a role for UNESCO and other concerned agencies, governments, NGOs and interest groups, to advocate the need for a sustainable funding mechanism for universal access to information which is a global public good.

Role of Information Institutions

What are the distinctions and interplay between electronic and traditionally published public domain information? What is the role of traditional information institutions in respect of the development of virtual (digital) libraries and archives?

Libraries are part of the social strategy in democratic societies and have a mission to promote learning and knowledge creation, to support the information needs of their user communities, and to provide the means for an informed citizenry. These "public good" objectives are in conflict with the philosophies of economic rationalism which underlie the debate on the global knowledge economy.

This trend has serious implications for the conservation and growth of the information commons, "historical democratic premises for providing open access to information through libraries are being challenged as information resources become a form of capital and as more aspects of information infrastructure are privatised." Libraries and archives are a key source of public domain information, yet they are coming under increasing pressure in the digital era.

There are competing predictions about the future of virtual or digital libraries and electronic publishing. The first scenario is one of radical transformation, where print-on-paper is replaced by electronic publication as the norm. Electronic access will result in an unprecedented breadth and multiplicity of information sources. There will be fundamental changes in the relationship between authors and publishers, information institutions and their constituencies; in particular, far less dependency on intermediation and on conventional channels of access and distribution. Information institutions (such as traditional libraries, archives and museums) and publishers, which rely on physical collections or print-on-paper, will have to transform themselves or face extinction.

The other view of the future is that, "we are in the process of evolutionary, not revolutionary, social change toward an information-oriented society. This chapter sees digital technologies as an extension or continuation of earlier technology (for example, computer networks are a continuation of earlier communication technologies such as the telegraph, telephone, radio and television)." The technology develops in response to people's social choices. Those institutions which had to manage these technologies will adapt their practices to the new generation of technology, "Electronic publishing will become ever more important, but only for certain materials that serve certain purposes. Print publishing will co-exist with other forms of distribution. Although relationships between institutions will evolve, publishers, libraries and universities serve gate-keeping functions that will continue to be essential in the future. More activities will be conducted online, with the result that face-to-face relationships will become ever more valued and precious."

Both scenarios (described respectively as the discontinuity and continuity theory) are an exaggeration. The third prediction which seems more plausible has been described as the, "co-evolution of information technology, human behaviour, and organisations". None of these exist in isolation; they influence the development or responses of the other, so that, "technology pushes, while demand pulls".

The co-evolution theory is supported by current trends in the print and electronic publishing markets. Demand continues unabated for print (on paper) material and the number of bookshops continues to grow. Various delivery mechanisms and media co-exist rather than replace or extinguish the older more traditional means of communication (whether this is oral tradition relying on human memory, hand worked manuscripts and other works, typesetting and print, radio or TV). If anything, the advent of digital information and electronic access promotes interest in information generally so both electronic and print media benefit.

Each has their own niche. There is also duplication with the availability of some information in both printed and online media. While electronic publishing will transform some information markets (especially due to the shifting economics of scholarly publishing and to the increasing array of formats), and while it will continue to occupy an important niche, it is unlikely that it will ever extinguish print. Similarly, the value-added services of editing, marketing and distribution should result in a continuing role for publishers.

The information overload of the information age will ensure there is also a place for librarians. However, their role will no longer be as gatekeeper but as interpreter. The advances in navigation tools may facilitate retrieval, but by opening up vast reservoirs of knowledge previously inaccessible, it has also ensured that there should be a role for those who have the skills to know how to maximise search potential and how to interpret the results of the search process.

This is because, "access to information does not of itself signify competitive advantage or guarantee the user becoming more informedÿÿ Tapping the unique items of useful information and (through synthesis and analysis) seeing the pattern in them—this is the art of online search today".

The development of digital technologies, particularly online services and electronic publishing, and their impact on conventional channels of distribution and access, are perceived as a threat by many scholars, librarians, print publishers and distributors. In particular, the move from print (on paper) to electronic publishing is seen as a major challenge.

The acquisition of research information (in the form of journals and scholarly collections) by universities and reference libraries is declining; this is despite an increase in the output of the world's research information. Meanwhile, there is a trend to cut the budgets of research libraries, yet the costs of maintaining their information infrastructure, particularly for science and technology journals, is escalating.

Librarians are under serious pressure as they struggle to maintain both print and electronic resources. In the case of journals, these often relate to the same body of information. The cumulative effect of these trends has been described as a "crisis" in scholarly communications.

The irony is that electronic publishing is well suited to scholarly works because, for example, research journals have a relatively small audience and therefore suffer from the lack of economies of scale (making the cost of these collections prohibitive). Electronic access becomes critical in a research environment where the number and price of scholarly journals are growing at a greater rate than these libraries can afford. The result is that libraries can only acquire an ever decreasing proportion of the scholarly literature which should be available to their user community.

This perceived crisis has prompted collaborative efforts among research organisations, and numerous initiatives among industrialised countries, which advocate a strategic rethink of their national research information infrastructure.

There has been much speculation about the impact of digital information, including the shift to electronic publishing, on the information market; particularly, its implications for different pricing models. Some of these impacts which are relevant to electronic publishing have been summarised as follows, "Some proprietary positions in simple distribution chains are likely to erode as a result of disintermediation and intense competition. Reduced production costs and pressure to avoid residual transaction costs may force vendors away from complex pricing models.

For example, usage-based pricing may give way to subscription pricing. Such dynamics will lead to new business models and, in small markets where users are also producers, may lead to new institutional arrangements for managing life-cycle costs of information. Similarly, as production decrease, the cost of information may be assimilated by the underlying infrastructure or assumed by advertisers and other interests.

This trend may be seen in the pricing of online services and in the massive volunteering of content on the World Wide Web. This applies to editorial and navigation functions traditionally performed by publishers and libraries to be performed increasingly by individual authors and users."

Print (on paper) publishers face very high fixed first copy costs. Competition creates pressures to price at marginal cost, but most publishers face similar cost structures. The significance of electronic publishing is that it introduces a medium with the potential to reduce significantly first copy costs.

While the above quote focuses on the changes brought about by digital media and electronic publishing, particularly on pricing models, in other respects there is much that remains unchanged. For example, publishing adds value to authoring.

The publisher provides services in the form of copy editing, proofing, typesetting, printing and binding. It may also be responsible for marketing and distribution. While some of these services are rendered obsolete by electronic access and electronic publishing, others remain relevant. For example, electronic journals will still require distribution skill in the form of server administration, backup maintenance and network management.

The conclusion, in economic terms, is that, "Publishing adds significant value to authoring. The digital revolution is changing sources and amounts of value added, but not eliminating it.

The costs of some functions are decreasing rapidly, but other costs are not. Meanwhile, as new information services are developed, new opportunities for publishing value-added are also created." This comment recognises that one of the most significant consequences of electronic publishing is the opportunity created by unlimited new formats and functionality. These include the ability to search, sort, display and to use hyperlinks between documents and from citations to original sources.

Accordingly, another consequence of electronic publishing and electronic access are the opportunities to find new value from different uses of content and to recover the cost of these services through differential charges. The presumptions which make this possible are that different users value different uses or content differently; electronic access makes it possible to retrieve various aspects of information and in different forms.

The economics of this result has been described as follows, "Electronic access enables both publishers and libraries to engage in new product bundling and non-linear pricing schemes. The first will often involve unbundling of traditional journal components, and then rebundling in a greater variety of packages, some of them customised for customers, or customisable by them. Non-linear pricing is facilitated by lower transaction cots for fine-grained purchases, and feasible direct usage monitoring by the publisher or library.

New bundling and pricing schemes are enabling technologies: they liberate previously unrealised sources of value from existing content and from new value-added services. For example, bundling can do a better job of extracting revenue from users who value the same content differently. Non-linear pricing can "sort" users by their preference for new services, and extract more of their differing values. Publishers earn returns on their innovations that can offset fixed publishing costs, and by spreading those fixed costs over more streams of revenue, can recover them with less quantity distortion and vulnerability to competition. In a competitive publishing environment, consumers get to keep most or all of the newly liberated surplus (excess of value over cost)."

Any consideration of the interplay between print and electronic publishing, such as cost comparisons, must recognise that electronic access changes the profile of available services and their quality.

Libraries are much more than information collections and inventories. They are also social institutions which support and serve the information needs of their user communities in a variety of ways, "A library is more than books and bricks. If it is successful, it supports a sense of community among its users, as an archive of its collective knowledge and as a resource for its future. Yet digital libraries thus far have tended to be digitised versions of card catalogs, books and journals, and as such do not evoke a sense of community."

One of the most successful features of the Internet has been the use of its networking capabilities (the World Wide Web, e-mail, bulletin boards and chat rooms) to develop virtual user communities. Many libraries currently take advantage of this facility to extend their library community into the networked or virtual world.

We can expect the next phase of development for digital libraries to make the link between facilitating access to digital collections which are of relevance to a particular constituency and the networking ability provided by the Internet. Another observation concerning the importance of personal human interaction is that the strongest sense of virtual community develops when network communications are reinforced with face-to-face meetings. Therefore, it is reasonable to assume that physical libraries, or libraries as institutions, will never disappear, but will evolve so that digital libraries become an extension, rather than a replacement, of the current information infrastructure.

An important distinction between print media and electronic publishing has its origin in the tangible nature of print-on-paper. A book is a physical item, a product. There is a tendency to treat digital information as a service. This could have long lasting effects on access to information. By paying for a book, the purchaser owns it forever. By paying for the right to access information online, such as under a licence or a subscription service, there is no guarantee that the user (purchaser) will retain access to the previously available information, "Complex and difficult balances will need to be established, as information increasingly becomes an event to be viewed or experienced, rather than packaged as an artefact to be kept and archived."

The other consequences of the widespread trend towards user pays licensing models have already been referred to in paragraph, in respect of the undermining of the fair use doctrine. There are strong reasons as to why knowledge creators and the holders of intellectual property rights need to retain a degree of control in many (but not all) circumstances.

However, "There also needs to be a place for the capture of cultural history and social memory - at some point events are both common enough (widely enough available to the public) and important enough to become part of that record. Social agreements need to be developed about the status of information as event, and these agreements need to be reflected in the law and in practice; the legitimate interests of artists, commerce, and society must all be balanced."

The circumstances in which information can be considered a "publication" has significant consequences for public access to information. Public access to facts and ideas in published works is regarded in many jurisdictions as part of the copyright normative structure. When information is published in a public way, there are public access expectations. There is therefore a body of law, fundamental to the current intellectual property rights regime, which relies on the distinction between information which is published or unpublished, which is public or private.

For print (on paper) information, the distinction between what is published, as opposed to unpublished, has historically been reasonably clear. In the digital environment, these distinctions have become blurred, creating concerns about the IPR status of certain information. Examples include the situation where information is posted to a closed user site, requiring password access, or else via an intranet. Another difficult situation is where the control systems of the computer allows multiple layers of conditional access.

The use of hyperlinks has prompted debate over the rights to access and link other sites. The dynamic nature of postings is another issue, where it can be unclear as to whether or not a work is still evolving or is a completed draft. As a result of these features of the technology, it has becoming increasingly difficult to determine what information is unconditionally available as public domain information, "What appears to be a relatively simple distinction in the print world—published vs private - becomes complex in the digital world The concern also exists that more informational works will be distributed in ways that will be labelled as private, keeping them inaccessible to the public and out of our cultural and intellectual heritage."

The problems associated with the preservation of digitised archives pose a major challenge to the fate of historical and cultural records in the digital era. Under the doctrines of first-sale and fair use, and the copyright deposit schemes, libraries have been able to purchase a book or journal for inter-library lending and can take steps to preserve it indefinitely so that it can continue to be made available to the public.

With electronic publishing, a vast amount of digital information is never formally published, with the result that these works are not caught by the legal requirement to ensure that a number of copies are deposited in the national public library. As discussed previously, there is an unresolved problem of the line between publication and limited distribution becoming quite blurred or ambiguous. It is no longer sufficient to rely on deposit rules which are dependent on a criterion of "publication".

Another difficulty is that with a printed book, a legal (copyright) deposit scheme is manageable in that it requires a finite number of copies to be deposited in the relevant library or archive. The problem is how to ensure the same certainty can be achieved with electronic access to digital information, as this cannot be open-ended access; and especially if access is more complex, due to the linking of texts, than just allowing access to a single document or journal format.

There are many technical barriers to preserving digital public domain information. The long term archiving of this information necessitates storage on media which have a long life span, can be easily retrieved and viewed, despite changes to the technology There is an additional dilemma of how to capture dynamic and interactive digital works, and at what point during their evolution or creation process.

As storage media deteriorate, it must be possible to allow the systemic copying, for conservation and preservation purposes, of digital material from older media to the current generation. This needs to be permissible under copyright laws. This issue is not just limited to the copyright of the digital information itself, but also to the intellectual property status of its medium.

If digital information can only be read through the use of proprietary software, then this medium must also be migrated from one generation of equipment to the next. Quite apart from the impact on the availability of information, the use of automated rights management systems (which can control subsequent reuse of that information), will complicate and impede the ability to preserve information which has been protected or is controlled in this way.

The strategies to combat obsolescence may require copyright changes to allow migration from one storage technology to another and to resolve the tension between reformatting and the creation of derivative works. The technical problems of managing digital information must be addressed because of their serious impact on the amount and availability of information which becomes part of the information commons, through libraries, archives and other information institutions.

The traditional physical notion of an information institution places more certain boundaries on its form and services. The ability of the global network to link digital resources will result in many different models and hybrid forms of information institutions and services. The role of the conventional library includes selecting, collating, organising, conserving and providing access to information on behalf of a community of users. The particular practices of the library have evolved through the centuries, adapting to changes in information media. The libraries of the future will follow the same evolutionary pattern in modifying their design and capabilities to respond to the latest generation of digital media and electronic access.

The future design of the digital library will be of critical importance to its role of conservator, promoter of and conduit to public domain information. The debate over the future design of digital libraries has moved beyond the early emphasis on data bases and information retrieval, to view them, "as an extension, enhancement, and integration of information retrieval systems and of multiple information institutions."

Despite the emphasis of such definitions on the full lifecycle of creating, seeking, using, preserving and disposing of information resources, the World Wide Web is still not seen as a "global digital library". There are a number of reasons for this view, including: the incompleteness of its content (with available digital content being only a tiny proportion of the total of printed materials available); its lack of coherence and cataloguing; its lack of standards of validation; the ineffectiveness of its tools for information retrieval; and, lack of a specific user community.

The key influence on the emergence of digital libraries is intellectual property policy. It will shape the future design of the virtual or digital library. The reason is that it is the modes of access and use of the information by users that creates the value in respect of information, and this is controlled by intellectual property policy.

There are parallel systems of intellectual property, resulting in the parallel emergence of digital libraries. There are three very different kinds of digital libraries which have been described by Peter Lyman as follows: copyright, where collections have been placed online by research libraries and individual academics (by digitising their paper collections and placing them in the public domain on the World Wide Web); gift exchange, where authors volunteer their own intellectual property by placing it directly on the World Wide Web and into a type of global public domain; contract, where publishers create an electronic commerce library by charging online fees for service to access information protected by password and encryption technologies (and in that sense the information is on the private domain of the Internet).

Lyman also comments on the implications of this third model, contract-based access ("the e-commerce library"), for the future of public domain information. He notes that the primary unsolved problem is the social inequality implied in this model and draws a disturbing inference from any concept of "universal access" which is modelled on telecommunication concepts of universal service, "The use of contracts formalises the transition from an information policy-based on public libraries to a system of "universal access", modelled after American telecommunication policy. With universal access, public access to the network is subsidised, but the consumer must pay for the information used. Previously, the fair use exemption to copyright has subsidised information access for education purposes. Today, "universal access" is being defined as access to the Internet itself rather than to educational information on the Internet. Thus information flows in the digital library of the future will likely be governed on a per capita or fee for service basis; on the other hand, the argument goes, these revenues will fund the development of vast high quality online libraries."

Another factor in the design of the digital library of the future is the need to know the psychological, sociological, economic, political and cultural factors that motivate people to create, use, seek and acquire information. What are the users' criteria for selecting and evaluating digital information? Of particular importance are judgements about quality. For example, one of the key findings of the writings on the economics of scholarly information is that, despite the problems of high fixed costs and relatively low marginal costs, it is the perceived value of the scholarly journal which is the most important differentiator in determining price. Factors such as the prestige and quality of the journal and the requirement on academics to publish as a measure of their academic performance, are significant influences on price and demand.

Documents are created for a purpose and often within a community context, therefore its very important to understand the "social life" of a document or particular information. This is necessary in order to design digital libraries that support the behavioural context of their information collection.

In order for digital libraries to become more than a metaphor, and to evolve into a virtual information institution capable of conserving and providing access to public domain information, there is a need for strategies on a number of issues:

— How to manage the co-evolution process in collections where libraries are required to maintain both print and electronic versions, and collections are becoming more hybrid and distributed.

— How to ensure that information systems are useable and able to serve large and diverse communities; this will require initiatives ranging from rules and standards for metadata, new methods of autoindexing, more sophisticated searching and navigational tools (other than based on word frequency or source type).

— The organisational requirements of the move from independent to linked systems, and from supporting isolated individual access to knowledge networking.

— The need to consider the social context and to make digital libraries and networks relevant to, and able to serve, multiple communities; in particular, how to achieve the balance between libraries tailored to a specific user community and the need for interoperability within the global information infrastructure.

— The need to enable users to bridge the numerous formats, representations and languages of individual digital libraries; this highlights the importance of standards for data exchange, portability, interoperability and for physical connections among devices.

— The importance of libraries and librarians remaining highly visible, despite being part of a well-functioning information structure, in order to emphasise their critical role in maintaining an information commons and facilitating universal access.

— How to scale up from the current level of ICT and the Internet to a truly "global digital library" that is much more complex with more diversity and greater numbers of users. In addition to the connectivity issues of more bandwidth and speed, "scaling requires new methods for seeking, creating, using, managing, preserving, and delivering information. It requires new economic models for allocating network resources. New policy models are needed for protecting and managing intellectual property, privacy and security, both domestically and internationally."

— Digitisation is still very expensive due to the labour costs of handling each page for scanning. The preservation of the electronic record is also an expensive process due to the deterioration of the media, obsolescence of the equipment and the need for software upgrades, and the need to maintain dynamic links to other systems.

— The above references to standards, bridging and interoperability include the many issues to be resolved in terms of future formats of metadata. This is information about what exists, in what form and where it can be located. As well as being descriptive, metadata may also have a functional purpose. It has a critical role to play in facilitating access to public domain information. There is a tension between the need for specialised formats serving specific user communities and the need for sufficiently generic formats to enable search and retrieval of information despite it being located in different discipline areas or across various domains.

The role of the librarian must change in response to electronic publishing and electronic access. Librarians are an example of value-add, however, with the by-passing inherent in online access, the concept of value-adding becomes blurred and there is the threat of disintermediation. Librarians could lose much of their gatekeeper role, due to the multiplicity and availability of databases and systems, and the increasing sophistication of search tools and retrieval processes.

However, there will be an increasing need for information intermediaries to make sense of the vast array of resources and information overload. The digital library will move beyond the collection of content on behalf of a user community and facilitating information retrieval, to the cycle of creating searching and using information, with the development of the services that are implicit in this role.

There will also be technical roles in the development of information infrastructure for standards, interoperability, document and reference linkage, and collating the digital sources for specific user communities. In the future, the role of librarians will evolve: "from collection builder to knowledge prospector,from classifiers, cataloguers, indexers to metadata developers and publishers. from information retrieval specialists to knowledge navigators and expedition guides. from reference librarians to information analysts and knowledge interpreters. librarians will need to become effective collaborators as well as teachers."

In terms of rethinking the role of librarians in the information age, the focus should not be on digital libraries but on universal access (to information). The relevant questions are, "What resources and services are needed, and by whom? Which are essential and which are desirable? What infrastructure is needed to support information resources and services? Who should provide them?" In the context of an Information Society for All and the debate over universal access, the "public domain" has evolved into a term of art. What we understand by this term is that the public domain is an intellectual commons which is the essential foundation for an informed and participatory society. It is critical for education, research and knowledge-creation. Therefore, the public domain has come to represent that body of information resources and knowledge where it is perceived that there are greater public benefits to be derived from sharing and disseminating that information to the broadest possible audience; the corollary is that any implied exclusivity (in terms of control over this process) is to be actively resisted. The concept of a public domain is readily transportable to the global environment and is captured by the phrase "global public good".

The hope and promise of the knowledge society is that it will ultimately enhance the quality of life for its citizens, reinforce social cohesion and result in economic opportunity and inclusion. The caution is that the profound changes brought about by the communications technologies of the information age, are resulting in increased inequities. The erosion of that body of knowledge and cultural and social heritage, which is captured in the information commons, takes us down the path of a deepening digital divide.

We are also at a critical stage in the formulation of the policies, regulatory frameworks, and infrastructure, that will comprise the future global knowledge society. This is despite a lack of understanding about the dynamics of the information economy and the social and global impacts of the emerging information and communications technologies. For these reasons, there is an urgent need to advocate the special role that public domain information must play in the future fabric of the knowledge society.

It is therefore essential to promote a concept of "public domain information" and to ensure its recognition in information policy, law and ICT design. This means resisting measures which create a "pay-per-view digital library", thereby resulting in the "enclosure of the information commons".

5

Responsibilities of Information Systems

A range of potential information systems (IS) responsibilities arises in the public sector, from which eight can be identified:

— *Information systems planning*: the priorities set for new information systems, for the applications of new information technology (IT), and for other IS-related changes.

— *Organisational structures and staffing*: the organisational structures used to support the information systems function, and the staffing of that IS function.

— *Data management*: the way in which data is structured and controlled in the organisation.

— *Computing and data management architecture*: the way in which IT is spread and connected throughout the organisation, and the way in which data structures and processing are divided across the IT.

— *Information systems development*: the who and how by which new information systems are analysed, designed, constructed and implemented.

— *IT acquisition*: what information technology is procured and how it is procured.

— *Training*: what skills are required in training, how that training is to be delivered, and to whom.

— *Technical support*: the way in which IT is installed, maintained, repaired and otherwise supported in its operation.

There are three possible approaches to these IS responsibilities which will be discussed in this chapter:

— *Centralised*: decisions are taken at the most senior or central level.

— *Decentralised*: decisions are taken at some level lower than the most senior; typically by individual work units within the organisation or even by individual staff.

— *Core-periphery*: decisions are taken at *both* senior and lower levels, either separately or in an integrated manner.

Centralised Approach

Many public sector organisations began their 'computing careers' by adopting a centralised approach, and there are continuing drives to maintain centralisation. These drives include particularly the desire of senior public managers to control the costs, pervasive impacts, and potential failures associated with information systems. Managers are also driven by the desire to achieve the potential benefits of centralised approach, including those listed below.

A well-planned centralised system holds data used across the organisation in one place, allowing all staff to access it. This makes it both faster and easier to undertake organisation-wide activities. Central planning and operation also allows compatible technology and skills to be introduced. Exchange of hardware, software and staff between organisational systems and units therefore becomes much easier.

One main intention of centralised approaches is to have a single version of any particular information system for the whole organisation, and to store any item of data once and only once. As a result, there is no wasted effort, no wasted storage capacity, and no inconsistency of data. A centralised approach to information systems provides an organisational focus for learning and for control. This is likely to produce higher quality information systems and can also reduce costs by:

— avoiding the decentralisation problems of non-functioning or malfunctioning systems,

— avoiding the decentralisation problems of inadequate security, maintenance and documentation, and by

— allowing technology purchases and system developments that are not organisational priorities to be blocked.

Achievement of scale economies

Centralised approaches allow most activities to be undertaken more cheaply per unit. Items purchased externally – computers, software packages, consumables, staff training, etc. – can be decided upon once and then bought in greater bulk. Activities undertaken internally –

from system development to implementation and maintenance, and management of all these processes – cover a greater number of staff.

However, centralised approaches are beset by problems, some of which are outlined in this and the following section. First, there are constraints: most public sector organisations encounter considerable barriers if they attempt to develop a centralised approach to information systems, as described below.

Technical constraints

Where decentralised information systems, manual or computerised, are already in place, technical barriers to centralisation may be immense. Indeed, computerisation may create 'electronic concrete' that increases these barriers. The barriers include differences between existing decentralised IS in everything from data definitions to software to computing and network systems. Technical barriers also include the need to create some form of interconnection – typically a computer network – between the different organisational units whose systems are to be centrally controlled.

Resource constraints

Centralised approaches require the commitment of four key resources: money, time, people, and skills. For many public organisations, a centralised approach may not be possible because of financial constraints; because staff are too busy on other things; or because no-one has the confidence or capabilities to undertake the necessary planning and co-ordination tasks.

Perceptual constraints

The perception of information itself is a constraint to centralised approaches. Information is intangible, and public managers rely heavily on informal information in their decision making. Information is therefore perceived in a way that makes it hard for senior public managers to appreciate some of the key tenets of a centralised approach: that information is an organisation-wide resource; that it has a cost; that it can provide value for the public sector; that it needs to be managed; and so on.

Partly related to this is the perception of costs and benefits. The costs of decentralised approaches – of wasted efforts, of organisational inflexibility, of user time diverted from other activities – are frequently hidden. The benefits, such as managers being able to do what they like, are fairly obvious. For centralised approaches, by contrast, the equation is often the other way round. The resources required for the implementation of centralised approaches require an overt, 'up-front' commitment. The benefits, though, may be rather intangible, and it can be difficult to shift the perceived cost-benefit balance in favour of centralisation.

Political constraints

Information is a component of power. Any attempt to alter the pattern of information flows – which adoption of a centralised approach invariably involves – means a possible loss of power that will be resisted.

This is a particular problem for the public sector given the political antagonisms caused by the need to fight over limited resources. Resistance manifests itself most often in an unwillingness to share data with other individuals or groups. Differing political agendas that create barriers to data sharing also exist. People find it hard to think of "my data" or "our data" becoming "the organisation's data".

Political barriers to the centralised allocation of other information system resources such as money, equipment and staff, can also arise.

Cultural constraints

Barriers and antagonisms between decentralised units can undermine any hope of drawing them together for a centralised approach to information systems. At times, these barriers seem to derive from a 'them and us' attitude that is akin to modern-day tribalism. These cultural barriers are seen in the different mindsets that create quite different views of the world between groups; in the different jargon they use in communication; and in the different issues and people they value. This makes it hard to centralise.

Lack of trust deriving from such barriers is seen to prevent the type of co-operation required for centralised approaches to information systems. It is, indeed, the IT business which has helped to spread *NIH*: the *not invented here* mentality that rejects information systems for the simple reason that someone else developed them.

Structural constraints

Structural barriers to centralised approaches in the public sector are found both within and between public sector organisations:

— *Top managers*: do not understand IT or its possible uses in their organisation. They will resist centralised approaches they fear they cannot understand or control.

— *IT staff*: do not understand the public organisation's business and are only really interested in the technology. This prevents centralised approaches being business-led, and leaves them being technology-led. Such approaches, if developed at all, therefore address only IT, not data or information systems or business objectives.

— *Mainstream staff* can be divided into:

— *Computer illiterates* who feel threatened by IT, its jargon and its association with change and the unknown; they will resist centralised approaches because of their fears, and

— *Computer literates* who want to pursue their own agenda without seeing the need for co-ordination of IT activities or for 'interference' from IT staff; they will undermine centralised approaches by trying to develop their own information systems.

In addition, there may be members of the most difficult staff group – *semi-literates* – who think they know all about IT, are vocal in expressing their opinions, but who in practice understand little about the technology and nothing about information systems.

The gaps are partly those of objectives, of knowledge, and of culture, with each group talking a different 'language', holding different worldviews and/or interests, and not trusting the others. However, gaps also relate to the public organisation's structures for information systems responsibility. For example, a centralised IS unit may remain independent with little involvement from mainstream managers unless it is explicitly staffed and structured to create that involvement.

These structural problems – especially when combined with political and cultural barriers – seem likely to increase during reform processes of decentralisation, privatisation and outsourcing that lead to fragmentation of public sector organisations. We are then faced with the paradox that public sector reform simultaneously increases the requirement for, but decreases the possibility of, centralised approaches to IS.

Some of these barriers also exist to decentralised approaches, and we should recognise them as *barriers to change in general* rather than to one or other approach. However, the barriers to centralised approaches appear greater and, the more strategic and centralised the approach, the greater these barriers are likely to be.

Disadvantages of centralised approaches

Even if the listed constraints were to be overcome, centralised approaches can produce some disadvantageous outcomes. One obvious disadvantage of a centralised approach – as already noted above – is the high level of overt resource costs. Other disadvantages are described below.

Heavy time consumption

Centralised decisions and actions are more time-consuming than a decentralised approach because of: the additional time it takes for information to flow up the organisation as an input to centralised decisions; the additional time it takes to collate information from a variety of different decentralised locations as an input to centralised decisions; and the additional time it takes for implementation information to flow down the organisation. The result can be inordinate delays in the process of information systems development.

Limited ability to meet user needs

Centralised approaches necessarily mean that priority goes to those systems which are seen as important by some select and centralised staff group. The priorities of the periphery – both individuals and individual work units – may not be addressed. Consequences of this failure to meet user requirements may include:

— a backlog of user applications awaiting development,

— limited use or even total failure of centrally-planned information systems, and

— poor quality of data within these systems, since users will not be motivated to maintain data quality.

The frequent outcome is that end users subvert central controls and impose a *de facto* decentralisation.

The greater the amount of central planning that has gone into an information systems decision, and the longer that decision is therefore intended to provide guidance for the organisation, the less flexibility it offers the organisation to cope with internal or external changes. The British Army fell into this trap when it produced its first IT strategy. The strategy document ran to 800 pages and created a 'strait-jacket of detail' that meant managers 'felt like prisoners of over-rigid procurement methodologies and ... over-rigid IT strategies and management structures.'

Increased dependence and vulnerability

In general, centralised approaches to information systems make public sector organisations more dependent and more vulnerable for a number of reasons:

— greater numbers of staff rely on single information systems,

— greater reliance on a few key staff who plan, develop and run those systems,

— greater technical complexity that makes problems harder to diagnose, and

— greater potential impact of data security breaches.

As a consequence management controls have to be far more rigorous (hence costly) with centralised systems.

It would seem that centralised approaches to public information systems are highly problematic. What, then, of decentralised approaches? As technology has become smaller, cheaper, easier-to-use, more reliable, and more powerful, so decentralised approaches seem to be an increasing possibility. Decentralisation may also be driven by a desire to remove control from central IT units, or by its perceived advantages, which include those listed below.

The closer the proximity of user and developer, the less the communication gap and the more likely it is that the developed system meets the users' real needs. At the extreme, where users are able to develop their own information systems, these are far more likely to meet their requirements than those developed by someone else.

Higher usage of computerised systems

This flexibility to fit local needs helps to explain the dramatic growth in computer use associated with decentralised approaches, such as end-user computing. Users are better motivated by such approaches and are far keener to take up computing when it directly supports their own interests and work.

Faster system development

The less the organisational distance between system user and system developer, the faster development of that system is likely to be. Again taking the extreme of end-user development, there will be no delay for the development of mutual understanding and no clash with higher priority information systems developments. This can help to overcome the staffing constraints and systems development backlog that often afflict centralised IS units. Other aspects of system use such as implementation, operation, troubleshooting and maintenance are also likely to occur more quickly under a decentralised regime.

Perceived lower costs

The 1990s have been characterised by a growing realisation that the costs of decentralised approaches are greater than anticipated because of many initially-unrecognised indirect costs. Nevertheless, some still argue that decentralised approaches present lower costs than centralised approaches. This is thanks to faster development, less miscommunication, greater fit to local needs, the greater emphasis on smaller computers, the greater emphasis on buying software packages rather than developing software in-house, and so on.

Decentralised approaches

However, just like their centralised counterparts, decentralised approaches are also beset by problems, some of which are outlined below and in the following section.

Many of the constraints to centralised approaches described above are, in fact, constraints to change in general. They are therefore also constraints to a decentralised approach and will not be reiterated in detail. Examples include:

— *Technical constraints,* such as heavy existing investments in a centralised system.

— *Resource constraints,* such as a lack of skills to support decentralised decision making and action on information systems.

— *Political constraints,* such as the unwillingness of those at the centre to change information flows, resource flows and associated organisational power.

However, it is rare for these constraints to be completely insurmountable, partly because of the great motivation of staff and individual work units to take some control over IT. At least some elements of IS decentralisation are therefore found in almost all public sector organisations.

Disadvantages of decentralised approaches

Even if the listed constraints are overcome, decentralised approaches can produce some disadvantageous outcomes.

Decentralised approaches can create information systems in different work units that are mutually incompatible. The resulting 'electronic concrete', like its centralised counterpart, constrains the scope of activities that organisations can undertake, or imposes substantial additional time and financial costs on those activities. In particular, strategic, organisation-wide activities are constrained. This can lead to anything from a difficulty in aggregating basic financial information across the organisation, to an inability to implement any strategic plans.

Barriers to sharing other resources, including human resources

There may also be an inability to share resources other than data if work units are allowed to set up their own separate systems. It may be hard to exchange hardware and software. Perhaps more importantly, each individual information system requires a unique set of skills for system development, implementation and operation. This makes it much more difficult for staff to move between different systems.

Duplication of effort

Apart from constraining what public organisations can do, decentralised approaches also tend to be very costly because units will often duplicate what others are doing. Duplication may cover:

— analysis, design and implementation of information systems,

— gathering and administration of data, and

— system operation, support and maintenance.

In addition, computer input, output, storage and processing capacity will all have to be duplicated. The unnecessary duplication of data (known as *data redundancy*) tends to be particularly problematic, yet it is quite common. For example, public organisations often store basic details of their employees many times over:

— on paper and on computer, and

— for personnel, for payroll, for training, and for other records.

This imposes additional costs in gathering, maintaining and updating data. In addition, because data about similar entities is held simultaneously in two or more different locations, it tends to become inconsistent. No-one then knows which, if any, version of the data is the most accurate or up-to-date. Trying to put together a reliable record involves a lot of chasing around and cross-checking.

Lack of learning and control

In addition to the extra direct costs that duplication imposes, there is an indirect cost of lost learning opportunities and limited cross-fertilisation of ideas. Decentralised approaches also necessarily mean limited central ability to plan and control, leading to a tendency for some decentralised systems to be developed and used without due care. The result may be a system that never works or does not work properly, with compromised data quality or system security.

Failure to achieve scale economies

As already noted, there are scale economies in information systems covering data, people, hardware and other resources. Decentralised approaches make all activities more costly, from buying computers to gathering data to training staff to system operation and maintenance. All of these problems can be largely summarised as: higher-than-desirable costs or a lower-than-desirable scope of public sector activities. The intangibility of many of the problems means that costs are not always recognised. For example, only in recent years have the true costs of end-user microcomputer ownership begun to emerge, with estimates up to US$10,000 or more per computer per year. Much of this is the cost of staff time taken up when users provide support to other users and when PCs are used for non-job-related or other unproductive activities. Training, maintenance and administration costs also contribute.

Both the centralised and the decentralised approach can provide benefits for public organisations. Yet, at the same time, such approaches can be hard or impossible to implement, and can produce serious disadvantages for the organisation.

What is the way out of this quandary? One way forward is the adoption of a core-periphery approach that attempts to reconcile the push of the centralised approach with the pull of the decentralised approach. It does this in two ways.

First, through *integration*: drawing the centralised and decentralised approaches together into some kind of unified or compromise approach. Second, and more commonly, through *division*. This accepts that both centralised and decentralised approaches will be found, and then attempts to set some demarcation lines that will keep the two separate, thereby allowing them both to be accommodated.

A decentralised approach may be most economic for public organisations, because it saves on overt input costs. A centralised approach may be most efficient, because it avoids waste and duplication. But a successful core-periphery approach may be most effective because it can simultaneously provide:

— the control necessary to share key resources (including data), to avoid duplication, and to achieve economies of scale; and

— the freedom necessary to meet user needs, and to overcome blocks to IT usage and IS development.

Core-Periphery Approach

A core-periphery approach to IS planning involves strong and active participation of users and local units in the formulation of strategy.

The planning process may then involve decisions about other elements of the core-periphery approach: planning which data items are generic and which are specific; dividing out responsibilities for information systems development; and so on.

In line with other core-periphery elements, such plans may also aim to guide more than dictate. The successor to the UK Army's 800-page strategy document cited above, for example, was only 30 pages long. It provided a guiding framework, allowing for flexibility and local initiative.

Organisational structures and staffing

A core-periphery approach may involve a separation of central and local responsibilities, as described below for areas such as data management and IS development. However, another strand can be an attempt to close the 'ITernal triangle' gaps identified above. For example, there is likely to be some central IS unit with a co-ordination role in this approach. It may have a management structure that involves end users and senior staff as well as IT staff. It may also be underpinned by a relatively open philosophy that looks outside the unit and regards the end users as its customers. This, for example, has been the philosophy adopted in restructuring IT structures across the South African public sector.

One common application of the customer-oriented philosophy is to create an 'end-user support centre'. This is essentially an internal extension/outreach unit. It reaches out from the centre to support users on the periphery and to help them make best use of their information systems and technology.

Another example of core-periphery approaches is the attempt to hire or create *hybrid staff*. They understand both the context and work of a public sector organisation *and* the role, management and jargon of information systems.

Data management

A core-periphery approach to data management typically involves a division of responsibilities, such as that which has been adopted across the Canadian government.

This division defines the centre's role as being the management of 'generic' data items (i.e. those used across all or most of the organisation). Typical generic data items would include those about organisational employees, finances, projects and services.

The periphery's role would be to:

— make use of generic data,

— alter generic data only within certain centrally-determined controls, and

— control 'specific' data items (i.e. those used only by individuals or small groups), for example, those within a database of personal contacts.

Computing and data management architecture

The most common core-periphery computing architecture is the client/server model, in which computing power is divided between the central servers and the local client workstations. This architecture has now been adopted by vast numbers of public sector organisations worldwide.

For organisations moving straight from a manual or stand-alone system to a client/server model, the main decisions to be made concern how power and resources are to be divided between the server core and the client periphery. Organisations moving from a centralised to a client/server architecture have an additional decision to make: what to do with the centralised system, which will often be mainframe-based.

There are three main choices:

— scrap the mainframe and move over fully to the client/server system,

— run two architectures in parallel, or

— make the mainframe part of the client/server architecture.

Information systems development

A core-periphery approach to systems development can involve a division of responsibilities, for example, defining certain types of information system as suitable for central development, and others as suitable for decentralised/end-user development. Decisions about how to classify project proposals for particular information systems can be made by a joint team of managers with technical staff input. This team will allocate central resources only to projects meeting agreed criteria.

Candidates for central development might be those systems where one or more of the following applies:

— the system is critical to the functioning of the organisation,

— the system is to be used by more than one department,

— data is drawn from several different sources, and/or

— there are particular technical issues such as a very large database or a need for a fast response time.

Such systems are seen as too important, too cross-cutting, and/or too skill-intensive to be appropriate for decentralised development.

Candidates for decentralised development might be those systems where one or more of the following applies:

— the system is relevant only to the individual user or department,

— data is drawn only from an existing centrally-managed database or from a proposed locally-managed database, and/or

— processing or reporting requirements are subject to frequent change.

Such systems are seen as too small and/or too specific to be appropriate for central development.

A slightly different perspective would aim to create a division of responsibilities within the development of each individual information system. Decentralised users might be responsible for systems analysis, training, documentation, and ongoing support. Centralised IT staff might be responsible for design, construction, implementation, operation and maintenance of the system.

In the development of a new management information system to support reform of materiel requirements planning, for instance, the US Air Force Logistics Command involved users throughout the IS development lifecycle. Users were made responsible for current system analysis, requirements specification, review and acceptance of detail design, preparation of test data, setting of acceptance criteria and user acceptance. They were also involved with the testing and data conversion processes. Coupled with formal project management procedures, this helped to ensure a good fit between user needs and system outcomes.

Alternatively, the central role may just be one of quality assurance: end users or work sections are responsible for developing an application, but quality is assured in some way by the central IS unit. This may involve central guidelines on anything from development methods to data structures, or central testing of programs or documentation. Finally, a core-periphery approach may also attempt to bridge internal divisions and have shared responsibilities for systems development. It might do this by creating structures that bring different groups together or through processes that allow these groups to communicate with each other. Such structures may involve participatory or prototyping techniques of systems development. The Royal Netherlands Air Force adopted this last method through the mechanism of a management game involving the simulation of the entire organisational information system for a planned air base. Not only did this create a shared vision for change among participants, it also facilitated discussion of key issues, and created a sense of unity between those involved. As a result, this has been recommended as a standard approach to public sector change.

IT acquisition

Standards for IT acquisition bring many immediate and obvious benefits to organisations. Unfortunately, they may be resented by users and can be circumvented relatively easily by users who have any local control over finances. This is a sensitive area because those who control the information technology tend to control the information held by that technology. As we know this, in turn, is a component of organisational power.

A core-periphery approach to acquiring information technology therefore typically involves a mixture of 'carrot and stick': encouraging users to follow standards, and providing some limited sanctions for those who do not. It also typically involves a flexible approach to standards that allows users some local leeway within a set of boundaries.

The US General Services Administration and the UK's CCTA/Government Centre for Information Systems both make use of this approach, essentially providing public agencies with a shopping list of discounted items via central framework agreements. There is an 'opt in' model by which agencies can use these channels if they wish, but are not bound to do so.

Other elements of this approach may include:

— Reserving purchase of certain types of hardware (i.e. servers or all network hardware) for central decisions, or reserving purchases above some financial threshold for central approval, but allowing other purchases to be made by users. One intention here is to retain central control over the hardware that will form an organisation-wide technology infrastructure, such as telecommunications, but to relax other controls.

— Limiting the size of decentralised IT budgets. This avoids the extreme of a wholly centralised budget, which antagonises users and leads them to spend other budgets on IT. It also avoids the extreme of a wholly decentralised IT budget, which can lead to an unwillingness to fund any central services.

— Disseminating a set of minimum functional requirements (memory, disk size, chip, operating system capability, etc.) that all computers should meet, but allowing freedom of choice of model and supplier.

— Providing central advice, bulk purchase, installation assistance, training, and maintenance and repair services only for standardised hardware and software, but allowing users to diverge from this if they are willing to support themselves.

— Requiring that all networked IT conform to a certain specification, but allowing greater freedom for stand-alone information technology.

— Setting organisational standards for IT on a committee with strong user representation.

Other components of a core-periphery approach may include training and technical support.

Training

A common core-periphery approach is to centralise the planning of training for core information systems. Other training needs may be met, as requested, by end-user support centres or by informal training methods. There may also be central provision of access to open and flexible learning systems such as CD-ROM- or Internet/ intranet-based training packages or videos.

Technical support

Given the very specialist nature of many repair and maintenance tasks, there are very high costs in leaving them to individual end users. Many organisations, therefore, have at least one IT support employee per department who takes on this role. Centralising this role even further can lead to response times and prioritisation that may seem poor from a user perspective. However, the more specialised the role, the more the arguments for centralisation.

In the case of both training and technical support (and other activities), consideration will have to be given to charges levied on work units or users for centrally-provided services. The benefit of charging (even a nominal sum) is that it induces users to take the services seriously. It will also transfer resources to the central IS unit. The problem of charging is that users may decide not to use the service, possibly creating additional costs for the organisation if equipment is then not used properly or wrongly repaired or left in an unusable condition.

6

Internet : A Unique Communication

The rights to freedom of expression, information, privacy, and free association under international law apply as much to online communication as to other forms of individual communication. While international treaties and instruments do not address electronic speech specifically, their assertion of the right to "seek, receive and impart information and ideas *through any media and regardless of frontiers*" (emphasis added) is clearly applicable to expression via the Internet.

Article 19 of the Universal Declaration of Human Rights proclaims:

Everyone has the right to freedom of opinion and expression; this right includes freedom to hold opinions without interference and to seek, receive and impart information and ideas through any media and regardless of frontiers.

Article 19 of the International Covenant on Civil and Political Rights (ICCPR) reaffirms that everyone's right to freedom of expression "shall include the freedom to seek, receive and impart information and ideas of all kinds, regardless of frontiers, either orally, in writing or in print, in the form of art, or through any other media of his choice." Article 19 states, furthermore, that restrictions on this right "shall only be such as are provided by law and are necessary: (a) For respect of the rights or reputations of others; (b) For the protection of national security or of public order (*ordre public*), or of public health or morals."(2) The ICCPR has been ratified by Algeria, Egypt, Iran, Iraq, Israel, Jordan, Lebanon, Kuwait, Libya, Morocco, Syria, Tunisia, and Yemen. It has not been ratified by Bahrain, Oman, Qatar, Saudi Arabia, and the United Arab Emirates.(3)

The Open Internet Policy Principles, declared in March 1997 by a working group of European and North American experts, point out:

The Internet does not exist in a legal vacuum. For the most part, existing laws can and should regulate conduct on the Internet to the same degree as other forms of conduct. Such laws may differ from country to country, but should conform with the applicable binding human rights obligations contained in the Universal Declaration of Human Rights, the International Covenant on Civil and Political Rights and the European Convention on Human Rights.

Under international law, governments are allowed to restrict the free flow of information to protect certain narrow interests such as national security or public morals. But any prior censorship of material before it is published should be subjected to the strictest level of scrutiny in line with international standards, which normally includes inquiry into the interest sought to be protected, the seriousness of the threat, and whether there are alternate means of protecting that interest that are less restrictive of the right to free expression.

Indeed, the American Convention on Human Rights states in Article 13 that the right to freedom of expression "shall not be subject to prior censorship." Filtering or blocking access to Internet material by a government amounts to pre-publication censorship. Virtually all governments in the Middle East that block content on the Internet suppress some material that is unquestionably legal. Moreover, none of the governments in the region make public how censorship is actually practiced and what sites are blocked, insulating their actions from any scrutiny or evaluation under international human rights standards. The decision of what to block, and what technology to use to block it, should be in the hands of end users, rather than governments. A variety of software programs is readily available to users for this purpose.

The Right to Privacy

The freedom from arbitrary and unlawful interference with one's privacy and correspondence is protected in international law, and applies to electronic communications. A capricious, unjust or disproportionate interference would be "arbitrary," as would one that was for a purpose inimical to the protection of human rights more generally, such as inhibiting peaceful dissent. States may not randomly or freely intercept or monitor e-mail or Internet usage; in the narrow circumstances where surveillance can be justified, it must be subject to limitation and control to avoid infringing these rights. Moreover, the International Covenant on Civil and Political Rights requires states to act positively to protect individuals from such interference with privacy or correspondence on the part of third parties such as non-state actors. Encryption, as a technology that protects communications and correspondence from arbitrary interference, should be lawful and accessible to individual users.

Free expression encompasses a right to communicate anonymously. Anonymity in communications is critical to the right to express political beliefs, and to seek and impart information without fear of retribution. Anonymity has served persons who wish to provide anonymous tips to journalists or "blow the whistle" on improprieties in their workplace, authors who wish to write under assumed names, and participants in sensitive discussions, such as an AIDS support group. The role of anonymous speech in fostering freedom of expression was eloquently defended thus:

Despite readers' curiosity and the public's interest in identifying the creator of a work of art, an author generally is free to decide whether or not to disclose her true identity. The decision in favor of anonymity may be motivated by fear of economic or official retaliation, by concern about social ostracism, or merely by a desire to preserve as much of one's privacy as possible. Whatever the motivation may be, at least in the field of literary endeavor, the interest in having anonymous works enter the marketplace of ideas unquestionably outweighs any public interest in requiring disclosure as a condition of entry.

Encryption

Encoding electronic communications (encryption) is growing more commonplace, and indeed, is commonly recognized as essential to facilitating the growth of electronic commerce. "Strong" encryption software, that is, coding that is nearly impossible for third parties to decipher, is widely available now to individuals and businesses, where once it was solely used by governments. Encryption protects privacy of communications, but even more importantly, it enables the free expression of ideas and information, particularly where there has been a record of government surveillance and repression. By guaranteeing privacy of communications and authenticating the identity of communicators, encryption also enables free association between individuals in cyberspace, an important extension of a traditional right in the new circumstances of globalization.

While there are legitimate law enforcement concerns that must be taken into account in any national policy on encryption, there is no justification for either banning individual use of encryption or licensing users. Encryption should be viewed as a vehicle of expression like a language; the use of encryption alone should not subject an individual to criminal sanction, any more than should the use of Esperanto or Swahili to communicate. Individuals should not be required to obtain authorization from the authorities in order to send or receive encrypted communications, nor should they be compelled to provide in advance to law enforcement authorities access to key recovery or other mechanisms that would permit the decoding of their communications. These are all over-broad policies that penalize law-abiding persons.

Liability for Online Content

The right to free expression is best served by laws that

focus liability for speech on the originator of the offending content, rather than on its conduit. ISPs do not fit neatly into any existing media paradigm and should not be subjected to regulatory structures that may be suitable for other technologies or media, such as a newspaper that can be held liable for articles appearing in its pages. ISPs act most of the time merely as conduits of information (data carriers, akin to telephone companies), offering the technical means for users to receive and disseminate information. In most cases, ISPs have no knowledge of the content of the messages they transmit, or even of the web sites they host—many of which are revised daily by their authors. The situation is arguably different when the offending content is contained in material over which the ISP exercises editorial control, such as a proprietary opinion column; or when the ISP is made aware that offending content has been posted on a web site it hosts and does not remove it.

To hold ISPs presumptively liable for all content they host or carry would pose a regulatory burden on providers that would drastically reduce and slow the flow of information—if the burden could be carried at all. The Global Internet Liberty Campaign (GILC) argues, "No one can monitor the enormous quantity of network traffic, which may consist of hundreds of thousands of e-mails, newsgroup messages, files, and Web pages that pass through in dozens of text and binary formats, some of them readable only by particular proprietary tools." Second, GILC points out, "ISPs cannot provide material in one country while blocking it in another; such a distinction would require an enormous new infrastructure on top of the current network."

The Johannesburg Principles on National Security, Freedom of Expression and Access to Information, put forward on October 1, 1995 by a group of experts in international law, national security, and human rights, state that restrictions on freedom of expression should be permitted only when "the government can demonstrate that the restriction is prescribed by law and is necessary in a democratic society to protect a legitimate national security interest".

According to the Principles, the burden of demonstrating the validity of the restriction rests with the government. Criticism of the government or its leaders is protected. In addition, a government must demonstrate that "the restriction imposed is the least restrictive means possible for protecting that interest".

The Universal Declaration of Human Rights affirms in Article 12, "No one shall be subjected to arbitrary interference with his privacy, family, home or correspondence." The International Covenant on Civil and Political Rights states in Article 17, "No one shall be subjected to arbitrary or unlawful interference with his privacy, family, home or correspondence..." The language of this provision is broad enough to encompass online communications, including electronic mail and newsgroup postings.

Encryption involves encoding a text prior to transmission, through the use of mathematical logarithms, so that it can be read only by the sender and the intended recipient, who are in possession of "keys" that decrypt the encoded text and present it in its original form.

Requiring that laws restricting the content of on-line speech distinguish between the liability of content providers and the liability of data carriers. Insisting that on-line free expression not be restricted by indirect means such as excessively restrictive governmental or private controls over computer hardware or software, telecommunications infrastructure, or other essential components of the Internet.

Including citizens in the Global Information Infrastructure (GII) development process from countries that are currently unstable economically, have insufficient infrastructure, or lack sophisticated technology. Prohibiting discrimination on the basis of race, color, sex, language, religion, political or other opinion, national or social origin, property, birth or other status. Ensuring that personal information generated on the Internet for one purpose is not used for an unrelated purpose or disclosed without the person's informed consent and enabling individuals to review personal information on the Internet and to correct inaccurate information. Allowing on-line users to encrypt their communications and information without restriction.

"Everyone has the right to freedom of opinion and expression; this right includes freedom to hold opinions without interference and to seek, receive and impart information and ideas through any media and regardless of frontiers."

Universal Declaration of Human Rights, Article 19 (emphasis added). For the first time since this 1948 proclamation of the international human right to freedom of expression, the citizens of the world have the ability to exercise that right on a truly global basis, "regardless of frontiers." With the advent of the Internet, methods of accessing and disseminating information have been fundamentally changed, with profound implications for individuals, civil society and governments.

Like no medium before it, the Internet permits any individual with a computer and a gateway to the Internet to communicate instantaneously with others worldwide. The Internet offers educational institutions, businesses, and non-profit organizations an opportunity to exchange ideas and promote scientific, cultural, and economic progress. Traditional forms of media can greatly expand their audiences at nominal cost. The Internet is global in its reach. To a degree that no other technology can, it transcends national borders and eliminates barriers to the free flow of information.

These unique features of this new technology, if properly supported, can foster the freedom of expression essential to democratic rule and civil society in ways previously impossible.

Governments, however, have already begun to impose controls on the Internet, threatening the potential of this new medium. Some governments have enacted laws prohibiting certain content on the Internet and have sought to prosecute users and service providers. Others have tried to control access, by insisting on the installation of national "proxy servers" and requiring the blocking of targeted web sites. And in other countries, governments have encouraged forms of "self-regulation" that are in fact intended to enlist service providers to control the behavior of their customers.

An increasingly well-established body of international law protects the right to freedom of expression. As we shall see, various human rights instruments are diluted by exceptions and may be difficult to enforce. Moreover, not all countries are parties to a binding human rights agreement. But international human rights law undoubtedly has advanced the cause of free expression and undoubtedly applies to the Internet and other digital media. Given the broad language of international and regional human rights documents, there is no doubt that government measures to control the Internet are subject to challenge under international law.

The purpose of this report is to lay the groundwork for the proposition that the unique qualities of the Internet support an even more robust application of international free expression principles to online communications. The technology itself both demands and can support fuller protection of free expression: The borderless nature of the Internet requires that the phrase "regardless of frontiers," which appears in the key international human rights instruments, be applied with a fresh eye. The concept of a right to "impart" information takes on new meaning when anyone can be a publisher.

Since censorship in one country may constitute a direct infringement on the right of persons in other countries to "impart" information "without regard to frontiers," the traditional deference given to local norms should be less relevant to the Internet. The decentralized nature of the Internet makes government controls less effective (even futile), because Internet users have numerous ways of circumventing them. At the same time, the user-controlled nature of the technology means that government controls are less necessary in some contexts. Furthermore, given the essentially unlimited capacity of the Internet, there is less need for government intervention to ensure fairness or balance or to protect reputation. On the Internet, the marketplace of ideas can function with less regulation since good ideas can always achieve the space they deserve. Mistakes can be corrected and the right of reply can be effectuated instantaneously. Under international law, necessity, proportionality, and efficacy are key concepts in judging the validity of restrictions on freedom of expression. If government regulation of content on the Internet is not likely to succeed and not necessary, then it becomes less supportable under international rules.

This paper is merely a beginning, intended to spark further action. A closer examination of the caselaw of the international tribunals is required. A fuller effort is needed to educate judges of the international tribunals, staff of the human rights commissions, and policymakers at international bodies on the unique elements of the Internet and the special significance of user control. Ultimately, free expression cases involving the Internet will be brought before the international human rights tribunals. With further development of the principles outlined here, the Internet could serve as a fulcrum for the expansion of free expression principles.

This chapter is addressed both to governments and to Internet activists. To governments, it says, "Don't try to censor the Internet because your efforts may well violate international human rights law, especially given the unique nature of the Internet." To activists, the chapter says, "Consider how to use international human rights documents to challenge Internet censorship. Here are some arguments why the Internet is entitled to even greater protection that other media."

Applying international human rights principles to the Internet requires an appreciation of the fundamental characteristics of the digital on-line media. The unique qualities of the Internet justify according the strongest protection to free expression on-line and should prompt a new vision of the right to receive and impart information "regardless of frontiers."

The Internet is really a network of networks and is comprised of a number of different technologies and infrastructures. Viewed as a whole, it is uniquely:

Global: The Internet provides immediate access to information from around the world. With simple e-mail, it is as easy to send a message to another continent as it is to the building next door. Through the World Wide Web, thousands of newspapers and tens of thousands of other information sources are available from around the world. While access is still not available to most of the world's population, the fastest rates of growth are in less developed countries.

Decentralized: The Internet was designed by purpose to be decentralized, to work without gatekeepers, and to accommodate multiple, competitive access points. The absence of gatekeepers of the kind that exist in broadcasting, cable television, or satellite transmission, the availability of numerous hosting sites, and the irrelevance of geographic location mean that material can almost always be published outside the control of governments, monopolies or oligopolies.

Open: The Internet has low barriers to access. Service can be priced very inexpensively. The costs of creating and disseminating content are extremely low. Because of the Internet, anybody who has a computer and a modem can be a publisher — a digital Gutenberg.

Abundant: The digitization of information and the ability to transmit it over the telephone network, combined with the decentralized nature of the Internet, mean that the Internet has essentially unlimited capacity to hold information. In economic terms, the marginal cost of adding another web site, sending another email message, or posting to a newsgroup is essentially zero.

Interactive: The Internet is designed for bi-directional communication: All Internet users can be both speakers and listeners. The Internet allows responsive communication from one-to-one, from one-to-many, and from many-to-one.

User-Controlled: The Internet allows users to exercise far more choice than even cable television or short wave radio. The user can skip from site to site in ways that are not dictated by the content providers or by the access provider. User can control what content reaches their computers. Users can encrypt their communications to hide them from government censors.

Infrastructure independent: The Internet is not linked to any infrastructure other than the telephone system. Dial-up access is available from any telephone that can make an international call. Access to the Internet can also be wireless and satellite based and therefore further removed from effective control of governments.

Courts and other institutions that have considered in depth the question of Internet regulation have recognized these unique features. In a 1996 Communication, the European Commission noted: "A unique characteristic of the Internet is that it functions simultaneously as a medium for publishing and for communication. Unlike in the case of traditional media, the Internet supports a variety of communication modes: one-to-one, one-to-many, many-to-many. An Internet user may "speak" or "listen" interchangeably. At any given time, a receiver can and does become content provider, of his own accord, or through "re-posting" of content by a third party. The Internet therefore is radically different from traditional broadcasting. It also differs radically from a traditional telecommunication service."

The European Commission Legal Advisory Board, which advises the European Commission on legal matters concerning the European information market, also recognized the uniqueness of the Internet, calling it "a positive instrument, empowering citizens and educators, lowering the barriers to the creation and distribution of content and offering universal access to ever richer sources of digital information." The United States Supreme Court, in ruling that the Communications Decency Act was unconstitutional and that the Internet merited the strongest protection of free expression, based its judgment on the conclusion that the Internet was "a unique and wholly new medium of worldwide human communication."

The vast new potential of the Internet for expanding access to information and participation in government and civil society has already begun to show itself with concrete contributions to democracy and human rights.

Facilitating participation in government

The bi-directional nature of the Internet has tremendous potential for fostering democratic participation, giving voice to the voiceless. The Internet could allow citizens to communicate with their government, to pose questions to their elected representatives, and to submit comments on pending issues.

While many governments have been slow to take advantage of the democratic potential of the Internet, some harbingers of progress can be seen. In January 1995, the municipality of Bologna created the Iperbole system — a free-of-charge "civic network" offering citizens and businesses an opportunity to send requests, suggestions, claims and complaints by email to more than 1,300 municipal offices. The system also includes discussion and newsgroups dealing with specific topics, suggested by citizens, business enterprises, public and private institutions, and by the municipal administration itself. The UK conducted a one-time on-line consultation on the government's freedom of information proposal.

Western governments are not the only ones that have begun to respond. In Hungary earlier this year, Hungary's iNteRNeTTo held an online debate between politicians from the two leading parties. The Costa Rican government, to make voting more convenient, is working to shift to an electronic voting system. Taking advantage of a literacy rate of 94% and the fact that about 50% of grade schools have Internet-connected computers, Costa Rica hopes to run an entirely electronic balloting in 2002. International bodies also use the Internet to promote public participation in their activities. For example, last year the EU conducted an online forum regarding illegal or harmful content on the Internet.

Grassroots organizations can use the Internet to mobilize voters to be active on issues. One example is the Adopt your Legislator campaign developed by CDT in the US.

Expanding access to government information

One of the most important potential benefits of the Internet is the ability to provide rapid access to the full text of government documents. If a government is willing, it can provide its citizens access to enacted and proposed laws, regulations, government reports and statistics, transcripts of parliamentary debates, judicial decisions, all searchable by word or concept. Information previously available only to experts, usually only in the capital city, and often only with great expenditure of time and money can now be made available to individuals in the smallest rural town and at public libraries in the poorest neighborhoods. This vast openness need not be the luxury of only wealthy nations. In almost every country in the world, most government information is now created by word processing, meaning that the information is already digitized. Again, if the government is willing, the information can be rapidly and inexpensively put on-line, even using simple Gopher technology.

Many nations have begun to use the Internet, nations as diverse as the United Kingdom, the Czech Republic, and South Africa. The European Union is a most effective user of the Web to make its voluminous publications available to a wide audience. Some examples from the U.S. include THOMAS, the Website of the Library of Congress and GPO Access providing access to materials from the Government Printing Office, including all proposed federal regulations, and transcripts of daily Congressional debates.

Civil society through the building of networks among individuals

The Internet has opened up new opportunities for discourse, on matters political, intellectual, and personal. The Internet's architecture allows for a diversity of views and exchange of information that is simply not possible in any other media. As of August 1998, one service identified 29,000 IRC (Internet Relay Chat) channels, 30,000 Usenet newsgroups, and 90,095 mailings lists — each one representing a network of individuals worldwide interested in a particular subject.

Among the first to use the Internet were human rights activists. In 1992, the International Freedom of Expression eXchange (IFEX) was established to provide accurate and timely information regarding censorship and attacks on journalists. The primary method of transmitting information is by e-mail: whenever there is a serious threat to freedom of expression, the IFEX action alert network sends out detailed information on the case via e-mail to participating organizations and individuals, who in turn mount international protests from their own regions. GILC member "Derechos" is an on-line human rights organization focusing on Latin America that exists largely through the Internet.

The Internet has been at the forefront of democratic uprisings. In Indonesia, "Bypassing the government-controlled television and radio stations, dissidents shared information about protests by e-mail, inundated news groups with stories of President Suharto's corruption, and used chat groups to exchange tips about resisting troops."

Traditional media and promoting pluralism

The Web has become a place where there is ready access to newspapers and other publications. A wide range of print publications are available on-line, and many broadcast media now have on-line services that allow searching of past broadcasts, a capability previously available only to governments and a few research institutes. The Radio Free Europe/Radio Liberty Newsline illustrates the use of old-fashioned e-mail to disseminate information to a dispersed audience very inexpensively.

The Internet makes it possible for more organizations to distribute news and commentary, increasing the diversity of voices. The Association for Independent Media in Bosnia has made use of the Internet, both e-mail and the World Wide Web. AIM operates on the principle of a mail-box system. Information is exchanged via a central computer located in Paris. AIM texts are available in Serbian, Croatian, Bosnian, and a choice of texts is available in English. Subscribers to AIM regularly receive the whole production of AIM via e-mail. The China News Digest makes available news from non-official sources. While the site is sometimes blocked by the Chinese government, users in China have found ways to access it. The service also uses e-mail to disseminate its news within China.

The Internet is Uniquely Resistant to Government Controls

With the Internet, it is increasingly difficult for governments to control content. The Internet offers creative ways to disseminate information around the controls of censors. Radio B92 in Belgrade is one of the leading examples of this. When authorities shut down the radio station, it put its programming on the Internet through RealAudio, using a Dutch service provider; Radio Free Europe, Voice of America, and Deutche Welle picked up the station off the Net and rebroadcast it back into Serbia, where it served as the source of independent reporting and a focal point for democratic opposition. Faced with this strategy, the government allowed the station back on the air.

In June of 1997, Chinese dissidents founded *Tunnel,* a Chinese language journal of dissent. Tunnel is managed and edited in China. Once an issue is ready to be published, it is secretly delivered to the United States and then emailed back to China from an anonymous address. "Thus its staff remains safely hidden in cyberspace, and all of its contributors, both in China and abroad, write under pseudonyms."

The Digital Freedom Network, was created with the primary objective of publishing on-line material that has been suppressed. When the government of Belarus suppressed the independent newspaper Svaboda, Radio Free Europe/Radio Liberty made its reports available in three different ways: the Belarus service of RFE/RL featured materials from Svaboda journalists, its website posted their articles, and the daily live RealAudio news broadcast of RFE/RL's Belarus service carried Svaboda content.

The technology of the Internet frustrates control in other ways. Proxy servers purportedly block access to web sites known to contain objectionable content and thus preclude such content from being accessed. Such servers fail to achieve their goal, however, because web site operators whose sites are targeted as containing undesirable content can simply change their web site address; and an Internet user in a country imposing controls can simply dial into a server outside the country and access the desired information, thereby avoiding the proxy server altogether.

An "Anti-Censorship Proxy" has been created that allows users to evade filters. Even if the telephone company is state-owned, it cannot differentiate a telephone call to a foreign server from an international fax. Furthermore, encryption allows determined users to create "tunnels" to banned foreign sites in ways that completely evade government control. And while access through an Internet Service Provider is desirable, dial-up access is available from any telephone that can make an international call. Access to the Internet can also be wireless, making it even harder for governments to exercise controls.

The creation of mirror sites is one practice that helps assure the free flow of information, even against government censorship efforts. Given the global nature of the Internet, content can be published from anywhere in the world. When a government tries to prosecute a content provider or force the withdrawal of material, there are others around the world prepared to copy or mirror the information on their own sites, in countries where the information is legal.

One example involved the site of a Basque organization hosted by an American service provider. The site was supporting Basque independence, although it did not promote violence. Nonetheless, from Spain, there came an apparently orchestrated campaign of "mailbombing" — flooding the site's service provider with e-mail in order to disrupt service. The service provider publicized the problem and soon a number of organizations, one in Holland, one in England, several in the U.S., installed mirror websites, which were perfectly legal in the host country.

With so many sites, the harassment campaign fizzled out. The Internet Freedom Campaign, an English group hosting one of the mirror sites, set up an on-line bulletin board for surfers to post their opinions about the issue, showing how the Net is the perfect place for controversial information to appear, Similarly, when a local governmental body in the UK, the Nottinghamshire County Council, sought to suppress the publication of the so-called JET Report, an official report on the hysteria that has attended certain child abuse cases, the report was immediately mirrored on numerous sites, ultimately totaling 35, as a result of a campaign organized by GILC member Cyber-Rights & Cyber-Liberties (UK), When an issue of a Zambian newspaper carrying an article critical of the government was banned, the issue was mirrored outside the country.

Governments Have Sought to Impose Various Controls on Internet Content and Access

Despite the power of the Internet — or perhaps because of that very power — governments have sought to restrict it. Government actions infringing freedom of expression on the Internet take many forms:

— *Internet-specific laws:* Some governments have criminalized certain types of speech on the Internet. Such criminal penalties may come in the form of laws whose expressed intent is to protect minors from certain material regarded as "harmful." However, as the United States Supreme Court recently found, requiring that Internet speakers shield certain populations from their speech is effectively a total ban on that speech.

— *Application of existing laws:* Governments can act to restrict speech without specifically enacting laws targeting Internet-based speech. For example, German government action against CompuServe for providing access to material illegal under German law did not require enactment of new law, merely the assertion by government agents that certain Internet speech violated the existing laws.

— *Content-based license terms applied to Internet users and service providers:* Several countries have already established licensing systems that require Internet users and/or service providers to agree to refrain from certain kinds of speech, or block access to speech as a condition of having a license to use the Internet or provide access to the Net. China has issued rules requiring anyone with Internet access to refrain from proscribed speech. And the Singapore Broadcasting Authority requires all Internet Service Providers to abide by licensing terms demanding that they block access to foreign web sites and newsgroups deemed harmful to national morals.

— *Compelled use of filtering, rating or content labeling tools:* Blocking, filtering, and labeling techniques can prevent individuals from using the Internet to exchange information on topics that may be controversial or unpopular, enable the development of country profiles to facilitate a global/universal rating system desired by some governments, block access to content on entire domains, block access to Internet content available at any domain or page which contains a specific key word or character string in the address, and over-ride self-rating labels provided by content creators and providers. Where any such mechanisms are required by public authorities or otherwise forced on users, they constitute serious threats to human rights.

Regional Agreements Manifest a Universal Commitment to the Right to Free Expression

Over the past half-century, international human rights law has enshrined the rights to free expression, access to information, and privacy of communications, creating a strong presumption against governmental intrusions. These rights are reflected both in the provisions of numerous international and regional agreements and in decisions rendered by human rights tribunals. These human rights doctrines protecting freedom of expression are fully applicable to the Internet. Indeed, these protections may offer especially strong protection to the Internet, given its unique features.

These human rights instruments have their limitations. The Universal Declaration has been accepted in effect by all 185 Member States of the United Nations, but not all of its provisions have become binding. The International Covenant on Civil and Political Rights is binding, but its enforcement mechanisms are limited. While there are binding regional agreements for the Americas, for Europe, and for Africa, there are none for Asia or the Middle East. Enforcement mechanisms are available under these regional agreements, but they are limited too. Where individual review is available, the time required to pursue a case all the way to the international level may be substantial. Most importantly, these instruments, particularly the European Convention, are burdened with exceptions that have been seriously criticized as over-broad.

Nonetheless, these human rights agreements have served to expand freedom of expression worldwide, becoming part of international law and affecting the domestic laws of many nations. The numerous international and regional instruments discussed herein provide substantial evidence that the principle of free expression is a well-settled principle of international law. The collection of treaties, agreements, and international tribunal decisions also evidences an international consensus on the scope of this right: it applies to all forms of media, it applies to the ability to receive and to impart information, and it is subject to only limited restrictions.

The advent of the Internet raises the question of how these human rights instruments apply to the new communications media. The answers are in some respects encouraging: the instruments are drafted with very forward-looking language, with powerful implications for a medium that operates "regardless of frontiers."

International Agreements

The international community has stated its commitment to the right to free expression in a series of fundamental agreements, including the Universal Declaration of Human Rights, the International Covenant on Civil and Political Rights, and the International Covenant on Economic, Social and Cultural Rights.

Universal Declaration of Human Rights

The right of free expression was first proclaimed an international norm by the then-members of the United Nations in the 1948 Universal Declaration of Human Rights ("Universal Declaration"). Taken together, Articles 19, 12, and 27 of the Universal Declaration constitute a blueprint for the protection of free expression on the Internet.

Article 19 of the Universal Declaration proclaims: "Everyone has the right to freedom of opinion and expression; this right includes freedom to hold opinions without interference and to seek, receive and impart information and ideas through any medium and regardless of frontiers."

Article 12 of the Universal Declaration provides: "*No one shall be subjected to arbitrary interference with his privacy, family, home or correspondence.*" The language of this provision is broad enough to encompass all communications directed to an individual or group of individuals, including electronic mail and newsgroup communications. Finally, the right to seek, receive and impart information guaranteed in Article 19 of the Universal Declaration is reinforced by Article 27, which upholds the right of each individual "*freely to participate in the cultural life of the community, to enjoy the arts and to share in scientific advancement and its benefits.*" Given that the Internet's roots are in the exchange of scientific information, Article 27 seems particularly apt to the protection of communications on the Internet.

The foresightful language of Article 19 ("*through any medium*") makes it clearly applicable to expression via the Internet. The rights to "seek" and "impart" information seem particularly relevant to "surfing" the 'Net and posting information on Web sites for all to read, while the right to "receive" information encompasses the exchange of electronic mail and the downloading of information.

The Universal Declaration is subject to exceptions. Article 29(2) provides:

"In the exercise of his rights and freedoms, everyone shall be subject only to such limitations as are determined by law solely for the purpose of securing due recognition and respect for the rights and freedoms of others and of meeting the just requirements of morality, public order and the general welfare in a democratic society."

Enforcement

The Universal Declaration is not a treaty. It was adopted by the United Nations General Assembly as a resolution having no force of law on its own. However, over time the Declaration has become a normative instrument that creates some legal obligations for Member States of the UN. Many of the principles established by the Universal Declaration have since entered the corpus of international law as evidenced by an overwhelming consensus of opinion and practice among states. This consensus is illustrated in subsequent international and regional treaties and agreements, decisions of international tribunals, and domestic constitutions and legislation. Further, the Declaration has served as an inspiration for other human rights agreements of more direct effect.

The United Nations Commission on Human Rights was created in 1946 under Article 68 of the UN Charter.

States name representatives to the 53 member Commission, where they serve as instructed governmental delegates. The Commission prepares reports and coordinates an expansive network of working groups and rapporteurs with thematic or country mandates. It has been criticized for being politically motivated and selective in approach, but it serves as the principal UN forum for addressing charges of human rights violations and as a focal point for broadening the human rights agenda of the UN.

In 1993, the Commission established the position of Special Rapporteur on the promotion and protection of the right to freedom of opinion and expression. In his 1998 report to the Commission, the Special Rapporteur specifically commented on the impact of new communications technologies and governmental efforts to regulate them:

"The Special Rapporteur is of the opinion that the new technologies and, in particular, the Internet are inherently democratic, provide the public and individuals with access to information sources and enable all to participate actively in the communication process. The Special Rapporteur also believes that action by States to impose excessive regulations on the use of these technologies and, again, particularly the Internet, on the grounds that control, regulation and denial of access are necessary to preserve the moral fabric and cultural identity of societies is paternalistic.

These regulations presume to protect people from themselves and, as such, they are inherently incompatible with the principles of the worth and dignity of each individual. These arguments deny the fundamental wisdom of individuals and societies and ignore the capacity and resilience of citizens, whether on a national, State, municipal, community or even neighbourhood level, often to take self-correcting measures to re-establish equilibrium without excessive interference or regulation by the State."

In its resolution of April 1998 on the right to freedom of expression, the Commission welcomed the Special Rapporteur's report and specifically invited him to "assess the advantages and challenges of new telecommunications technologies, including the Internet, on the exercise of the right to freedom of opinion and expression,... taking into account the work undertaken by the Committee on the Elimination of Racial Discrimination on racism, racial discrimination, xenophobia, and related intolerance."

International Covenant on Civil and Political Rights

The principles first enunciated in the Universal Declaration are reiterated and expanded upon in the 1966 International Covenant on Civil and Political Rights ("ICCPR"), which took effect in 1976 and has now been ratified by 140 nations. Article 19 of the ICCPR restates Article 19 of the Universal Declaration almost verbatim. It declares: *"Everyone shall have the right to hold opinions without interference. ... Everyone shall have the right to freedom of expression... ."* In words somewhat more expansive than the Universal Declaration, Article 19 of the ICCPR expressly states that the freedom of expression extends to all forms of media: *"this right shall include freedom to seek, receive and impart information and ideas of all kinds, regardless of frontiers, either orally, in writing or in print, in the form of art, or through any other media of his choice."* The ICCPR also reiterates the crux of Article 12 of the Universal Declaration: *"No one shall be subjected to arbitrary or unlawful interference with his privacy, family, home or correspondence."*

The ICCPR defines the scope of limitations that could be imposed on the freedom of expression. Consistent with the law of most if not all nations, the ICCPR recognizes that freedom of expression may be curtailed under certain circumstances. The ICCPR requires, however, that restrictions on free speech be narrowly defined and not arbitrary. Article 19(3) of the ICCPR provides that restrictions on the freedom of expression are valid only where such restrictions are *"provided by law and are necessary: a. For respect of the rights or reputation of others; [or] b. For the protection of national security or of public order, or of public health or morals."*

The essence of applying the ICCPR involves interpreting this limitation. It has been urged that this provision means that laws restricting freedom of expression must be "accessible, unambiguous, drawn narrowly, and with precision." Moreover, the burden of demonstrating the validity of a restriction on free speech should lie with the government. The key hurdle for governments is the requirement that restrictions be "necessary;" this has generally been interpreted as a high standard.

The ICCPR includes several other provisions relevant to freedom of expression. Article 17 provides, *"No one shall be subjected... to unlawful attacks on his honour and reputation. ... Everyone has the right to the protection of the law against such... attacks."* Article 20 states, *"Any advocacy of national, racial, or religious hatred that constitutes incitement to discrimination, hostility or violence shall be prohibited by law."*

Under the Covenant, States Parties are required to submit reports every five years on the measures they have taken to protect and advance human rights. The Covenant established a Human Rights Committee, one of the principal functions of which is to examine these reports. The Committee makes conclusions on individual state reports and also issues general comments, which serve as advisory opinions on the Covenant. (The Committee also has had since its inception jurisdiction over complaints filed by one State Party against another, but few states declared their acceptance of the mechanism and it has never been used).

In 1976, an optional protocol went into force which enables private parties to file individual complaints against States Parties that have ratified the covenant. The protocol is itself a treaty, and therefore binds the states that have ratified it. Complainants must exhaust domestic remedies first. Once a complaint has been admitted as properly drawn, the Committee brings the matter to the attention of the state involved, which has six months to respond. The Committee, after considering all the written communications on the matter, issues its "views."

The Committee has no power to enforce its findings, but it does require States Parties to indicate in their periodic reports what measures they have taken to give effect to the Committee's recommendations. "In particular, the State Party should indicate what remedy it has afforded the author of the communication whose rights the Committee has found to have been violated."

Economic, Social and Cultural Rights

Restrictions on the Internet also implicate rights established by the International Covenant on Economic, Social, and Cultural Rights ("ICESCR"). Echoing Article 27 of the Universal Declaration, Article 15 of the ICESCR recognizes the important *"benefits to be derived from the encouragement and development of international contacts and cooperation in the scientific and cultural fields."* Accordingly, the 136 signatories pledge to *"diffuse science and culture"* and to *"respect the freedom indispensable for scientific research and creative activity."* These provisions articulate that free expression across borders must be respected to realize social, scientific, and cultural advancements.

To take advantage of such progress, Article 15 of the ICESCR establishes that all individuals are entitled "to enjoy the benefits of scientific progress and its applications." One of the most effective means of doing so is through Internet communication, which enables people in distant and diverse countries to share valuable scientific research and social insights.

The ICESCR does not establish any interstate or individual complaint system. It only requires the States Parties to submit *"reports on the measures which they have adopted and the progress made in achieving the observance of the rights recognized herein."* Art. 16(1). There is a Committee on Economic, Social and Cultural Rights, which reviews the country reports and issues General Comments and analyses, which serve as a platform for the Committee to try to advance awareness of human rights issues arising in the social context.

Regional Agreements

Regional human rights agreements in Europe, the Americas, and Africa establish the right of free expression for all individuals and privacy in their communications with others. Such freedoms are protected in all forms of media and "regardless of frontiers." These regional agreements are especially important because of the opportunities they offer for international judicial review of actions restricting free expression.

European Convention of Human Rights

The European Convention for the Protection of Human Rights and Fundamental Freedoms ("European Convention") was adopted in 1950 by members of the Council of Europe. Article 10 states in full:

— "Everyone has the right to freedom of expression. This right shall include freedom to hold opinions and to receive and impart information and ideas without interference by public authority and regardless of frontiers. This Article shall not prevent States from requiring licensing of broadcasting, television or cinema enterprises.

— "The exercise of these freedoms, since it carries with it duties and responsibilities, may be subject to such formalities, conditions, restrictions or penalties as are prescribed by law and are necessary in a democratic society, in the interests of national security, territorial integrity or public safety, for the prevention of disorder or crime, for the protection of health or morals, for the protection of the reputation or rights

> of others, for preventing the disclosure of information received in confidence, or for maintaining the authority and impartiality of the judiciary."

The European Convention thus establishes that the right of free expression pertains to cross-border communication, which naturally applies to much of the content available on the Internet. Closely linked to freedom of expression are additional rights in the European Convention: the right to respect for correspondence and privacy, contained in Article 8; the right to freedom of peaceful assembly and freedom of association, contained in Article 11; and the right to manifest one's religion or belief, contained in Article 9.

Article 10 is not stated in absolute terms. The second paragraph specifies that freedom of expression can be curtailed in furtherance of a series of enumerated interests. It has been widely debated whether these exceptions are too broad. But even in the U.S. and other countries with constitutional free speech provisions, restrictions are permitted through judicial interpretation. Supporters of Article 10's approach argue that Article 10 is preferable because the catalogue of possible restrictions is limited and because Article 10 also establishes that any restriction on the exercise of the freedom of expression must be "prescribed by law" and "necessary in a democratic society" to serve one of the enumerated interests.

Application of the exceptions in the second paragraph will always turn on the factual and legal context, considered case by case. In specific situations, it has been found that there was no violation of Article 10 in: the application of blasphemy laws to seize a film, the UK's ban on broadcasting interviews with representatives of the IRA, prohibitions on Nazi material, laws against obscenity, even state disciplinary measures against a lawyer who used aggressive or insulting language.

Article 10 must be interpreted in light of other Articles, notably Article 17, which states that nothing in the Convention creates a right to engage in activities *"aimed at the destruction of any of the rights or freedoms set forth in the convention."* Article 17, it has been held, was intended "to prevent totalitarian groups from exploiting, in their own interests, the principles enunciated in the convention." Accordingly, for example, the Court has concluded that it was not a violation of the Convention for the Netherlands to convict extremist right-wing Dutch politicians for distributing racist leaflets. Other provisions affecting the freedom of expression include Article 6, which guarantees the right to a fair trial, and the right to personal privacy in Article 8, which protects a person's honor and reputation against attack, both of which concepts are also reflected in Article 10(2) itself.

Most European countries that are party to the Convention have made it part of their national law, meaning that it can be invoked in the national courts. For many years, the UK declined to do this, but the Convention will be fully incorporated in UK law when the Human Rights Bill 1998 is enacted.

The European Convention has an explicit enforcement mechanism based on judicial review by an independent regional tribunal, the European Court of Human Rights, located in Strasbourg. The most important feature of the Court's jurisdiction is that individuals can bring complaints against Contracting States alleging violations of the Convention. The procedures of the Court are well beyond the scope of this paper. It is sufficient to note that individuals may bring their cases before the Court after exhausting local remedies and that an application must first be presented to the European Commission on Human Rights. The Commission decides on the admissibility of the complaint. If the Commission decides that the case is admissible, it issues a report (which is not binding), and there is a procedure for referring cases to the Court. The Court's judgments on the merits are binding but declaratory in nature. The Court has no power to quash the impugned decisions of the national authorities. The Court may, however, award "just satisfaction" in the form of financial compensation. In most cases, States have been reasonably swift to make the changes in their laws and practices necessary to bring them into conformity with the Court's decision.

Case Law of the European Court Relevant to the Internet

The European Court described the scope and importance of the right of free expression under Article 10 in its landmark decision in *Handyside v. UK:*

— "Freedom of expression constitutes one of the essential foundations of [a democratic society], one of the basic conditions for its progress and for the development of every man. Subject to paragraph 2 of Article 10, it is applicable not only to 'information' or 'ideas' that are favourably received or regarded as inoffensive or as a matter of indifference, but also to those that offend, shock or disturb the State or any sector of the population. Such are the demands of that pluralism, tolerance and broadmindedness without which there is no democratic society."

The Court applies a three-part test. Any restriction on the freedom of expression must be prescribed by law; have as its aim a goal that is legitimate under paragraph 2 of Article 10; and be "necessary in a democratic society" to achieve that goal. The Court has stated that the exceptions in paragraph 2 "must be narrowly interpreted and the necessity for any restrictions must be convincingly established."

At the same time, the Court has concluded that states are allowed a "margin of appreciation" to determine whether a restriction is necessary in light of local circumstances. This means that what can be prohibited can vary from country to country. This is particularly true in the area of morals. Thus, in the *Handyside* case, the Court held that it was permissible for the UK to prosecute the publisher and seize and destroy copies of a certain book even though the book was acceptable in most other countries. In *Sunday Times v. UK*, the court found that states were not entitled to such a margin of deference regarding the "far more objective notion of the 'authority' of the judiciary."

Much of the interpretation of Article 10 turns on the interplay between the concept of "appreciation" and the requirement that any restriction be "necessary in a democratic society." The unique elements of the Internet require a reconsideration of both concepts.

The Court has made it clear that the free expression principles of Article 10 apply differently to different media. The nature and extent of permissible restrictions depends on the nature of the medium. In particular, "the potential impact of the medium concerned is an important factor" to be considered in applying Article 10. The Court has noted that material that might not be proper for broadcast could not be banned from print. The Internet, for all its power, tends to be a less immediate, less inflammatory medium. For example, offensive or heated language that would pose a threat to public order in front of a crowd poses no danger on the Internet when readers are dispersed in location and may even be dispersed over time.

The necessity test has several elements: First, the European Court has made it clear that any government action must be effective, in that it must be reasonably likely to in fact serve one of the permitted governmental interests. Second, the Court has made it clear that any restriction must be proportional, meaning that it cannot be overbroad. Third, the concept of proportionality implies that a government restriction should not be permitted if a less restrictive alternative would serve the same goal while respecting other values such as the primacy of the family.

Various forms of government Internet censorship would violate Article 10 under one or more of these tests. First, none of the proposed methods of control (short of denying access to the Internet altogether) are likely to be effective, given the very nature of the Internet. Users will almost always be able to find ways around the censor, both to post banned material and to access it. As demonstrated by the examples of mirroring and anti-censorship given the borderless nature of the Internet, a user in a repressive country can usually find a host in another country that will host banned content. In addition, to further protect themselves from government controls, speakers can render themselves anonymous/ unidentifiable. Efforts to block offensive material at the national level have proven to be very spotty at best —

even the simple changing of a URL can frustrate a filter. Unencrypted email is extremely difficult to filter, while it is absolutely impossible to filter email if it is encrypted, even at a very low level of security.

Government censorship also will not meet the proportionality test. For example, government bans on information deemed harmful to minors will result in making the same information unavailable to adults, who are entitled to see it.

Finally, in some contexts, the user-controlled nature of the Internet makes government control unnecessary because user control offers alternative means of achieving certain goals. This point could be especially relevant in the area of protection of morals, where the Court has granted states the widest margin of appreciation. Many of the proposed governmental controls on content on the Internet are put forth in the name of protecting children from content that is permissible for adults. But the unique user-controlled nature of the Internet makes government control for this purpose unnecessary, because parents are in a better position than the government to control what their children see, by supervision, training, and, if they chose, by using filtering software. While the use of filtering, labeling and rating tools raises serious freedom of expression concerns, both the US Supreme Court and the European Commission have relied on the availability of filtering software as a reason not to pursue governmental censorship.

This argument does not assume that filtering is effective. GILC members have documented the flaws in various filtering programs, including their overbroad blocking of perfectly appropriate material. So this argument is not in any way an endorsement of filtering software. Further, any government-mandated filtering by schools, libraries or ISPs is censorship and would violate the free expression principles discussed here. See section V.C below. The argument here simply recognizes that filtering software is available to users. Families can use it if they want. If government tried to require families to use it, that would constitute impermissible censorship and probably infringe on other human rights principles protecting the sanctity of the family. But the values supposedly promoted by government censorship in the area of protecting children are already reflected in products available to the end user. The fact that filtering is available to individuals is not a reason for the government to mandate its use; rather, under free expression principles, the availability of filtering software to parents is one reason why governments should not mandate it or otherwise restrict expression on the Internet. It is not necessary for governments to regulate the Internet to protect children because parents can exercise control.

A family's choice to use filtering preserves their moral values without limiting the options of other users. Since there is an alternative means of satisfying the government's goal that also empowers families, the government restriction on speech should violate Article 10. Particularly relevant to the Internet, given the practice of mirroring, are a number of Court decisions holding that prohibition on publishing certain content was not "necessary in a democratic society" if the information was otherwise available. Perhaps the most important case on this subject is the famous "Spycatcher" case, involving the memoirs of a former member of the British Security Service.

The Court held that the injunction against publishing the book was no longer appropriate under Article 10 after the book was published in the United States. (It is noteworthy that the government's interest lost its force when the information was published in another country.) From that point on, since the confidentiality had been breached, the injunction in the UK violated Article 10. In *Weber v. Switzerland*, the Court unanimously found that the sentencing of Mr. Weber to a fine for having breached, at a press conference, the confidentiality of a judicial investigation was not "necessary" for the protection and impartiality of the judiciary because the information had already been disclosed at a prior press conference. In *Vereniging Weekblad Bluf! v. the Netherlands*, the Court followed the same approach with regard to the seizure and withdrawal from circulation of a magazine article on the activities of the Internal Security Services of the Netherlands.

In that case, after the magazine had been seized, the publishers quickly reprinted a large number of copies and sold them on the streets of Amsterdam. Since the information in question had already been made public, the Court concluded that preventing its disclosure was not "necessary in a democratic society." While there was a dispute as to the number of people to whom the information had been made accessible, the court noted that those people "were able in their turn to communicate it to others."

The Court has also recognized a distinction between those who make certain offensive statements, and those who serve as the conduits for that information to the public. The distinction arose in a case concerning the liability of a journalist, but it may have relevance to the question of ISP liability. The Court said that a journalist could not be prosecuted for publishing racist remarks uttered by others. The Court said: "The punishment of a journalist for assisting in the dissemination of statements made by another person in an interview would seriously hamper the contribution of the press to discussion of matters of public interest and should not be envisaged unless there are particularly strong reasons for doing so." Substitute "ISP" for "journalist" or "the press" and one has a good statement of the importance of not holding ISPs liable for content they did not create. Other cases has also drawn a distinction between the author of statements and the conveyor of those statements.

Finally, in *Informationsverein Lentia v. Austria,* the Court concluded that Contracting States are under a positive obligation under Article 10 to take measures to ensure pluralism in the media. The case concerned applicants to set up a radio station and a television station. In Austria, that right was vested solely in the Austrian Broadcasting Authority. The Court found that as a result of technical progress, restrictions in the form of a public monopoly could no longer be justified and therefore violated Article 10.

The Court has decided very few cases based on Article 10's right to "receive" ideas and information and those have focused on claims of access to government files. In *Leander v. Sweden,* the Court held that the right to receive information under Article 10 "basically prohibits a Government from restricting a person from receiving information that others may wish or may be willing to impart to him." In *Z v. Austria,* Application no. 10392/83,

56 DR 13, admissibility decision of 13 April 1988, the Commission held that freedom to receive information is "primarily a freedom of access to general sources of information which may not be restricted by positive action of the authorities."

While the Convention does not apply to private actions, the Court concluded, however, in one case that an official reprimand by a professional association qualified as a public action. This raises the question of whether a "self-regulatory" code of conduct adopted by an association of ISPs would rise to the level of action covered by the Convention. The answer will depend on a country-by-country understanding of the nature of the association, its relationship with the government, the circumstances under which a particular "code of conduct" was adopted, and the mechanism, if any, for enforcing the code and sanctioning an ISP that did not comply. Given governments' increasing reliance on "self-regulation" to achieve public objectives, a broader interpretation of what constitutes public action may be needed.

Declaration on the Freedom of Expression

European countries also manifested their commitment to free speech in the Council of Europe's 1982 Declaration on the Freedom of Expression and Information ("Council of Europe Declaration"). This Declaration reaffirms Article 10 of the European Convention and proclaims that the freedom of expression is *"a fundamental element [of] the principles of genuine democracy, the rule of law and respect for human rights."* The Declaration also provides that the freedom of expression and information is *"necessary for the social, economic, cultural and political development of every human being, and constitutes a condition for the harmonious progress of social and cultural groups, nations and the international community."* The Council of Europe Declaration thus recognizes that the freedom of expression serves not only an individual interest, but the interests of nation states and the international community as well.

Significant in the context of Internet communication, the Council of Europe Declaration recognizes that *"the continued development of information and communication technology should serve to further that right, regardless of frontiers, to express, seek, to receive and to impart information and ideas, whatever their source."* To achieve this high level of protection, the Council of Europe member states agreed to the following objectives:

— "absence of censorship or any arbitrary controls or constraints on participants in the information process, on media content or on the transmission and dissemination of information;

— "the availability and access on reasonable terms to adequate facilities for the domestic and international transmission and dissemination of information and ideas; [and]

— "to ensure that new information and communication techniques and services, where available, are effectively used to broaden the scope of freedom of expression and information."

New Europe and other OSCE Instruments

The 55-member Organization for Security and Co-operation in Europe ("OSCE"), formerly known as the Conference on Security and Co-operation in Europe, sponsored the 1990 Charter of Paris for a New Europe. Signed by 31 countries from Europe, Russia, Canada, and the United States, the Charter proclaims: *"We affirm that, without discrimination, every individual has the right to freedom of thought, conscience and religion or belief, [and] freedom of expression."*

The OSCE's 1994 Budapest Summit Declaration, "Towards a Genuine Partnership in a New Era," complements the Charter by asserting that participating members *"take as their guiding principle that they will safeguard"* *the right to freedom of expression and recognize that "independent and pluralistic media are essential to a free and open society."* The Internet is the most "independent and pluralistic" of all media; it should therefore benefit from the strongest protection against restrictions on the free flow of information.

OSCE member states also have committed to making *"efforts to facilitate the freer and wider dissemination of information of all kinds [and] to encourage co-operation in the field of information."* In accordance with this commitment, and in recognition of commitments made under the Universal Declaration and the ICCPR, the OSCE declared that its member states *"will ensure that individuals can freely choose their sources of information."*

Finally, countries of the OSCE reaffirmed the ICCPR's limitations on the scope of permissible restrictions on the right of free expression. The 1990 Conference on the Human Dimension concluded that any restrictions on fundamental rights and freedoms must be

1) provided by law;

2) consistent with obligations under international law, particularly those made pursuant to the ICCPR and the Universal Declaration; and

3) must relate to one of the objectives of the applicable law and be strictly proportionate to the aim of that law.

The American Declaration of the Rights and Duties of Convention on Human Rights

Regional agreements from the Americas also explicitly embrace the freedom of expression. The American Declaration of the Rights and Duties of Man was the first international human rights instrument, predating even the Universal Declaration. Article IV of the American Declaration states: *"Every person has the right to freedom of... expression and dissemination of ideas, by any medium whatsoever."*

The American Convention on Human Rights ("American Convention") was adopted in 1969 and entered into force in 1978. It is worth quoting in full, for several of its provisions are of particular relevance to current debates concerning the Internet:

— "Everyone has the right to freedom of thought and expression. This right includes freedom to seek, receive, and impart information and ideas of all kinds, regardless of frontiers, either orally, in writing, in print, in the form of art, or through any other medium of one's choice.

— "The exercise of the right provided for in the foregoing paragraph shall not be subject to prior censorship but shall be subject to subsequent imposition of liability, which shall be expressly established by law to the extent necessary to ensure:

a. respect for the rights or reputations of others; or

b. the protection of national security, public order, or public health or morals.

— "The right of expression may not be restricted by indirect methods or means, such as the abuse of government or private controls over newsprint, radio broadcasting frequencies, or equipment used in the dissemination of information, or by any other means tending to impede the communication and circulation of ideas and opinions.

— "Notwithstanding the provisions of paragraph 2 above, public entertainments may be subject by law to prior censorship for the sole purpose of regulating access to them for the moral protection of childhood and adolescence.

— "Any propaganda for war and any advocacy of national, racial, or religious hatred that constitute incitements to lawless violence or to any other similar action against any person or group of persons on any grounds including those of race, color, religion, language, or national origin shall be considered as offenses punishable by law."

As is the case with the international and European counterparts to these agreements, the plain language of the American Convention is clearly applicable to the Internet.

Notably, the American Convention has several features that go beyond other human rights instruments. For one, the American Convention explicitly states that the exercise of the right of freedom of expression *"shall not be subject to prior censorship."* The rule against prior censorship is also reinforced by Article 14, which provides for a right of reply by anyone inured by inaccurate or offensive statements or ideas disseminated to the general public.

In a provision that may be relevant to the problems posed by Internet "self-regulation," the American Convention applies to private action and makes it clear that the right of expression may not be restricted by indirect methods or means. Article 13(3) provides that the *"right of expression may not be restricted by indirect means, such as the abuse of government or private controls over newsprint, radio broadcasting frequencies, or equipment used in the dissemination of information, or by another means tending to impede the communication and circulation of ideas and opinions."*

The American Convention, in language identical to the ICCPR, sets forth a list of permitted grounds for restriction, a list narrower than that in the European Convention: restrictions on speech must be *"expressly established by law to the extent necessary to ensure [either] [r]espect for the rights or reputation of others... or [t]he protection of national security, public order, or public health or morals."*

Article 11 of the American Convention, like other international agreements, protects the privacy of personal communications: "No one may be the object of arbitrary or abusive interference with his private life, his family, his home, or his correspondence."

Enforcement of the American Convention

The protections of the Convention are enforced by the Inter-American Commission on Human Rights and by the Inter-American Court of Human Rights.

The Commission is an institution of the Organization of the American States. It has the authority to conduct investigations and make recommendations to both the OAS and to Member States. It can "prepare such studies or reports as it considers advisable in the performance of its duties." It can issue advisory opinions to governments. And it is required to take action on petitions by individuals or NGOs and "communications" by Member States.

The Inter-American Court of Human Rights is the principal judicial organ of the inter-American system. Only the Commission and the States Parties have standing before the Court; individuals cannot directly institute proceedings. The Court hears cases of an adjudicatory (or "contentious") nature and also can issue advisory opinions. Proceedings are instituted by the filing of an application either by a State Party or by the Commission. An individual wishing to bring his or her case before the Court must file at the Commission (after exhausting domestic remedies). The Commission then takes the case to the Court

The Inter-American Court has noted that the American Convention is more generous in its guarantee of freedom of expression than the corresponding provisions of both the European Convention and the ICCPR. The Court stated in one case:

"Freedom of expression is a cornerstone upon which the very existence of a democratic society rests. It is indispensable for the formation of public opinion. ... It represents, in short, the means that enable the community, when exercising its options, to be sufficiently informed. Consequently, it can be said that a society that is not well-informed is not a society that is truly free."

One of the leading opinions of the court has to do with the indirect means of controlling freedom of expression, and specifically with a form of self-regulation. The Compulsory Membership case involved a United States citizen who was working in Costa Rica as a journalist without being a member of the Association of Journalists as required by Costa Rican law. He was convicted of the illegal exercise of the profession of journalism in the absence of membership in the Association. The Court said that any restrictions on the freedom of expression must meet four requirements: the existence of previously established grounds for liability; the express and precise definition of these grounds by law; the legitimacy of the ends sought to be achieved; a showing that these grounds are necessary to ensure the ends.

The Court placed considerable emphasis on the requirement of necessity, in terms that have relevance to attempts to censor the Internet. Following the rulings of the ECHR, the Court concluded that necessity implied the existence of "a pressing social need." It was not enough to demonstrate that the regulation was simply useful, reasonable or desirable. The necessity and hence the legality of restrictions "depend upon a showing that the restrictions are required by a compelling governmental interest." Furthermore, the court held that in accordance with the principle of proportionality, the restriction must be "closely tailored to the accomplishment of the legitimate governmental objective necessitating it."

The Court noted that the Inter-American Convention prohibited private controls on the freedom of expression. It indicated that the type of private controls prohibited by the Convention might arise when monopolies or oligopolies instituted practices that restricted speech. The association of journalists was another form of private control, albeit one backed up by a law compelling membership. In defense of the rule, it was argued that compulsory membership was the normal way to organize a profession in order to guarantee adequate standards, thus better serving the community. The Court found this argument unpersuasive. In order to demonstrate that the restriction was necessary, it had to be shown that the same results could not be achieved by less restrictive measures.

The Commission in a 1994 report adopted and reiterated the principles expressed by the court. The Commission proceeding involved "desacato" laws, which criminalized expression that offended, insulted or threatened a public official in the performance of his or her duties. The Commission found that such laws did not serve a legitimate purpose and were not necessary. The Commission also adopted a test similar to the Brandenburg test in the united States, stating that "criminalization of speech can only apply in those exceptional circumstances when there is an obvious and direct threat of lawless violence."

The African Charter on Human and Peoples' Rights ("African Charter"), adopted by 50 countries of the Organization for African Unity, declares in Article 9: *"Every individual shall have the right to receive information .*

. . *[and] to express and disseminate his opinions within the law."* The plain language of this provision clearly establishes that the African Charter protects the full range of modes of communication among people, including communication on the Internet, as well as access to information on the Internet. The African Charter also provides that the parties "have the duty to promote and ensure through teaching, education and publication, the respect of the rights and freedoms contained in the [African Charter] and to see to it that these freedoms and rights as well as corresponding obligations and duties are understood." Finally, the African Charter circumscribes any potential restrictions on the fundamental right to free expression; instead, Article 27 provides that individuals should exercise protected freedoms "with due regard to the rights of others, collective security, morality and common interest." The African Charter also has an enforcement mechanism that hears individual cases.

Opportunities for the Human Rights Community

Undertaking a judicial case in order to advance the cause of human rights is always a risky business. It requires careful selection of the complainant, the respondent, and the forum. It calls for a clear-eyed weighing of the chances of success. A poorly conceived case can yield an adverse decision that represents a set back for the cause of liberty.

Mindful of these concerns, it is clear that the international human rights instruments offer opportunities to NGOs seeking to challenge governmental regulation of Internet content and access. In some cases, the most promising venues may be under the regional agreements.

Europe: Individuals or other private parties may seek to take their cases before the European Commission and the European Court, after they have exhausted their domestic remedies. Therefore, an NGO concretely affected by a law or practice could bring a case challenging Internet censorship to the Commission and then to the Court. Complaints in the abstract are excluded, however.

The ECHR also allows the submission of amicus briefs. (Amicus briefs are not accepted by the Commission, although with an applicant's consent it is possible to contribute arguments before the Commission as part of an application.) Article 36(2) of the Rules of the Court provide that "The President of the Court may, in the interest of the proper administration of justice, invite... any person concerned who is not the applicant to submit written comments or take part in hearings." The Council of Europe's Explanatory Report notes that the "person concerned" referred to in Article 36(2) may be a natural or legal person. A person wishing to participate should fax a request to the President of the Court as soon as possible after a case has been brought before the court. A number of NGOs (including Amnesty International and Article 19) have filed such briefs before the Court, and the Court in its judgments has explicitly referred to the arguments and information supplied by amici.

Americas: Under the Inter-American system, while individuals do not have standing to bring their cases directly before the court, they can ask the Commission to take up their cases. Indeed, according to Article 44 of the Inter-American Convention, petitions containing denunciations or complaints of violations of the convention by a State Party may be lodged at the

Commission by any person, any group of persons, and any non-governmental organization legally recognized in one or more Member States of the OAS. These categories of potential complainants with standing are considerably broader than those in most other international human rights instruments. There is no requirement that petitioners be the actual victims of a Convention violation. "Furthermore, there is no requirement that the complainant be within the jurisdiction of the respondent state. ... The reference to [NGOs] clearly recognizes the important role which they may discharge in the protection of human rights. ... It should be noted that it matters not that an NGO be legally present and recognized in the territory of the respondent State Party; it is enough that it is recognized in one or more OAS Member States."

United Nations: In preparing its annual reports, the UN's Commission on Human Rights regularly draws on information provided by NGOs. Likewise, the Human Rights Committee, which oversees compliance with the ICCPR through the reporting mechanism, also accepts submissions from NGOs. Both the Commission and the Committee should be educated on, and urged to examine, Internet issues.

National Laws Restricting Freedom of Expression on the Internet

In the past, it was assumed that a country could control content within its borders, subject to free expression principles, and that publishers had some ability to control and direct the distribution of their materials. (Even in the broadcast realm, there were limits to the reach of most transmitters. But satellite transmission of television signals is forcing a parallel breakdown of borders in the broadcast field.) Thus, in *Handyside,* even though the book at issue was legal in most countries of Europe, Article 10 of the European Convention was not violated by the UK's efforts to prohibit its sale in the UK. If a restriction was justified in a particular country, then it applied to both domestically produced and foreign produced material, even if the foreign material was legal where produced. A magazine printed legally in the Netherlands would have to be tested by German standards if someone wanted to distribute or possess it in Germany.

But this margin of appreciation doctrine — clearly in tension with the language "regardless of frontiers" — was based in large part on the physical nature of the media by which information and ideas were produced and disseminated. Respect for differing legal norms — even though freedom of expression was raised to the level of an international right — was based on the premise that a country had a reasonable chance of success in keeping material out of its territory, at least things like books or reels of film or paintings on canvas, and that publishers had a reasonable chance of success in controlling distribution of their materials.

On the Internet, neither governments nor publishers have this type of control over information, for information is no longer tied to physical objects. The global nature of the Internet should give new relevance to the concept "regardless of frontiers" found in human rights instruments. As Judge Martens said in a separate opinion in the Spyçatcher case, "in this 'age of information' information and ideas cannot be stopped at frontiers any longer." Judges Pettiti and Farinha made the same point in their separate opinion: "In the era of satellite television it is impossible territorially to partition thought and its expression or to restrict the right of information of the inhabitants of a country whose newspapers are subject to a prohibition."

Under human rights principles, expression on the Internet will still be subject to restriction, but without the "margin of appreciation" that has supported restrictions in so many cases. The Internet requires the adoption of a true international standard of review, one that must look to consensus rules generally.

The rise of the Internet also requires a reexamination of the meaning of the concept to "seek and receive" and to "impart" information. National restrictions on local speech have a direct and negative impact on the ability of Internet users around the world to "seek and receive" information and ideas, as well as their right to "impart" information. For example, if citizens of one country are prohibited from discussing political issues critically online, then not only are their rights infringed upon, but also the right of others around the world to "seek and receive" that information is directly implicated. Similarly, a country's efforts to block certain content from outside its border implicates the right of those in other countries to "impart" the information. A new rule is called for: only that content can be prohibited which all (or virtually all) countries agree is prohibited.

Indirect Methods of Control are just as Dangerous as Direct Government Censorship

Internet Service Providers (ISPs) play a special role in the operation of the Internet. While ISPs differ in nature from country to country, most people most of the time access the Internet through an ISP. The crucial role ISPs play in providing access to the Internet has made them the target of some governments' efforts to regulate content on the Internet. Those countries have assumed that if they can control ISPs, they can control content on the Internet.

ISPs do not fit any of the existing media paradigms. They are very distinct from broadcasters. For this reason, it is not legitimate to subject them to regulatory structures designed for other technologies.

There are two sets of arguments against making ISPs responsible for content they do not create. First, trying to make ISPs responsible for information that flows over their systems (but which they did not create) would fundamentally change the nature of the Internet and could destroy its power. Second, there is growing recognition that ISPs cannot technically assume responsibility for content they did not create. The task of sifting information is impossible. It would be so easy to encrypt content, to change addresses, to send images by email.

Technical factors prevent a service provider from blocking the free flow of information on the Internet. First, an Internet service provider cannot easily stop the incoming flow of material. No one can monitor the enormous quantity of network traffic, which may consist of hundreds of thousands of emails, newsgroup messages, files, and Web pages that pass through in dozens of text and binary formats, some of them readable only by particular proprietary tools. As the European Commission noted recently, "it is as yet unclear how far it is technically possible to block access to content once it is identified as illegal."

A second technical problem is that a provider cannot selectively disable transmission to particular users. Electronic networks typically do not allow for the identification of particular users or their national region. ISPs cannot provide material in one country while blocking it in another; such a distinction would require an enormous new infrastructure on top of the current network. Some networking technologies, such as newsgroups, may allow individual operators to select some groups or items and block others. But many technologies, such as the World Wide Web, currently do not support such selectivity.

A number of countries have recognized, after considerable study and debate, that ISPs should not be liable for content they did not create. This reflects a judgment that while ISPs ought to provide law enforcement reasonable assistance in investigating criminal activity, confusing the role of private companies and police authorities risks substantial violation of individual civil liberties. In 1997, Germany adopted a Multimedia Law (the Information and Communications Services Act) which provides that access providers are not responsible for any third-party content to which they only provide access. Providers also are not responsible for "any third-party content which they make available for use unless they have knowledge of such content and are technically able and can reasonably be expected to block the use of such content."

In the United States, section 230 of the Communications Act, 47 United States Code sec. 230, states "No Provider or user of an interactive computer service shall be treated as the publisher or speaker of any information provided by another information content provider." In adopting this provision, Congress specifically found that "the Internet and other interactive computer services offer a forum for a true diversity of political discourse, unique opportunities for cultural development, and myriad avenues for intellectual activity," and it said that its goal was "to promote the continued development of the Internet."

The European Commission also has concluded that regulation of ISPs was not the best way to address content regulation. In its 1996 Communication to the European Parliament, The Council, The Economic and Social Committee and the Committee of the Regions on Illegal and Harmful Content on the Internet, the Commission stated that "Internet access providers and host service providers play a key role in giving users access to Internet content. It should not however be forgotten that the prime responsibility for content lies with authors and content providers."

The Commission stated that blocking access at the level of access providers would go far beyond the limited category of illegal content and "such a restrictive regime is inconceivable for Europe as it would severely interfere with the freedom of the individual and its political traditions." Therefore "the law may need to be changed or clarified to assist access providers and host service providers, whose primary business is to provide a service to customers."

"Therefore, the position of the ISPs should be clarified, and they should not be targeted by the individual governments and law enforcement bodies where the ISPs have no control of the Internet content." The European Parliament in its decision of 13 May 1998 and the Council of The European Union in it recommendation of 28 May 1998 both agreed with the

Commission and concluded, in effect, that ISPs should not be liable for content they did not create.

The "Bonn Declaration" of European Ministers likewise underlined the importance of clearly defining the relevant legal rules on responsibility for content of the various actors in the chain between creation and use. The Declaration recognized the need to make a clear distinction between the responsibility of those who produce and place content in circulation and that of intermediaries such as the Internet Service Providers.

In the EU and in a number of other countries, "self-regulation" has been offered as a viable alternative to governmental control of Internet content. The use of the term "self-regulation" is a misnomer in the context of controlling speech on the Internet. In the normal sense of the phrase, "self-regulation" is when a group of people or companies decide that, in their own best interest, they should themselves regulate how they go about their joint interests. However, what is being suggested by the term "self-regulation" as applied to the Internet is not that ISPs as a group should regulate their own behavior, but rather that ISPs should regulate the behavior of their customers by taking down offensive websites or blocking offensive content.

Under international law, privatized control may be harder to challenge. However, in a number of cases, it may be clear that the ISP is acting under pressure from the government and has, in essence become the agent of the government for carrying out a government policy. What is often promoted as Internet "self-regulation" is actually "privatized censorship." It is consistent with the fairly common occurrence of having a formerly direct government function turned over to a private business.

The backing is still state power and government threat, but the actual implementation and mechanics of the suppression of material is delegated to a trade group.

GILC member Cyber-Rights & Cyber-Liberties (UK) wrote in its report "Who Watches the Watchmen: Internet Content Rating Systems, and Privatised Censorship"

"The current situation at the UK does not represent a self-regulatory solution as suggested by the UK Government. It is moving towards a form of censorship, a privatised and industry based one where there will be no space for dissent as it will be done by the use of private organisations, rating systems and at the entry level by putting pressure on the UK Internet Service Providers. One can only recall the events which took place in the summer of 1996 and how the ISPs were pressured by the Metropolitan police to remove around 130 newsgroups from their servers."

If it can be shown that "self-regulatory" measures are mere proxies for more direct government control, they may be vulnerable to challenge under human rights law. For one, they do not meet the test of proportionality. When ISPs come together to self-regulate certain classes of content in exchange for some limit on their liability for that content, the overwhelming tendency will be to censor more material, rather than less, in an effort by the ISPs to be certain that they have removed any material that might be illegal. Where ISPs are dependent on government grants of liability limitations, their "self-regulating" actions must satisfy the perceived demands of law enforcement, even if this results in removal of legal, protected speech.

Initial reports from "self-regulatory" systems cast doubt on their effectiveness and suggest that the only effective way to combat crime such as child pornography is with well trained police. The two most important hotlines in Europe, the Dutch hotline and the UK hotline, have observed that despite the large amount of complaints they receive, this amount is tiny compared to the vast volume available on the Internet. The effects these hotlines have on dissemination of illegal content is also tiny. The Dutch Hotline, in its annual report, warned that it had absolutely no effect on distribution of illegal content in chat-boxes and E-mail, and that its influence on such distribution in newsgroups was very limited. According to the Internet Watch Foundation Annual Report, of the 4,300 items blocked by private action, "[o]nly the few articles appearing to have originated in the UK are suitable for investigation and action by the UK police." Thus with little measurable law enforcement impact, thousands of presumably legal items were nevertheless removed from the Internet.

Blocking, filtering, and labeling techniques can restrict freedom of expression and limit access to information when used or mandated by governments or their agents. Specifically, such techniques can prevent individuals from using the Internet to exchange information on topics that may be controversial or unpopular, enable the development of country profiles to facilitate a global/universal rating system desired by governments, block access to content on entire domains, block access to Internet content available at any domain or page which contains a specific key-word or character string in the URL, and over-ride self-rating labels provided by content creators and providers.

Government-mandated use of blocking, filtering, and labeling systems are subject to the same limitations under basic international human rights protections as other Internet restrictions: No matter what the means, government restriction on speech or access to speech of others violates basic freedom of expression protections. Filtering is inappropriate in public educational institutions and libraries.

In its statement to the OECD in March 1998, GILC articulated several policy principles related to filtering and labeling:

Global rating or labeling systems squelch the free flow of information: Efforts to force all Internet speech to be labeled or rated according to a single classification system will distort the fundamental cultural diversity of the Internet and will lead to domination of one set of political or moral viewpoints. Such systems will either be easy to use and not have enough categories for all cultures or they will have so many categories to cater to all cultures that they will be unusable. These systems are antithetical to the Internet and should be rejected.

Infrastructure distortions to force labeling must be rejected: Extra-legal means of forcing individuals to use filtering, labels or ratings such as ratings requirements in search engines or default settings in browsers restrict the free flow of information online and distort the basic openness of the Internet.

Transparency must be maintained: Users must be made aware if their Internet access is being filtered, and, if so, based on what filtering system. They must also be able to disable the filtering at any point.

White lists are preferable to black lists: Access to a variety of tools which make positive suggestions (white lists), pointing to certain content, rather than blocking content (black lists), should be encouraged.

Diversity is essential: To the extent that individuals choose to employ filtering tools, it is vital that they have access to a wide variety of such tools.

An Important Guarantor of Free Expression

Central to free expression and the protection of privacy is the right to express political beliefs without fear of retribution and to control the disclosure of personal identity. Protecting the right of anonymity is therefore an essential goal for the protection of personal freedoms in the online world.

Anonymity has been an integral part of the growth and development of the Internet. Some governments are working to extend techniques for anonymity. The Netherlands and the Canadian province of Ontario are pursuing studies on anonymity. The German government has recently adopted legislation that would encourage the adoption of anonymous payments systems for the Internet.

But other efforts are underway to establish mandatory identification requirements and to limit the use of techniques that protect anonymity. For example, in December 1997, the Interior and Justice Ministers of the G-8 endorsed a proposal to require identification for Internet users. Some governments have also tried adopt legislation that would prohibit access to the Internet without the disclosure of personal identity.

Governments should not require the identification of Internet users or restrict the ability to express political beliefs on the Internet anonymously. Efforts to develop new techniques to protect anonymity and identity should be encouraged. The governments of Canada, Germany, and the Netherlands are to be commended for their recent efforts to support anonymity. ISPs should not establish unnecessary identification requirements for customers and should, wherever practicable, preserve the right of users to access the Internet anonymously.

The vast majority of Internet use is for legitimate and indeed positive purposes. The effect of access and use of this global interactive medium has been to promote democracy and civil society worldwide. On the Internet, citizens are not mere consumers of content but also creators of content.

The Internet is a unique communication medium. It is more than a mere industry. Like no other medium before, it allows individuals to express their ideas and opinions directly to a world audience, while allowing them access to other ideas, opinions and information to which they may not otherwise have access.

While the mass media usually responds to the economic and political interests of those who control it, such controls do not presently exist on the Internet. Here, citizens from the most repressive regimes are able to find information about matters concerning their governments or their human rights records that no local newspaper may dare print, while denouncing the conditions under which they live for the world to hear. The Internet allows us an intimate look at other countries, other people and other cultures which few before were ever able to attain. This power to give and receive information, so central to any conception of democracy, can be truly achieved on the Internet, as nowhere before.

Restrictions on the free flow of information on the Internet should be subject to the strongest protections under international law. The free flow of information and ideas is the very essence of the Internet. One state's restrictions on Internet content infringe upon the rights of all Internet users around the world to benefit from a free exchange of social, political, economic, cultural, scientific, and personal information.

Technology surely will outpace states' efforts to restrict the free flow of information on the Internet. New methods of accessing the Internet, for example by satellite, will make territorial boundaries even less relevant to the Internet than they are today. Attempts to suppress information and communication on the Internet, therefore, not only violate international human rights laws, in the end they are likely to be futile.

The Internet industry continues to expand in China, the government continues to tighten controls on on-line expression. As recently as July 11, 2001, President Jiang Zemin condemned the spread of "pernicious information" on the Net and called existing legislation "inadequate." Since 1995, when Chinese authorities began permitting commercial Internet accounts, at least sixty sets of regulations have been issued aimed at controlling Internet content. The broadly-worded regulations represent a clear violation of the right to freedom of expression, and the government is devoting considerable time and resources to trying to implement them.

As of January 2001, sending "secret" or "reactionary" materials over the Internet became a capital crime. Generally, however, persons convicted for their use of the Internet have received sentences of between two and four years, and we are not aware of anyone having been charged under Internet-specific regulations. Instead, they have all been found guilty of violating provisions of the Criminal Code. The elaborate regulatory framework serves, however, as a statement of policy, a justification for monitoring and surveillance, a set of guidelines for what constitutes "illegal" activity, and a deterrent to Internet users.

The government's determination to censor on-line content has grown with Internet usage. Improved infrastructure, introduction of mobile phones, and other low-cost methods of connection to the Internet, as well as increased local language content, have fueled that growth. The main contact points connecting China's Internet system with the worldwide system consists of nine so-called Internet Access Providers controlling the physical lines to the outside world. By July 2001 these access providers accommodated some 620 Internet Service Providers (ISPs) who served in turn some 1,600 Internet Content Providers (ICPs) and an estimated 26,000,000 users by the government's own conservative estimates.

This backgrounder examines the development of China's repressive regulatory framework, its surveillance and closures of Internet cafés, and the detention of Internet users.

Between 1994 and the present, China's rules and regulations on the Internet became progressively more comprehensive, moving from efforts to regulate Internet business to restrictions on news sites and chat rooms. These regulations give the government wide discretion to arrest and punish any form of expression. For example, "topics that damage the reputation of the State" are banned, but an Internet user has no way of knowing what topics might be considered injurious. As the regulatory framework evolved, the Chinese government shifted primary responsibility for control of the Internet from the Ministry for Public Security to the Internet service providers themselves.

In 1994, one year before the Internet became commercially available for individuals in China, the State Council issued the "PRC Regulations for the Safety Protection of Computer Information Systems" which gave the Ministry of Public Security overall responsibility for supervision of the Internet. According to the regulations, Public Security is entitled to "supervise, inspect and guide the security protection work," "investigate and prosecute illegal criminal cases" and "perform other supervising duties." In February 1996, the State Council issued rules on the connection between China's domestic network and the international Internet. These regulations began to shift some of the responsibility for control of content to the Internet companies themselves.

Units providing international inward and outward channels and interactive and interfacing units shall establish a network management center to strengthen the management of their own units and their consumers according to the relevant laws and state regulation, to improve network information security management, and to provide good and safe services to consumers.

Units and individuals engaging in Internet business shall strictly enforce safety and security control systems according to relevant state laws and administrative regulations, and shall not make use of the Internet to conduct criminal activities - including activities prejudicial to state security and the leakage of state secrets - or to produce, retrieve, duplicate, and disseminate information prejudicial to public order or pornographic materials."

Public Security then issued a decree that all Internet users register with a police bureau in their neighborhood within thirty days of signing up with an ISP. Police stations in provinces and cities followed up on this almost immediately. They also set up computer investigation units. In December 1997, the "Computer Information Network and Internet Security, Protection and Management Regulations," issued by the Ministry of Public Security, states:

No unit or individual may use the Internet to create, replicate, retrieve, or transmit the following kinds of information:

1. Inciting to resist or violate the Constitution or laws or the implementation of administrative regulations;
2. Inciting to overthrow the government or the socialist system;
3. Inciting division of the country, harming national unification;
4. Inciting hatred or discrimination among nationalities or harming the unity of the nationalities;
5. Making falsehoods or distorting the truth, spreading rumors, destroying the order of society;
6. Promoting feudal superstitions, sexually suggestive material, gambling, violence, murder,
7. Engaging in terrorism or inciting others to criminal activity; openly insulting other people or distorting the truth to slander people;

8. Injuring the reputation of state organs;

Other activities against the Constitution, laws or administrative regulations.

Units and individuals engaged in Internet business must accept the security supervision, inspection, and guidance of the Public Security organization. This includes providing to the Public Security organization information, materials and digital document, and assisting the Public Security organization to discover and properly handle incidents involving law violations and criminal activities related to computer information networks.

The main two sets of regulations that foreign investors such as AOL will have to confront are the "Telecommunications Regulations Of The People's Republic Of China" and the "Measures For Managing The Internet Information Services," both issued by the State Council and effective from September 25, 2000.

The Telecommunications Regulations state that:

No organization or individual may use telecommunications networks to make, duplicate, issue, or disseminate information containing the following:

1) Material that opposes the basic principles established by the constitution;
2) Material that jeopardizes national security, reveals state secrets, subverts state power, or undermines national unity;
3) Material that harms the prosperity and interests of the state;

4) Material that arouses ethnic animosities, ethnic discrimination, or undermines ethnic solidarity;
5) Material that undermines state religious policies, or promotes cults and feudal superstitions;
6) Material that spreads rumors, disturbs social order, or undermines social stability;
7) Material that spreads obscenities, pornography, gambling, violence, murder, terror, or instigates crime;
8) Material that insults or slanders others or violates the legal rights and interests of others;
9) Material that has other contents prohibited by laws or administrative regulations.

Meanwhile the "Measures For Managing The Internet Information Services" make service providers responsible for content they display. The service providers must record their subscribers' access to the Internet, their account numbers, the Web addresses they call up as well as the telephone numbers they use, and store this information for sixty days. The eight categories of information that is not to be produced on the Internet. Article 16 then goes on saying that if material under these categories is discovered, "it shall immediately stop the transmission, keep the relevant records, and report the situation to the relevant state authorities."

Other regulations that content providers have to face include the "State Secrets Protection Regulations For Computer Information Systems On The Internet" issued by the Bureau for the Protection of State Secrets (State Secrets Bureau) on January 25, but applied retroactively from January 1, 2000.

The management of secrets concerning information on the Internet shall be based on the principle of "whoever places materials on the Internet takes the responsibility." Information provided to or released on Web sites must undergo a security inspection and approval. Inspection and approval should be carried out by related departments. Related units shall, in line with state laws and regulations on guarding secrets, establish and improve a leadership responsibility system for the examination and approval of information intended for the Internet. Units that provide the information shall establish a security system for information examination and approval in accordance with certain work procedures.

Units and users that establish electronic bulletin boards, chat rooms or network news groups shall be verified and approved by the relevant organizations to clarify the requirements and responsibilities concerning the protection of secrets. No unit or individual shall release, discuss or disseminate information about state secrets on electronic bulletin boards, chat rooms or network news groups.

For electronic bulletin boards, chat rooms or network news groups that are open to the public, the host or its higher level competent department shall strictly carry out its responsibilities concerning the protection of secrets, establish a complete management system, and strengthen supervision and inspection. If information related to secrets is discovered, it shall take timely measures and report this to the local authorities for the protection of secrets.

The regulations demand that Internet Access Providers:

> Shall provide instruction about protecting secrets as an important part of the Internet related technical training. Agreements and user rules signed between the controllers of national trunk lines and Internet access providers, and between Internet access providers and users shall stipulate clearly that state laws on protecting secrets must be obeyed and that state secrets shall not be leaked.

Article 15 states:

Controllers of national trunk lines, Internet access providers and users shall accept the supervision and inspection conducted by departments in charge of protecting secrets and shall cooperate with them. They shall assist such departments in investigating illegal actions that divulge state secrets on the Internet. They shall also delete information on the Internet that concerns state secrets, as required by the departments in charge of protecting secrets.

Violation of the regulations mentioned above can lead to severe punishment. Content and service providers may face fines or closure, but users found in violation may face the death penalty for posting material that is not to the government's liking. On December 2000, the "Decisions Of The National People's Congress Standing Committee On Safeguarding Internet Safety" stipulated that:

> in order to maintain national security and social stability, one who commits any of the following acts, which constitute a crime, will be prosecuted for criminal liability in accordance with relevant regulations of the criminal law.

1) Fabricating rumors or slander, or publishing or disseminating other harmful information through the

Internet to instigate subversion of state power, overthrow the socialist system, or incite the splitting of the country to damage national reunification;

2) Stealing or disclosing state secrets, information or military secrets through the Internet;

3) Instigating national hostility and discrimination through the Internet to damage national unity;

Organizing evil cults and contacting cult members through the Internet to damage the implementation of state law and administrative laws and regulations.

In January 2001, possibly as a result of the imminent publication of the Tiananmen Papers, the collection of documents about decision-making by senior Chinese officials with regard to the student protests of 1989, the Supreme People's Court set the ultimate punishment:

Those who illegally provide state secrets or intelligence for units, organizations and individuals outside the country through Internet with serious consequences will be punished according to stipulations of the Criminal Law.... in especially serious cases, those who steal, make secret inquiries or buy state secrets and intelligence and illegally provide gathered state secrets and intelligence to units outside the country will be sentenced to ten or more years of fixed-term imprisonment or imprisonment for life and their properties may concurrently be confiscated by the state. In cases of a gross violation of law and where especially serious harm is caused to the state and people, law offenders may be sentenced to death and their properties will be confiscated by the state.

Internet Cafes

In practice the regulations have led Internet service and content providers and Internet cafés to set up their own monitors. In organizations like Sohu.com, a Nasdaq registered portal based in Beijing, appointed censors are monitoring the chatrooms and the bulletin boards and deleting material mentioned under the eight categories under the September 2000 "Measures For Managing The Internet Information Services." In Internet cafes, managers have appointed people who patrol the monitors checking what material appears on the screen. Both Internet content providers such as Sohu.com and Internet Cafes have issued their own sets of guidelines for users. Sohu.com, for example, gives the following message to clients who want to enter chatrooms: Please take note that the following issues are prohibited according to Chinese law:

1. Criticism of the PRC Constitution
2. Revealing State secrets, and discussion about overthrowing the Communist government
3. Topics that damage the reputation of the State
4. Discussions that ignite ethnic animosity, discrimination or regional separatism
5. Discussion that undermines the state's religious policy, as well as promotes evil cults and superstition
6. Spreading rumors, perpetrating and disseminating false news that promotes disorder and social instability
7. Dissemination of obscenity, sex, gambling, violence, and terror. Cyber-sex is not permitted within the English chat-room.

8. Humiliating or slandering innocent people
9. Any discussion and promotion of content which PRC laws prohibit.

If you are a Chinese national and willingly choose to break these laws, Sohu.com is legally obliged to report you to the Public Security Bureau.

Personnel of the Beijing-based Feiyu Internet Cafe routinely check screens by walking along the 800 computer units and reading over the shoulders of the clients. A note which is placed on a user's monitor to indicate the start of his or her login time, says "The Feiyu Web Bar Warns its Clients: Please do Not Download Web Pages with Illicit, Violent or Reactionary Content..." Content considered "reactionary" can include Falun Gong-related material, dissident web pages or sites promoting the independence of Taiwan or Tibet. Feiyu's website has a link to all major Internet regulations and added some additional ones. Under these rules, mostly issued by the Bureau of Industry and Commerce, Feiyu management is obliged to turn violators in to the local police station. In December, the China Daily reported that police raided the Feiyu Cafe and found some "illegal content," but the management was only fined, and business was back to normal after some hours.

On April 10, 2001, the State Council announced a three-month investigation into Internet cafés and other public Internet service providers. A conference, jointly held by the Ministry of Information Industry, the Ministry of Public Security, the Ministry of Culture and the State Administration of Industry and Commerce, then issued an order saying that within this period, no new Internet cafés would be approved. The moratorium was accompanied by an extensive checking of existing cafés nationwide during which the latter were obliged to re-register. The Legal Daily gave what it termed an "incomplete" progress report on June 14, 2001. By that time, police had investigated more than 56,800 "web bars," of which 6,071 were ordered to disconnect from the Internet. Between April and July 2001, over 2,300 cafés had been closed down altogether. Special measures were taken in some provinces. Police in Liaoning province installed software in 13,500 computers in the province's 5,000 Internet cafes to automatically filter pornographic, illicit and other harmful information. The raids were carried out "in order to rectify and standardize the order of the market economy" according to the paper.

Several individuals have been detained as a result of posting material on the Internet. In all known cases they were sentenced under articles in the Criminal Code.

Qi Yanchen is one of the founders of the China Development Union, a quasi-nongovernmental organization which was banned in late 1998. Qi was detained in late 1999. In September 2000, the Intermediate People's Court in Cangzhou, Hebei Province sentenced him to four years in prison for posting articles and parts of his book, The Collapse of China, on the Internet. The book is critical of China's current social situation. Qi was charged with spreading anti-government messages on the Internet and was convicted after a trial that lasted four and a half hours.

Huang Qi, a computer engineer, was charged with the crime of "instigation to subvert state power." Huang, together with his wife Zeng Li, ran www.6-4tianwang.com, a website designed to find missing persons. On June 3, 2000, authorities in Chengdu,

Sichuan province, detained Huang after they deemed the content posted "subversive." On September 25, Huang Qi was reportedly beaten in detention by three policemen after notes he had taken were confiscated. During the beating, he lost one tooth and got a scar on his forehead, according to a letter he gave to his lawyer in November. On January 2, 2001, the Chengdu City Procuratorate accused Huang Qi of violating Articles 103 and 105 of the Criminal Law. The articles punish actions that involve "organizing national separatism, destroying national unity"; "organizing, plotting or carrying out activities aimed at subverting state political power"; and "overthrowing the socialist system." Huang's trial began on February 13, 2001, but the trial was suspended indefinitely after he reportedly fell ill. It was re-scheduled for June 27, but again postponed. No reason for the delay was announced, nor was a new trial date scheduled.

Jiang was a teacher with the No. 9 Middle School in Nanchong, Sichuan province and owner of the Silicon Valley Internet Cafe in Nanchong. He was detained on August 16, 2000, five days after posting a series of articles critical of the Chinese government on an Internet bulletin board. He was charged with "subverting state political power." The Nanchong Intermediate People's Court sentenced him to two years in prison. In May 2001, a higher court in Sichuan rejected his appeal.

Guo Qinghai, a freelance writer, was arrested on September 15, 2000. On April 3, a court in Cangzhou, Hebei province tried and sentenced him to four years in prison. Guo was charged with "inciting to overthrow state political power." Guo had posted some forty articles on the Internet and published in the Hong Kong based magazine Kaifang calling for political reform. No one informed the family before the two-hour trial began, and as a result no family member attended. Guo did not have a lawyer for his defense.

Lu Xinhua, the author of several articles published on overseas websites, was detained on March 11, 2001 for "subversion." According to the Information Center for Human Rights and Democracy, Lu was formally arrested on April 20.

Yang Zili, a Beijing based computer engineer, is the founder of the Internet site www.lib.126.com. He was detained on March 13, 2001. Authorities have not given an explanation for his detention as yet. Yang had criticized the crackdown against the Falun Gong on his website. He also used the site to teach people how to use proxy servers, a way to circumvent censorship and access sites blocked by the Ministry of Information Industry.

Xu, a reporter and a founding member of the "New Youth Study Group," was detained in Beijing on March 13, 2001 for subversion. He was reportedly targeted for his use of the Internet and his association with the study group, which focuses on political reforms.

Jin, a geological engineer and a founding member of the "New Youth Study Group," was detained in Beijing on March 13, 2001 for subversion. He was reportedly targeted for his use of the Internet and his association with the study group, which focuses on political reforms.

Zhang, a freelance writer and a founding member of the "New Youth Study Group," was detained in Beijing on March 13, 2001 for subversion. He was reportedly targeted for his use of the Internet and his association with the study group, which focuses on political reforms

On April 18, 2001, police detained Chi, a worker in Changchun, Jilin province. They found on him articles with political content which he had downloaded from overseas websites. As of April 2001, he was detained in Lingyuan Prison, Liaoning Province.

Wang was taken into custody on May 6, 2001 from his home in Lingyi, Shandong for "libeling police on the Internet" but it is not clear what the content was of his allegedly libelous remarks.

Hu Dalin was detained on May 18, 2001, apparently for helping his father, a leftwing essayist named Lu Jiaping, post his writings on websites. The authorities were particularly angry over an article by the father about the case of the U.S. spy plane forced to land in China. The article was posted on May 11, 2001.

In June 2001, authorities in Xinjiang Autonomous Region sentenced Liu Weifang, a small business owner, to three years in prison for posting "reactionary articles" criticizing the Chinese Communist Party and its leaders on Internet bulletin boards. He had used his Internet name, lgwf, but authorities traced the messages to him. The Xinjiang Daily said Liu got off lightly because he had admitted guilt.

Wang, a former assistant professor of psychology at Southwestern Normal University in Chongqing, Sichuan, was arrested on June 2, 2001 in Shenzhen for downloading and distributing by e-mail promotional material on the Falungong spiritual movement.

Li, a businessman from central Hunan, was reportedly detained after e-mailing the Chinese language version of The Tiananmen Papers to friends. He was detained in Shaoyang, Hunan, as of July 2001 according to the Hong Hong-based Information Center for Human Rights and Democracy.

1. Agence France Presse, "Jiang Renews Warning Against 'Pernicious' Internet," July 11, 2001.
2. Eight separate ministries or government agencies, led by the Ministry of Public Security, are involved in Internet monitoring and control. They include the Ministry of Information Industry, the Standing Committee of the National People's Congress, the State Council, the Supreme People's Court, the State Bureau for the Protection of Secrets, the State Administration for Press and Publications, and the State Copyright Bureau.
3. "China to Speed up Internet," People's Daily, July 11, 2001.
4. PRC Regulations for the Safety Protection of Computer Information Systems (Zhonghua renmin gongheguo jisuanji xitong anquan baohu tiaoli,) Fazhi Ribao (Legal Daily), February 24, 1994, issued by State Council Order No.147, signed by Premier Li Peng on February 18, 1994.
5. PRC Interim Regulations Governing the Management of International Computer Networks (Zhonghua renmin gongheguo jisuanji xinxi wangluo guoji lianwang guanli zanxing guiding), Fazhi Ribao (Legal Daily), February 12, 1996, issued by State Council Order No.195, signed by Premier Li Peng on February 1, 1996.
6. Management Measures of the PRC Regulations for the Safety Protection of Computer Information Systems (Jisuanji xinxi wangluo guoji lianwang

anquan baohu guanli banfa.), in Jisuanji Ji Wangluo - Falu Fagui (Computers and Internet Laws and Regulations), Falu Chubanshe, Beijing: 1999, p. 99. These regulations were published in full by some Internet cafés. See also the website of Feiyu, an Internet café in Beijing.

7. PRC Telecommunications Regulations (Zhonghua renmin gongheguo dianxin tiaoli),.October 11, 2000, issued by State Council Order No.291, signed by Premier Zhu Rongji on September 25, 2000. Measures for Managing Internet Information Services (Hulianwang xinxi fuwu guanli banfa.), Fazhi Ribao (Legal Daily), issued by State Council Order No.292; signed by Premier Zhu Rongji on September 25, 2000.

8. Regulations Regarding Management of Secrets in Computer Information Systems and International Internet.

9. Decisions of the National People's Congress Standing Committee on Safeguarding Internet Safety.

10. Explanations on Certain Questions Concerning the Specific Application of Law in the Trial of Cases of Stealing, Making Secret Inquiries of or Buying State Secrets and Intelligence and Illegally Providing Gathered State Secrets and Intelligence for Units Outside the Country, in "China: Supreme People's Court on Stealing State Secrets, BBC Monitoring, January 23, 2001, from Xinhua, January 21, 2001.

7
Internet Governance

The Internet has often been hailed as a domain of be nevolentanarchy, a place where free communication is securely in place. It is a "modern Hydra" capable of circumvent in regulation and a" space of no control". As Internetbard John Perry Barlow says, "Governments of the Industrial World, . . . You have no sovereignty where we gather".

Stated less colourfully, the Internet presents challenges to governance. By governance, the existence of some authority able to make globally applicable rules for Un receptive May 2000; accepted 13 August 2001. Research for this study was performed while the author was a resident at the Center for the Sociology of Innovation at the Ecole desMines, Paris, with support from a Chateaubri and Fellowship from the French Embassy in the United States.

The reasons for this lie both in characteristics of the technology, which make control difficult, and in the global reach of Internet communications, which creates jurisdiction all conflict among government regulators.

This "ungovernability " of the Internet, however, is changing. In his book *Code*, Lawrence Lessig documents various strategies to eliminate user anonymity and there by facilitate law enforcement. Likewise, in a recent court case over Internet auctions of Nazi memorabilia that was illegal in France, the Yahoo! Corporation was ordered to detect viewer's location and apply local content regulations to them. As with other technologies spreceding it, as the Internet becomes important to the society around it, attempts are made to integrate it with in existing regulatory structures.

The most significant development in the trend to render the Internet governable is the creation of the Internet Corporation for Assigned Names and Numbers (ICANN). Created in 1998, ICANN is a private, nonprotentity whose official mandate is to perform technical coordination of core Internet resources, most notably domain names (e.g., mycomputer.org). Its site of incorporation lies in California but its authority extends, directly or indirectly, overall users of the Internet.

ICANN has the potential to radically change the nature of the Internet. By putting in place all the mechanisms needed for the creation, promulgation, and enforcement of regulations, ICANN makes effective Internet governance possible for the first time. No longer is the Internet a Hydra that is impossible to control. ICANN's mechanisms for governance can serve any number of possible regulations. The frequency of past attempts to regulate the Internet suggests that the realization of these mechanisms could attract widespread interest in their utilization.

Depending on one's viewpoint, creation of a capability for governance holds the promise or the threat of taming the electronic frontier. For peacemakers and Internet users, this account can help inform policy. That the Internet has a point of central control and that ICANN makes global public policy possible are not widely admitted. Recognition of these governance capabilities justies the application of normative criteria of legitimacy, accountability, and equity to the institution and its processes. This study contributes to a growing body of policy literature that analyses ICANN from the perspective of its historical origins, its legal status, and its institutional design.

This account is also relevant to theoretical debates over the relationship between technological systems and their social context. Recent scholarship in the social construction of technology has emphasized the influence of social factors in shaping technological change. Writers on technology policy have likewise emphasized how designing systems is comparable to writing law, insofar as both activities create social structures that constrain human behaviour. ICANN offers stark evidence of such social structuring, with the domain name system defining important parameters of governance. In what follows, first consider the technological and institutional factors that have inhibited Internet regulation and then continue with a more general discussion of what governance is. Then examine the domain name system, both as a technological and administrative hierarchy, and characteristics that allow for governance. There then follows an analysis of the mechanisms of Internet governance as realized in ICANN. Then, as an illustration of how the governance mechanisms work inpractice.

The Problem of Internet Governance

Regardless of whether one supports or opposes special regulations, it is generally recognized that regulation of the Internet has proven difficult. Copying music, software, and other forms of intellectual property has become simple, and the growth in legal actions against property violators likely represents only a small fraction of incidents of unauthorized copying. Attempts by national governments to control content have foundered on the Internet's global nature and the inter jurisdictional conflicts in regulation.

Barriers to regulation arise in part from characteristics of the technology. Internet communications do not pass through a central channel but are instead passed between many independent networks, and even the messages themselves are broken into packets that may follow different itineraries from source to destination. With multiple independent parties sending multiple independent packets through multiple independent channels, there is no central communication channel that could serve as a control point for promulgating and enforcing regulations.

Regulation also founders on institutional factors. The Internet challenges established jurisdictions. Public authority resides in the state, whose foundational characteristic is the exercise control over a geographically defined domain. Yet the "spaceless" nature of the Internet violates the geographical underpinning of public authority. The mismatch between a network that is global and regulations that are national under mines many attempts at regulation. To make conceptual sense of this situation, it is useful to step back from the details and consider governance from a theoretical level. What is governance? What is needed in order to govern? What is needed for governance of the Internet?

In *Democracy and Its Critics,* Robert Dahl defines what governance is and what is needed to achieve it. He identies a set of "assumptions of a political order" that specify the minimal conditions for a system of governance. The first is an *authority* Governance requires a governor or a sovereign. An entity, be it an individual or a group, must make policy decisions that apply to the members of the polity. A second governance mechanism is *la*w. Laws implement policy decisions. They might take the form of a tax, a license, or simply a binding rule. Third, there must be some mechanism for imposing sanctions. This allows for punishment of those who violate laws. Finally, governance requires the definition of jurisdiction. Jurisdiction defines the space over which the authority makes decisions and within which the laws apply and are enforced by the threat of sanctions. These four mechanisms make governance possible: the governing *authority* can make a policy decision that applies within its jurisdiction, embodying that decision in *law* and imposing sanctions on whomever disobeys.

The Internet's vaunted ungovernability results from the absence of these four mechanisms. Regulation is difficult because authority, law, sanctions, and jurisdictions are noting place. ICANN realizes these four mechanisms through its control of the Internet's domain name system (DNS). Although Internet communication has no central control point, Internet addressing, as realized in the DNS, is centralized. DNS provides the control point from which to regulate users. Moreover, the DNS is also an essential resource, so it provides a means of sanctioning users: denial of access to domain names is the equivalent to banishment from the Internet. The DNS also defines jurisdictions on the Internet. The logical organization of the DNS allows authority to be mapped onto distinct zones. Finally, the contractual foundations of the DNS provide opportunities to promulgate regulations. Taken together, these features render ICANN capable of governance.

In order to understand ICANN, one must first understand the domain name system. The Internet really consists of two "systems," one for communications (the" TCP/IP" protocols) and one for addressing (the DNS). The communication system is the Internet as we commonly know it. It is extremely decentralized—so much so that it is really not a "system" at all but rather just a set of protocols by which independent computer networks can send data packets to each other. It is this decentralized system that informs most public understanding of the Internet and that underlies claims about ungovernability.

In marked contrast to this, the addressing system—the domain name system (DNS)—is centralized. Nearly all Internet communications rely on this single system. The DNS can be thought of as the Internet's telephone book and directory assistance service. Before one computer can communicate with another, it must do the equivalent of contacting directory assistance with a name of the party it wishes to call and receiving back the number to dial. This is a necessary prelude to communication.

Internally, the DNS consists of a database and a dynamic look up service. The database includes pairs of domain names and IP numbers. Domain names are alphanumeric (and hence human-friendly) identiers of computers on the Internet. IP (Internet Protocol) numbers (or addresses) are machine-friendly numeric identiers. For example, a given computer's domain name might be mycomputer.org, and its corresponding IP number might be 12.34.56.78. The DNS resolves domain names into IP numbers. In name resolution, the DNS accepts a domain name from a user and returns the corresponding number. The DNS computers performing name resolution are called *name servers. Only* after resolution has occurred can the user-to-user e-mail or web communication begin.

This two-step procedure is immediately visible on most web browsers (e.g., Net scape Navigator). Once a user enters a domain name, the browser will indicate that it is interacting with the DNS by posting a message like "Looking up host . . ." As long as a few seconds may pass before resolution is performed, and IP number is returned, and actual communication may begin. Sometimes name resolution fails, as when a misspelled name generates an error message like, "Unable to locate host . . . ," and no number is returned. By watching the status messages on a browser's screen, a user can observe the name resolution process. At the heart of the DNS is the Internet's *name space*.

The name space lists (nearly) all computers on the Internet. At the time of this writing the name space contains tens of millions of entries. When one reads statistics about the growth of the Internet, the numbers usually refer to the size of the name space. It provides a rough approximation of the number of individual users: Since most computers listed in the DNS are gateways into private networks with many users, the number of users is much greater than the number of entries in the name space.

In a manner of speaking, the name space *is* the Internet. In order to exist on the Internet, a computer must be listed in the name space. Without a listing (without a domain name and an IP number) a computer cannot be found by others. Removal of a computer's listing from the name space constitutes a kind of banishment, for a computer disappears from the list of addressable computers. Whatever entity controls the name space database effectively controls the Internet. These points are discussed in detail next.

As currently designed, the name space must obey certain design principles. The system's designers claim that the name space must be unique and it must be managed by a single entity. There can only be one database that constitutes the definitive listing of computers on the Internet. Copies may exist, but in dependent name spaces cannot, because they could evolve to have different contents. Were multiple, independent names paces to exist, a given domain name could resolve to different IP addresses depending on which name space was used, which would render communication unreliable. This technologica l imperative of uniqueness underlies the centrality of the DNS, for all communications must use a single, authoritative name space. The Internet's use of a unique name space (with a single administrator) "is a technical necessity, not a policy choice". (Were this design feature not necessary, then numerous possibilities for policy choices would be opened).

Administration

DNS is more than a technical system; it is also an

administrative and policy system. Continuing with our simplied view of DNS as a single, non distribute d database, we can examine the DNS in terms of a single administrator and a single policy authority. The *policy authority* entity makes general rules for changes to the name space, such as allowable domain names, cost of registration in the name space, and restrictions on the addition or deletion of names. The administrator implements these decisions, adding, deleting, and modifying the database entries to reflect the entry, exit, and changed status of computers. The administrator also ensures the reliable operation of the name server.

The DNS's uniqueness requirement means that the policy authority and the administrator exercise monopoly power. There must be a unique name space, and it must be managed by a unique administrator, who, in turn, must be subject to a unique policy authority. "Both the design and the implementation of the DNS protocol are heavily based on the assumption that there is a single owner ormaintainer". Only in this way can the name space be guaranteed to function reliably. Directly or indirectly, this one DNS administrator contracts with every network connected to the Internet. Thus, paralleling the DNS's technical centralization is administrative and policy centralization.

The DNS administrator is also called a *registry*. For a computer to be available on the Internet, the user must approach the administrator and request to be *registered. The* registry registers the computer by adding the user's name-number pair to the name space. The legal mechanism used to connect the central policy authority with users is the *contract*. The Internet is a network of networks; most computers registered in the name space are gateways to private networks managed by net work administrators. Each listing in the DNS is accompanied by a contract between the central DNS administrator and a *network administrato*r.

The contract species rules and conditions for inclusion in the name space, such as the provision of contact information, the payment of an annual fee, acknowledgment of the role of the DNS adaministrator, and so on. Thus, every network in the Internet has a contract with the single entity overseeing the DNS. These contracts implement policy centralization. In this simplied version of DNS it is easy to recognize the feasibility of implementing governance. Only relatively minor medications would be needed to realize the four mechanisms of authority, law, sanctions, and jurisdictions. The DNS defines a central authority for the Internet.

The uniqueness requirement of the name space requires a single central authority, and its decisions apply to all servers in the name space. To render the DNS policy authority a true regulatory entity, its domain of decision making would simply have to expand to public issues, such as intellectual property regulation or content control. Since there are few technical barriers to such an expansion, it would be a policy choice. Thus, realizing governance on the Internet would require simply broadening the range of topics regulated by the DNS policy authority.

The DNS also defines the second governance mechanism law. The law of the Internet is contained in the domain name registration contracts. The provisions of the contracts with network administrators specify the detailed regulations for their actions. To regulate on broader topics, the language in the contracts would simply have to expand. Third, DNS provided a powerful mechanism for sanctions: domain name denial (i.e., the deletion of a user's name–number listing from the name space). This is the power of banishment : Network administrators who refused to obey the regulations in their contracts could be delisted from the name space and made to disappear. Name registration could be treated as a privilege, revocable if a user violated the rules.

The DNS neatly solves the problem of jurisdiction as well. The jurisdiction of the DNS policy authority extends to every computer on the Internet but no farther. The registration contract is the manifestation of jurisdiction . Every network administrator is contractually bound to the DNS's policy authority. Thus, the domain name system provided the means to realize mechanisms of governance. Relatively minor changes to DNS could put each mechanism in place. The DNS policy authority would need to merely broaden its regulatory scope and include those broader regulations in contracts with network administrators. Domain name denial provides an adequate mechanism to sanction rule breakers. The jurisdiction of the policy authority would exactly cover the Internet, no less and no more. In order to fully realize Internet governance, two additional considerations would have to be addressed. The practical some means would be needed to extend policy authority to the individual user. Since the domain name registration contract is between the central authority and a network administrator, individual users are not immediately subject to regulations.

Regulation of individual users could be achieved using a *flow-down contract* administrators generally require users to sign an agreement when they obtain an account, and this user contract could repeat the provisions from the administrators' contract. In this way a single set of regulations could "'flowdown" from the central DNS administrator to network administrator sand from there to all users. Indirectly, all Internet users could be regulated by the central DNS administrator. Violation of the user contract could lead to loss of Internet access for the user account.

Network administrators who failed to enforce ' flow-down contracts on their users would" and themselves subject to domain name denial, that is, banishment from the Internet. A second consideration about governance is more normative in nature. Were the DNS policy authority to become a general-purpose regulator, then careful thought would have to be given to its *legitimacy*. As the scope of its policymaking expanded, its authority would have to be grounded on some appropriate principle. This could be realized by placing ultimate policy authority in the hands of governments or in the hands of a newly constituted representational institution. As discussed later, when policy authority was located in ICANN, it adopted a representational mechanisms to ensure legitimacy.

The discussion so far has built on one simplifying assumption: that the Internet name space is a single, centralized database. In the early phases of the Internet's development this was true. In the 1970s the entire name space was contained in one called "hosts.txt". By 1983, however, the continued growth of the network had led researchers to redesign the name space, and break up the name space into multiple, interconnected pieces. The name space is less centralized than has been presented here. Decentralization renders governance of the Internet much more complex.

DNS and Governance

In fact, the name space is a *distributed* database. In theory, all name–number pairs could be held in one central database as described in the simplied account just given. However, since thousands of name resolution queries occur each second, a centralized DNS computer might be over whelmed. Instead, the name space is distributed among multiple computers to share the workload. The name space exists as a collection of partial, separate databases running on separate computers. Each partial database is called a *zone* (or *zon*e). A zone contains a subset of the total list of name–number pairs. To each zone is associated a *name server* (or *serve*r—a software program for name resolution) and a *host computer* (or *hos*t—the hardware that hosts the zone and name server). Thus, the entire name space is a distribute d database-and-name-resolution system whose building block is the triad of a zone name server program, and host computer.

As in any distributed database, the relationship between the parts is carefully structured. The different zone are linked to each other to form a top-down pyramidal hierarchy or an inverted tree (with its root at the top). At the apex of the hierarchy is a single zone, the *roo*t. The root zone links to multiple zones just beneath it, and those zones in turn link to multiple zones beneath them, and soon. (This is the same structure as the file on a personal computer). The levels in the hierarchy are clearly identified: The root zone links to "top-level" zones, these link to "second-level" zones, then the "third-level" zones, and so on. While a given zone may link downward to multiple zones, it can link upward to just one zone. Directly or indirectly, all zones link upwards to the single root zone. The existence of one root in the name space full is the uniqueness condition.

Subtrees in this distributed database are called *domains. A* domain consists of a zone and all zones beneath it in the hierarchy. Domain names are often referred to by their level in the tree. Domains beginning at top-level zones are top-*level domains* or TLDs; domains beginning at the next level are *second-level domains*, and so on. The domain of the root is the complete name space. The entire system constitutes the domain name system or DNS. The terms zone and *domain* are often used interchangeably, but the former refers to one single "file and the latter refers to that single file and all lower "file in its subtree.

A domain has a name—which, not surprisingly, is called a *domain name*. Well-known top-level domain names are.com, .org, and .net. The largest domain in the name space.com links to millions of lower-level domains. An Internet address like mycomputer.com consists of a second-level domain (my computer) and a top-level domain (.com). A string of domain names, with the different levels separated by dots, uniquely identifies any computer in the name space.

This distributed hierarchy defines relationships of top-down control. Any zone file can be modified to link (include) or delink (exclude) the zones below it in the name space. This is the power of virtual life and death. When a name server is connected to the root via some series of links, then it exists in the name space. Should a zone eliminate a link, the computer or computers below it in the hierarchy will be cut off from the name space. Each server in the hierarchy controls the path to the root for the servers below it.

A registry in Virginia maintains a zone file called .com, a registry in England maintains a zone file called .uk, my parent company hosts a zone is called holding company (which is itself linked to the .com zone file). By my registering my host into an available zone file, it becomes part of the name space and exists in the Internet. Likewise, should my entry in the zone file ever be delinked (the domain name cancelled), my host would disappear from the Internet. The modication to the zone file that allows me to enter or exit from the Internet is not made by me but by the administrator of the next higher zone file.

In the simplified explanation earlier, DNS administration and policy authority were held by a single pair of organizations. In the distributed DNS, every domain has such an administration – policy pair. These organizations are organized according to the distributed structure of the name space: Total DNS administration is a multiorganization hierarchy, with each administrator exercising control over lower level administrators. At the apex of the hierarchy is the root administrator.

Each administrator exercises monopoly control over its immediate zone file (to ensure uniqueness of its portion of the name space). Moreover, each administrator has authority over the entire domain beneath it. When it registers a lower level host, it delegates some authority to the lower level administrator, who exercises monopoly control over that lower zone file. Authority flows down the hierarchy from the root zone administrator, with responsibility for the entire name space, to the individual host computers at the lowest level zones. Each administrator is subject to the policies of higher level entities. In this way, the policies made at the root can be transmitted down through the levels of the hierarchy to apply, directly or indirectly, to all administrators in the DNS. As a group, the administrators serve as the gatekeepers to the name space and hence to the Internet.

Just as zone are joined by links, administrators are joined by contracts. The root administrator formalizes its delegation of authority to top-level administrators in a contract. Some provisions of that contract may be required to be included in subsequent contracts. In this way, regulations may dow down the entire hierarchy to the individual network administrator or possibly even the individual user, as discussed earlier.

As one would expect, the administration of the root zone is particularly important. All other hosts on the Internet access the name space only with a delegation of authority directly or indirectly from the root. Policy authority over the root—the power to add or delete top-level domains—confers direct control over all top-level domains and indirect power over all lower level domains. Authority over the root zone extends to the entire Internet.

In summary, this more accurate account of the DNS reveals another order of magnitude of technical and administrative complexity. Seen as a whole, the DNS is a centralized control point for the Internet. However, because it is a decentralized system, the DNS has an internal structure that relies on hierarchical control and contracts to achieve unified policy capabilities.

Factors in DNS

At this point we can switch from technical analysis to historical analysis. The discussion so far outlined the functioning of the DNS and its structure as a distributed data-base. This historical analysis outlines evolution of the DNS name space and its administrative hierarchy.

The Internet began as a research project in the 1970s, and the computer scientists developing it shaped the evolution of its administrative and policy institutions. This research community was centered in institutions like the Internet Engineering Task Force (IETF), the Internet Architecture Board (IAB), the University of Southern California's Information Sciences Institute (ISI), and the Internet Society (ISOC).

One person, in particular, played a key role in the DNS development: Dr. Jon Postel, a computer scientist at the University of Southern California. Working under a research contract from the US government, Postel exercised policy authority over the root, a function eventually called the Internet Assigned Number Authority (IANA). In his IANA role, Postel maintained the root zone " le, authorized the addition of new top-level domains (TLDs), selected administrators to whom to delegate authority, and performed myriad other tasks. Postel had first assumed this task as a graduate student in the 1970s. As the Internet grew, the significance of Postel's decisions increased accordingly, and by the 1990s his decisions had global implications. Yet policy authority over the root continued to reside in him personally. Since he worked as a government contractor, final authority of officially lay with the U.S. government—but for most of the 1980s and 1990s, Postel exercised personal authority over the DNS.

In 1984, in a document known as RFC920, Postel and colleague Joyce Reynolds defined the evolutionary trajectory of the name space defined the number of top-level zones and the names they would bear. While the name space would always have just one root zone file, Postel and Reynolds announced in 1984 that the top level would consist of some 250 zone files. RFC920 served as the blueprint for the structure of the name space and its future growth. This number of zone files had no basis in technical necessity; it could have been smaller or larger.

RFC920 also specified the character strings to identify the zone files. The 250 TLDs would be divided into two naming classes: There would be six "generic" TLDs TLDs: .gov, .edu, .com, .org, .mil, and .net), and there would be some 244 "country code" TLDs. Again, the particular character strings used in the domain names had no technical significance; they merely had to be unique. However, as chosen, the strings had major policy significance, for their meaning simplied that different zones would have different uses. The 250 TLDs defined a name space partly based on function (.com for commercial, .mil for military, etc.) and partly based on geopolitical identifiers (country names). Decided long before the Internet's global significance emerged, the number of TLDs and the meanings attached to them would have lasting consequences.

While RFC920 defined the DNS structure and naming conventions, its implementation proceeded incrementally over many years. Implementation of the TLDs required selecting an administrator to maintain the zone file and to operate the name server. Furthermore, the implementation of the generic TLDs proceeded very differently than the country code TLDs: The U.S.

government selected the former, while IANA selected the latter.

While Postel/IANA possessed policy authority over the root, the administrator of the root was a private company: Network Solutions, Inc. (NSI). NSI took its orders from IANA, but ultimately operated under contract with the US government. NSI both administered and exercised policy authority over .com, .net, and .org.

Growth in .com made NSI both wealthy and powerful. After the U.S. government opened the Internet to commercial use in 1994, registrations in .comexploded. By the late 1990s, .com had grown to over 10 million registrations—more than half of the entire name space. This concentration of growth in the name space was not an inherent feature of the DNS, but rather occurred as an unfore seen development—a combination of good marketing by NSI and widespread acceptance of the DNS naming convention, which identified .com as the commercial domain.

Ultimately, the .com domain contained so much of the total name space that it rivaled the root for its importance for the overall network. Charging an annual fee of $35 per registered name, NSI collected hundreds of millions of dollars of revenue from its monopoly of the Internet's one commercially named domain. In contrast to NSI, administrators of country code TLDs resembled IANA: They were usually nonprotect organizations, often affiliated with university research centers. Since IANA had defined zone files in terms of country codes and had created just one zone file per country, there was just one administrator in each country. Each of them constituted an implicit national monopoly: the .fr registrywas France's only registry, the .uk registry was the sole UK registry, and so on.

Although there was no technical basis for national monopolies, the naming convention in RFC920 implied such a system. Organizationally, the system of national ccTLD monopolies was reminiscent of the system of national telephone companies (PTTs), which operated as national monopolies in many countries. By October 2000 the full name space consisted of over 30 million name–number pairs. Since IANA had not expanded the number of top-level domains since issuing RFC920, most growth in the name space occurred in second-level domains. Most of that was contained in a single TLD, .com, where NSI had registered over 18 million hosts. NSI's .org and .net TLDs contained another 5 million hosts. The rest of the name space was mostly distribute d in various country code TLDs. Aboveit all, Jon Postel at IANA oversaw delegations of authority to new administrators .

Thus the DNS as it existed toward the end of the 1990s was considerably more complex than the system described earlier. First, it was decentralized. The change from hosts.txt to the decentralized DNS occurred in 1983. Second, over the years numerous non technical developments had shaped the system. Most TLDs bore country code identifiers, which associated them with geopolitical entities (countries). One zone file in the hierarchy, .com, contained nearly the entire name space (thereby somewhat defeating decentralization). In the community of nonprotect DNS administrators , Network Solutions was emerging as a commercial giant. Most importantly, policy authority for the entire DNS lay with one person, Jon Postel. The DNS was complex—and rife with potential conflicts.

Nonetheless, the DNS could still be used to realize the mechanisms of governance. Although more complex arrangements would be needed than those discussed earlier, a decentralized DNS could still be used to realize authority, law, sanctions, and jurisdictions.

Decentralization would not significantly affect the realization of two mechanisms: law and sanctions. Even with the addition of multiple levels of hierarchy, 'flow-down contracts could still bring rules down to users. Decentralization would require a longer cascade of flow-down contracts but would not otherwise affect this mechanism. Likewise, domain name denial could still serve as a sanction. With each administrator in the name space, from the root on down, exercising monopoly control over its zone file, each one could delink lower level hosts from the name space. Name registration could still be treated as a privilege, revocable if a registrant violated the rules.

Decentralization would render the other two governance mechanisms considerably more difficult to realize, however. Decentralization fragmented authority and jurisdiction, especially in the country code domains.

Policy authority and jurisdiction would still be unified at the root. IANA could make rules for the entire name space and promulgate them down the hierarchy. However, at the top-level domains (TLDs) it would encounter another authority that might challenge it. The distinction between generic TLDs (gTLDs) and country code TLDs (ccTLDs) would inhibit unity of authority and jurisdiction.

ccTLDs are associated with countries, and most countries already have policy authorities: their national governments. National governments could claim jurisdiction in ccTLDs bearing their country code. Although national governments' domains were lower in the DNS hierarchy than IANA, it would be awkward for IANA to assert authority over them. An Internet governance institution would be in a poor position to challenge a national government's right to make public policy. Even if a national government was unaware of the DNS (as was often the case), the proactive exercise of policy authority by IANA might provoke a national government to act. Thus it would be difficult for the policy authority at the root to exercise policy authority in the ccTLDs.

Making matters more complex, among the ccTLDs there would be a plethora of authorities. Country code TLDs were independent from each other, and each could make its own policies in its domain, potentially resulting in a host of divergent and conflicting policies. Decentralization of the DNS had created hundreds of authorities, each with an implicit claim of jurisdiction over their ccTLD. Thus it would seem that integrated governance of the Internet would be impossible. The engineers' decision to organize the name space according to politic allines, as codified in RFC920, had fragmented authority and jurisdiction.

In the gTLDs, in contrast, integrated governance would be possible. IANA could regulate domains like .com, .org,and .net, because these domains had no accountability to authorities outside of the DNS. Any authority they possessed in the DNS was only by way of a delegation from IANA. Furthermore, although gTLDs were only a small number of the total set of domains, they contained the lion's share of all users. Effective authority in just these domains would still affect most Internet users.

Thus fully integrated governance would not be possible in the DNS—but a workable degree of governance would be. The realization of a single authority and a single jurisdiction in .com, .org, and .net would be straightforward. Moreover, such a jurisdiction would include most users, given the heavy concentration of registrations in the gTLDs. Policy authority at the root could regulate them by flow-down contracts backed by the threat of domain name denial. This would reduce but not overcome the problem of fragmented authority.

To further mitigate the fragmentation of authority, IANA and national governments could seek to coordinate policies. Although there were hundreds of ccTLDs, registrations were unevenly distribute d among them. Domains like.uk or .jp contained many more registrations than others like .bg (Bulgaria). Coordination between IANA and just the largest ccTLDs would bring the Internet much closer to integrated governance by bringing most of the outstanding users under the same policies.

One could speculate that additional policy coherence could be achieved by pressuring any recalcitrant ccTLD authorities. Were a small ccTLD to resist enforcing some policy backed by IANA and by large governments, the larger parties could challenge the policy authority of the smaller national governments. IANA could exercise its ability to delink a top-level domain or reassign it to a more compliant administrator. In this way, smaller ccTLDs might be coaxed or bullied into adopting policies agreed on by larger players. Overall policy coherence would be improved.

In closing this section, a final issue must be addressed: the role of the U.S. government. The U.S.

government employed Jon Postel and Network Solutions, and it claimed" final authority over the root zone file. Although IANA was the highest policy authority in the DNS, IANA itself operated under policy authority of the United States. Were Internet governance mechanisms to be implemented, and were the status of the United States not to change, then the United States would be the final authority over the Internet. This again might cause tensions with other national governments, which would find themselves subordinate to the United States.

In summary, a decentralized DNS would not allow for full realization of mechanisms of governance. Law and sanctions could be easily realized, but authority and jurisdiction would be fragmented. Located in the gTLDs, most users could be regulated by IANA. Bringing the entire name space under IANA's authority, however, would require negotiation with many autonomous national authorities.

ICANN

Having reviewed the DNS, we can now turn to the Internet Corporation for Assigned Names and Numbers (ICANN). Created in 1998 and still evolving at the time of this writing, ICANN realizes the governance potential in DNS, lever aging Internet addressing to achieve global governance. Not only has it created the capabilities for regulation, it has even employed them: In 1999 ICANN promulgated global public policy that defined intellectual property rights in domain names.

By the late 1990s the DNS had come under severe stress from a variety of sources. The Internet had rapidly outgrown its original institutions , most notably the very personal nature of IANA, whose legitimacy was based on the reputation of one man. Should something have happened to Jon Postel, IANA could have become unstable. Another source of stress arose from entrepreneurs wishing to compete with NSI's monopoly: They began proposing alternate name spaces, new TLDs (e.g., .web), and independent registries. This threatened to fragment the name space.

The global nature of IANA was another issue. The United Nations' International Telecommunications Union (ITU) became involved and sought to assume authority over the name space. National governments and the European Commission became interested, too; they perceived a threat to their sovereignty from U.S. control of this new global information infrastructure. Disputes over sovereignty and jurisdiction were heating up. Intense conflicts also began to emerge over domain names that matched trademarks (e.g., coca-cola.com). The United Nations' World Intellectual Property Organization (WIPO) and U.S. interest groups applied intense political pressure to install trademark regulations in domain names. Making this political mix all the more volatile was that these conflicts developed in "Internet time"; every passing month witnessed exponential growth in the size of both the network and the political stakes.

The process by which the research community, trade mark interests, communication businesses, and national governments came together to create a new institution tore place IANA is documented elsewhere. Here we are interested in the product of that long and contentious process: ICANN.

ICANN is best understood as a set of semi-autonomous institutions. That set includes not only

ICANN as a corporation but also some external entities like a committee of national governments and the TLD administrators. The four mechanisms of governance are mixed deep in ICANN's administrative system and so can be difficult to identify. In what follows, analyse ICANN's features in terms of their governance-related functions.

The new ICANN corporation replaced Jon Postel as the policy authority over the root. ICANN solved the problem of stability: A person was replaced by an institution, so that the IANA could function independently of any one individual. ICANN also partially solved the problem of intergovernmental conflict: ICANN was private, and its by law sex plicitly for bade government officials from serving on the board. Thus although its authority would extend globally, that authority was ostensibly nongovernmental and would not conflict with national governments' sovereignty. Furthermore, with a mission to engage in simple technical coordination of the Internet, ICANN claimed to have no public policy role.

The problem of legitimacy was addressed by the composition of the board of directors. A person, Postel, was replaced by a collection of representatives; legitimacy through expertise and personal reputation was replaced by legitimacy through accountability to stakeholders. ICANN's board represented different functional and geographic constituencies. Of 19 directors, 9 represented technical expert groups, another 9 represented users, and the final director was the organization's top staff person.

ICANN's board, however, was itself subject to a higher authority: the U.S. government. The U.S. Department of Commerce (DOC) retained ultimate control of the root, leaving ICANN policy decisions subject to a potentialve to. Despite the much-publicized privatization, the United States never completely ceded its hold over the Internet. As an official "fact sheet" of the DOC stated, "The Department of Commerce has no plans to transfer to any entity its policy authority to direct the authoritative root server". Thus the Internet was international and privatized but only under the watchful over sight of the U.S. government. (Whether the United States will eventually cede full authority to ICANN is not currently known.)

Beneath the root, contracts extended the authority of ICANN and the United States down to the administrators of the gTLDs and the ccTLDs. The generic TLDs proved more willing to sign on, since NSI administered nearly all of them and was under pressure from the United States to participate in ICANN. Following some bargaining over conditions NSI and ICANN reached agreement in 1999. ICANN thereby achieved policy authority in the most populous domains. The ccTLDs proved more circum spect, and as late as 2001 ICANN was still reporting small progress in this area. Top-down policy authority in these domains failed to be established and remained one of the most difficult issues in the system.

The implicit conflict of authority between ICANN and national governments manifested itself in the Governmental Advisory Committee (GAC). The GAC was an official ICANN advisory committee in which national governments could meet, discuss, and coordinate their actions. Individually, each national government could assert policy authority over the zone file bearing its country code .Together, in GAC, the national governments could coordinate policy.

GAC's first acts were to establish the legitimacy of members' claims to policy authority. First, GAC declared," The Internet naming system is a public resource in the sense that its functions must be administered in the public or common interest". By defining the DNS as a public good, similar to electromagnetic spectrum, GAC prepared they way for governmental oversight. Then GAC linked that public interest to national governments' authority: "ultimate public policy authority over the relevant country code domain] rests with the relevant government". This justified the claim by national authorities that ccTLD domains were under their jurisdiction.

Thus ccTLD administrators found themselves under two authorities—and they asserted a third of their own. ICANN claimed that ccTLDs' authority derived from its higher authority over the root; if administrators did not flow-low ICANN's policies, ICANN could redelegate authority to another party. For their part, national governments claimed that their zone file was a public resource under their authority. A third approach was backed by ccTLD administrators, who cited policy documents that located authority in the "local Internet community" rather than in ICANN or in governments. This prescription would render the administrator s accountable to Internet users in their home country rather than to their government or ICANN.

GAC members sought to resolve this ambiguity in their favour by requesting from ICANN a veto power over ccTLDs similar to the U.S. power over the root. GAC proposed that ICANN's power of redelegation be given to national governments: "when ICANN is notified by the relevant government or public authority that the [administrator] has contravened the terms . . . ICANN should act with the utmost promptness to reassign the delegation". Country code managers would have access to the root only as long as their national government allowed it. ICANN resisted this arrangement, which would have subordinated it to national governments. At the time of this writing the fragmentation of authority over the ccTLDs remained unresolved.

The GAC forum allowed national governments to coordinateon a variety of other policies. GAC began developing a "best practice" document for country managers, so that national authorities could standardize their operations. Once common policies were defined, each national government could promulgate and enforce those practices in its own jurisdiction.

Thus the multiplicity of authorities caused jurisdictional fragmentation. ICANN claimed jurisdiction over the entire name space and, hence, over all users. Likewise, the U.S. jurisdiction extended over ICANN and so over the entire name space. At the top level of the name space, however, jurisdictional conflicts merged. The jurisdictions defined by the generic TLDs posed little problem; there ICANN prevailed. In the country code TLDs, however, national governments claimed jurisdiction. This prevented ICANN and the United States from realizing one unified jurisdiction in the name space. Still, the vast majority of Internet users found themselves in ICANN's sole jurisdiction.

Although ICANN regulated users, it did not have direct contact with users. Instead, a four tiered system was implemented, with ICANN at the top, users at the bottom, and two kinds of organization—registries and *registrars* —in between. At the top ICANN used its authority to make regulations. Beneath it, registries maintained the zone files and operated the servers (as described earlier). Beneath the registries came the registrars, who served as the retail interface to users. They performed customer-oriented tasks of leasing and servicing domain names to users, often bundling these with additional services like Internet service provision. Finally, at the bottom tier were users (or network administrators, who, in turn, contracted with individual users).

Flow down contracts spanned these levels. ICANN's regulations were embodied in contracts with registries, which included the regulations in their contracts with registrars, who included them in their contracts with network administrators. Policies "flowed down" from ICANN to registries to registrars and ultimately to private networks. The terms of the contract defined the laws of the Internet.

At each level, ICANN backed up contracts with the threat of domain name denial. Registries who disobeyed could have their domain redelegated. Registrars who disobeyed could lose their access to registries, so they would no longer be able to offer domain names to users. Users who disobeyed could have their domain names removed from the name space or assigned to someone else.

ICANN's Registrar Accreditation Contract was the primary mechanism for promulgating law. Any organization that wished to serve as a registrar had too bey the terms of this contract. It included an open-ended requirement: "Registrar shall comply . . . with all ICANN- adopted Policies" As ICANN policies changed and the accreditation agreement evolved so could the conditions imposed on domain name usage. It was this contractual blank check that most clearly gave ICANN the right to exercise broad governance activities. The contract's provisions had to be repeated in lower level contracts between registrars and users, guaranteeing that regulations would flow from ICANN to the registrars and eventually to users. These regulations were enforceable with clear sanctions: "The [domain name] holder shall agree that its registration of the [domain] name shall be subject to suspension, cancellation, or transfer pursuant to any ICANN- adopted policy . . . for the resolution of disputes".

Thus the basic governance mechanisms were flow down contracts backed up by domain name denial. The accreditation contract stipulated the regulations for the Internet, and the power to revoke domain names provided the sanction for enforcement. Internet users could only enjoy access to the name space if they obeyed ICANN's rules; if they broke the rules, they could see their domain name suspended, cancelled, or transferred.

Global Public Policy

The preceding discussion of DNS, governance, and ICANN's institutional design has been largely descriptive and analytical. What is reviewed here is mostly established fact. If one accepts the four part definition of governance, and if one admits that those mechanisms are indeed present in ICANN, then it is not controversial to state that ICANN has the capability to engage in Internet governance. So far, little has been said about whether ICANN exercises that capability or whether the system of governance is legitimate.

ICANN not only has the capacity to govern, it has also done so. ICANN has made global public policy. Shortly after ICANN's governance capabilities were implemented, they were put into practice. In August 1999 ICANN promulgated its first major policy: the Uniform Dispute Resolution Policy (UDRP), which mandated a procedure for deciding who has intellectual property rights in a domain name (ICANN, 1999 b). The UDRP illustrates how ICANN's governance mechanisms work in practice. The UDRP also constitute s ICANN's first global public policy.

In the late 1990s domain names became valuable, with names like yahoo.com and amazon.com becoming important business assets. As the value of domain names rose, disputes arose over name rights. Some disputes arose when individual s allegedly registered trademarks in anticipation of selling them to their owner; other arose when owners allegedly attempted to wrest control over desirable characterstrings from other users. Sometimes ownership rights conflicted with rights of fair use or free speech. The trouble with such conflicts was that existing trademark law was inadequate for many disputes: Trade mark law was national, whereas many disputes were international. Legal mechanisms to settle international disputes in domain names were expensive and awkward to employ.

ICANN's UDRP defined procedures for resolving domain name disputes, thereby effectively setting rules of ownership and property. Disputes would be settled through an alternative dispute resolution procedure, in which certified private arbitrators would decide the question of rights based on criteria defined by ICANN. Arbitration decisions could be enforced by removal or transfer of the disputed name. It was a "voluntary" system in that parties who were unsatisfied by the outcome of arbitration could still resort to existing judicial forums for judgment. However, since existing forums were extremely costly, the UDRP would in most cases provide the final decision on property rights. The UDRP had de facto the force of law.

The implementation of the Uniform Dispute Resolution Policy (UDRP) illustrates ICANN's use of all four governance mechanisms. First, the UDRP was developed with input from staff and various parties and ultimately approved by the ICANN Board in an exercise of its authority. Second, the policy was codified into law through the Registrar Accreditation Agreement. ICANN made the UDRPa condition for registrar access to the name space, and registrars had to include the UDRP in their retail contracts with users (it had to flow down"). Third, the UDRP included sanctions: Users who refused to agree to the policy in advance were denied access to the name space, and users who were found to be in violation of the UDRP could have their names deleted or reassigned (banishment). Finally, the UDRP applied in ICANN's jurisdiction. The policy regulated domain name usage in the .com, .net, and .orgdomains. In country code domains, where ICANN's authority did not immediately apply, the decision to adopt the UDRP lay with country code administrators . At the time of this writing, the policy had been adopted in some domains but not in all.

In making the UDRP, ICANN made global public policy. The UDRP regulates something of public value: rules of property. Rules of property, such as trademark, copyright, and intellectual property, are traditionally made by governments. The U.S. Constitution , for instance, specifies rules of intellectual property protection in patents. At the global level, the reason for a lack of regulation is not that property rules are somehow less public, but that there has been no recognized public institution to make such rules. ICANN stepped into this void. By making global rules on property, ICANN made a decisions on public values. Although the UDRP may not have been a policy of enormous import—property rights in domain names is a relatively small area of regulation—it was a significant first step into policymaking.

If ICANN makes global public policy, then it is appropriately evaluated by such policy criteria as legitimacy, accountability, and equity. Indeed, it is around issues like these that most controversies have erupted. Here, briefly review some of the issues that have arisen around the ICANN board's legitimacy.

U.S. policy for the creation of ICANN was laid out in the Department of Commerce "White Paper," which defined principles for ICANN. Two principles there were particularly relevant to legitimacy: ICANN should be committed to "private, bottom-up coordination," and it should be committed to "representation . . . [providing] input from the broad and growing community of Internet users". Some of these principles became embodied in ICANN's by laws, especially in the mechanisms for representation on the board.

In a number of instances these principles of legitimacy were not convincingly upheld. In a move that generated considerable public out cry (and hearings in the U.S. Congress), the first set of interim directors was appointed with no public participation or consultation. Instead, the selection process was conducted behind closed doors in a process later described even by Jon Postel as "undemocratic and closed". However, it was this board that promulgated the Uniform Dispute Resolution Policy.

The ICANN board was also implemented unevenly. The directors for the nine expert representatives were seated within approximately 1 year of ICANN's creation, and those directors quickly moved to weaken the seats reserved for Internet user representatives. In a series of board meetings in 1999 and 2000, the appointed and expert directors sought to eliminate, reduce, or delay the implementation of the elected directors (Klein, 2000a). In so doing, they repeatedly revised the corporate bylaws that constrained board actions. As one top government official declared to them at their meeting in July 2000, "the Board is increasingly giving the impression of being extremely cavalier in changes to the bylaws". Shortly thereafter, the board decided to modify the bylaws again to defer the final round of director elections until 2002—fully 4 years after the creation of ICANN.

Finally, ICANN's early board gave evidence of preferring industry professionals to represent Internet users. In the first, partial round of director elections, the board" labelled most of the nominee slots for user representatives with candidates of its own choosing, selecting individuals from telecommunications giants like France Telecom, Fujitsu, Deutsche Telekom, and Verizon. This tendency to favour the telecommunications supply industry over Internet users attracted the notice at ICANN's July 2000 meeting, of an Australian government official, who stated, "[ICANN] runs the risk of potentially becoming a de facto industry association". The legitimacy of the board to make decisions affecting all Internet users was again weakened by this tendency for some interest groups to seek (and arguably to achieve) disproportionate influence on the board.

With ICANN making global public policy, its lack of legitimacy was striking. Although the elections of 2000 brought some user representation to ICANN, they fell short of implementing the degree of representation called for in ICANN's original bylaws.

Institutions are not static entities; they grow over time and often expand their areas of activity. Such seems likely for ICANN. As an Internet governance entity, what policies might ICANN promulgate in the future?

Perhaps the most likely area of policy expansion is in intellectual property protection. Such expansion of rights has been actively championed since the beginning of the ICANN process and would be consistent with the initial direction of ICANN's activities. The UDRP could be expanded to give special registration rights to owners of celebrity names, famous marks, geographical names, and so on. ICANN could become a global regulator in the service of property and e-commerce.

Control over the name space could also be leveraged to promote social justice. ICANN and ccTLD monopolies could raise funds for a universal service fund to overcome the global digital divide, allowing poorer countries to pay less for Internet access than wealthy countries. In private conversations with this author, some ICANN directors from developing countries have supported such policies.

ICANN's capabilities could also be used for content regulation. Sites violating content regulations could be censored by having their domain names revoked or redirected. Domain name denial was used in this way in the case of voteauction.com, which operated a site containing illegal content (an online mechanism for the buying and selling of votes). The registrar for the domain cancelled the registration to suppress its content. In theory, ICANN could enforce regulations broadly using similar mechanisms.

ICANN could become a vehicle for taxation, perhaps serving as a means whereby governments collected commerce taxes or whereby ICANN funds its own initiatives. With domain names available from one sole source, users would have to either pay the fee or suffer denial of access. Indeed, both U.S. legislators and disgruntle d ccTLDs have accused ICANN of levying taxes.

Finally, ICANN could become a vehicle for U.S. national policy. In times of war or terrorism, countries opposing the United States could see their domains removed from the Internet. Individual registrations could be cancelled or redirected to reduce the effectiveness of hostile entities. The relationship between ICANN policy and U.S.national policy had already come up when the U.S. Department of Commerce had approved the addition of the.ps domain—for Palestine—to the root zone. Although the United States did not pursue its narrow national interest, the case attracted attention because of the potential for conflict.

8

Information Security

The need to protect sensitive and critical federal data has been recognized for years in various laws, including the Privacy Act of 1974; the Paperwork Reduction Act of 1980, as amended; and the Computer Security Act of 1987. However, information security has taken on new significance as both reliance on computers and vulnerabilities associated with networked systems have increased. This is because the same techniques that agencies are employing to help cut costs and improve service—interconnected systems, readily accessible information, and paperless processing—are also factors that increase the vulnerability of operations and data to unauthorized modification and disclosure and to potentially devastating interruptions in service. Agency managers have the primary responsibility for ensuring the security of their information resources, and they are in the best position to assess the risks associated with their programs and to develop and implement policies to mitigate these risks. However, since enactment of the original Paperwork Reduction Act in 1980, OMB has been responsible for developing government wide guidance on information security and overseeing agency practices.

Because of the breadth, significance, and complexity of this oversight challenge, it is important that OMB develop all possible strategies and assets—especially processes, staff expertise, and relevant information—to support its relatively small staff in fulfilling this responsibility.

Over the past 4 years, GAO has issued over 30 reports describing serious information security problems at major federal agencies, and agency inspectors general have issued numerous others. Our analysis of the most recent of these reports for the 15 largest federal agencies found that 10 agencies had serious information security weaknesses, some of which have existed for years. Material weaknesses were not reported for the other five agencies. However, independent reviews of computer-related controls at three of these five agencies were either not performed or were very limited.

The most common problems reported were (1) poor controls over access to sensitive and critical data and (2) incomplete and untested disaster recovery plans—weaknesses that essentially preclude an agency from reasonably ensuring the integrity, confidentiality, and availability of critical and sensitive computerized data, such as tax payer information and federal financial records. Examples include the following:

— Estimates by the Department of Defense indicate that attacks on unclassified computer systems and networks are a serious and growing threat to our national security, including Defense's ability to execute military operations and protect sensitive information. Defense data indicate that Defense may have experienced as many as 250,000 attacks in 1995 and that the number of attacks is doubling each year.

Successful attacks by outside intruders have shut down systems and corrupted sensitive data. However, estimates based on tests conducted since 1992 showed that less than 1 percent of attacks on Defense's systems were detected and reported. Although no summary costs have been developed, Defense officials estimate that the cost of such incidents is at least tens of millions of dollars per year.

— Annual audits since 1993 have found that due to poor computer controls, IRS cannot ensure that the confidentiality and accuracy of taxpayer data are protected and that the data are not manipulated for purposes of individual gain. Specifically, controls have not prevented users from unauthorized access to sensitive programs and data files, numerous users have been allowed powerful access privileges that could allow circumvention of existing controls, and security reports used to monitor and identify unauthorized access to the system are cumbersome and virtually useless to managers for monitoring activity.

— In March 1995, the Office of Personnel Management Inspector General reported that federal retirement program assets were "highly vulnerable to loss or misuse" because of electronic data processing weaknesses, primarily excessively broad user access privileges, related to systems that maintained 2.1 million annuitant files and generated $36 billion in benefit payments during fiscal year 1994.

Individual audit reports describe varying causes for specific weaknesses at individual agencies. However, our audits have shown that an underlying factor is poorly managed security programs that do not proactively and systematically assess risk, monitor the effectiveness of security controls, and respond to identified problems. Such programs are essential to ensure that management and technical controls, including actions to correct identified weaknesses, are effective on a continuing basis.

As part of its various efforts to explore and develop policies associated with a range of information security issues, in February 1996, OMB issued a revised version of its central guidance to agencies on developing an effective information security program. Like the previous version, issued in 1985. "Security of Federal Automated Information Resources," establishes a minimum set of management controls that are to be included in federal automated information security programs. These include assigning responsibility for security, developing a system security plan, screening and training individual users, assessing risk, planning for disasters and contingencies, and reviewing security safeguards at least every 3 years.

It also requires agencies to clearly define responsibilities and expected behaviour for all individuals with access to automated systems and to implement security incident response and reporting capabilities. OMB worked extensively with the National Institute of Standards and Technology, agency security managers Written comments submitted by numerous organizations and individuals and the remarks of agency officials that GAO interviewed indicate that the revised guidance is generally considered to be a valuable and necessary update that recognizes the increasingly open and interconnected computer systems that support agency operations.

Comprehensive oversight requires independently identifying management issues, focusing attention on these issues, and ensuring appropriate resolution of identified problems. Policy analysts in OMB's Office of Information and Regulatory Affairs and program examiners in OMB's Resource Management Offices have monitored selected security issues at individual agencies. However, the scope and depth of efforts intended to uncover critical information security issues vary among agencies, and these efforts are often reactive. GAO met with OMB program examiners for 11 agencies.

Of these, examiners for eight agencies essentially reacted to recognized problems, saying that they had little expertise regarding information resource management and related security issues. They said that they only considered security when it was raised as a significant issue by agency managers or auditors and, then, usually as it pertained to a specific program or system. Examiners for two other agencies had taken a somewhat more proactive look at the agencies' automated operations, including security; while the examiner for the remaining agency said that program examiners almost never considered systems-related issues, including security, as part of their examinations.

As for focusing on management issues, although OMB's revision of Circular A-130 focused general attention on the importance of information security programs, OMB has not systematically monitored compliance with its guidance or the effectiveness of security programs at individual agencies, even though problems in several agencies have been reported for years. While analysts in OMB's Office of Information and Regulatory Affairs have gained a high-level understanding of agency programs through informal discussions with agency personnel, most program examiners, who usually obtain more detailed information about individual agency operations, generally do not consider the effectiveness of an agency's overall information security program.

OMB obtains little documented information to help it proactively oversee agency information security programs. It has routinely obtained agency annual internal control assessments required under the Federal Managers Financial Integrity Act and Strategic Information Resource Management Plans. However, these documents vary significantly in level of detail regarding security issues and are often of little value for overseeing security practices. OMB generally does not obtain the more detailed self assessments of information security that agencies should be using as the basis for these summaries.

OMB program examiners cited independent audit reports as one of their most useful sources of information because they provided an independent assessment of agency operations. However, in the past, independent audits of computer security have not routinely been performed for all major agencies. Audits performed under the CFO Act of 1990 promise to make such independent audit information more routinely available because, in practice, such audits generally include evaluating and testing controls over information security. In the early 1990s, selected segments of federal operations became subject to annual financial statement audits under the Act, and in 1994, this audit requirement was extended to all major federal entities by the Government Management Reform Act. As a result, the percentage of federal expenditures that is audited has been steadily growing, and is expected to reach 98 percent by fiscal year 1997.

However, significant aspects of some agencies' operations, such as those involving sensitive medical records, are not likely to be covered by financial statement audits. For this reason, it is important for OMB, as well as agency managers, to coordinate their reviews of CFO Act audit reports and their reviews of other types of information security assessments, such as self assessments. When viewed together, these audits and assessments may provide a more comprehensive view of agency information security and allow OMB and agency officials to identify gaps in review coverage.

In light of the growing significance of information security and the widespread reported weaknesses, it is essential that OMB take advantage of all opportunities to leverage its resources and take advantage of available information. In this regard, OMB can analyse the increasing amount of audit information that is becoming available due to recently expanded requirements for annual financial statement audits of federal agencies, under the CFO Act. Although CFO Act audits pertain primarily to financial management systems, OMB's Office of Information and Regulatory Affairs and Office of Federal Financial Management could use them, in conjunction with agency self assessments, to determine if all key systems had been reviewed at an individual agency and to monitor actions to correct reported information security problems.

Also, the recently established CIO Council can serve as a forum for addressing government wide information security issues, raising security awareness, and developing a strategic approach to better understanding the security problems facing federal agencies and improving federal information security programs. The Council, established in July 1996 through Executive Order, is intended to be "the principal interagency forum to improve agency practices on such matters as the design, modernization, use, sharing, and performance of agency information resources." It is chaired by OMB's Deputy Director for Management, and its membership includes CIOs at all major federal agencies.

To enhance OMB's ability to oversee and improve federal information security programs, GAO is making the following recommendations to the Director of OMB:

— Advocate and promote the CIO Council's adopton of information security as one of its top priorities and development of a strategic plan for (1) increasing awareness of the importance of information security, especially among senior agency executives, and (2) improving information security program management government wide. Initiatives that the CIO Council should consider incorporating in its strategic plan include;

— developing information on the existing security risks associated with nonclassified systems currently in use;

— developing information on the risks associated with evolving practices, such as Internet use;

— identifying best practices regarding information security programs so that they can be adopted by federal agencies;

— establishing a program for reviewing the adequacy of individual agency information security programs using interagency teams of reviewers;

— ensuring adequate review coverage of agency information security practices by considering the scope of various types of audits and reviews performed and acting to address any identified gaps in coverage;

— developing or identifying training and certification programs that can be shared among agencies; and

Identifying proven security tools and techniques.

—Direct the Office of Information and Regulatory Affairs, the Office of Federal Financial Management, and the Resource Management Offices to (1) supplement their current reviews of audit reports to include reviewing audits conducted under the CFO Act in order to identify any findings related to information security and (2) use this information, in conjunction with reports on agency self assessments, to assist in proactively monitoring the scope of such reviews and the effectiveness of agency information security practices.

— Encourage the development of improved sources of information with which to monitor compliance with OMB's guidance and the effectiveness of agency information security programs. This could include engaging assistance from private contractors or others with appropriate expertise, such as federally funded research and development centers.

— Direct the Office of Information and Regulatory Affairs to develop and implement a program for increasing program examiners' understanding of information security management issues so that they can more readily identify and understand the implications of information security weaknesses on agency programs.

Agency Comments and Evaluation

In written comments on a draft of this report, OMB agreed that information security is an important management issue and stated that certain of the report's recommendations are meritorious. In particular, OMB said that it will encourage the CIO Council to adopt information security as one of its top priorities and that it will review (1) the training and related materials provided to program examiners and (2) the availability of improved sources of information. However, OMB disagreed with the report's tone, which it characterized as suggesting "that OMB has not been dedicating sufficient resources in the past to overseeing the agencies' information security activities, and that therefore OMB in the future should dedicate more of its resources to this objective." In addition, OMB stated its concern that the report overemphasizes OMB's role and that this could distract federal agencies from their responsibilities as the primary managers of federal information security.

GAO agrees that agency managers are primarily responsible for information security. GAO's audit efforts related to information security over the past few years have focused almost exclusively on individual agency practices, and it has made dozens of related recommendations to agency officials. Thirty products resulting from this work and containing these recommendations are listed at the end of this report. The results of this work led GAO to identify a pattern of government wide information security weaknesses.

In light of the pattern of weaknesses that GAO has identified and the increasing importance of information security in virtually every aspect of federal operations,

OMB has a vital leadership role to play in promoting and overseeing agency security practices. This role was recently reemphasized in the Information Technology Management Reform Act of 1996 and in revisions to the Paperwork Reduction Act, which together explicitly outline OMB's responsibilities for over seeing agency practices regarding information privacy and security. Information security has become a consideration in the management of virtually every major federal program and in billions of dollars in annual information technology investment decisions. For these reasons, GAO believes that information security, as well as other information management issues, merits a high priority relative toot her budget and management issues.

In this regard, GAO's recommendations are focused primarily not on increasing the amount of OMB resources but on increasing the impact of OMB's current resources by taking advantage of newly available audit information, discussed in chapter 4, and by expanding staff expertise. These actions, at a minimum, are needed to help address growing concerns over the adequacy of federal information security. GAO also believes that periodic oversight reviews of agency information security programs would be beneficial but that such reviews could be performed by interagency teams under the auspices of the OMB-chaired CIO Council.

As federal agencies expand their use of information technology, they face an increasing challenge to protect the integrity, confidentiality, and availability of information that is vital totheir missions. Like the nation as a whole, our government is becoming increasingly dependent on widely interconnected computer systems and the electronic data they maintain. These systems and data are essential to carry out critical operations, such as tax collections; safeguard billions of dollars in assets, such as military equipment and accounts receivable; and deliver basic services, such as social security payments and other benefits. Reliance on these systems and on electronic data is revolutionizingthe way that agencies collect, process, store, and disseminate information. However, without effective controls, such reliance also can increase the risks of financial loss, unauthorized access to sensitive information, and devastating interruptions in service.

To provide a government wide overview, this report summarizes the results of our reviews of information security at individual agencies and of similar assessments performed by others. The report also describes OMB's oversight of federal agency practices regarding information security and identifies opportunities for improvement. We performed this review in response to a request from Senator John Glenn, Ranking Minority Member, Senate Committee on Governmental Affairs, that we examine a broad range of federal information security issues. Subsequently, Senator Ted Stevens, Committee Chairman, also expressed interest in these issues.

Information security is a growing concern because the federal government, like the nation as a whole, is becoming increasingly dependent on computerized information systems and electronic records. These systems and records are fast replacing manual procedures and paper documents, which in many cases are no longer available as" backup" if automated systems should fail. The potential risks associated with reliance on electronic systems and records are exacerbated because more and more systems are being interconnected to form networks or are accessible through public telecommunication systems, making the systems themselves and the data they maintain much more difficult to protect from unauthorized users or outside intruders.

All major agencies rely on computer systems to provide critical support for their operations, and even greater reliance is planned for the future. In addition, agencies are increasing their use of inter connected systems and electronically transmitted data in order to streamline operations, make federally maintained data more accessible, and reduce paperwork.

Most notably, the Department of Defense has a vast information infrastructure that includes 2.1 million computers, 10,000 local networks, and 100 long-distance networks. The majority of the information maintained on Defense's computers is sensitive but non classified data essential to daily operations, such as commercial transactions; payroll, personnel, and health records; operational plans; and weapons systems maintenance records. In addition, Defense uses the Internet, a global network interconnecting thousands of computer networks, to exchange electronic mail, log on to remote computer sites, and obtain files from remote locations.

Civilian agencies are also increasingly reliant on interconnected systems, including the Internet, and on electronic data. The following examples illustrate just a few of the ways that agencies are expanding their use of information technology to support critical operations.

— Law enforcement officials throughout the United States and Canada rely on the Federal Bureau of Investigation's National Crime Information Center computerized database for access to sensitive criminal justice records on individual offenders. According to the Bureau's fiscal year 1997 budget submission, the system is available to 78,000 authorized users and processes an average of about 2 million transactions daily.

— The Internal Revenue Service (IRS), which relies on computers to process and store millions of taxpayer records, views electronic filing of tax returns as fundamental to its future operations. The number of individual income tax returns filed electronically increased from 4.2 million in 1990 to about 14.8 million for the first 3 and a half months of 1996. IRS goals include significantly increasing the number of electronically filed returns and eventually eliminating paper returns for a large segment of filers.

— The Customs Service relies on automated systems to process entry declarations, which totaled over 39 million in fiscal year 1994 and led to payment of over $20 billion in duties. Although many entry declarations are submitted as paper documents, a growing number are submitted electronically.

— The Department of Agriculture is reducing the use of paper food stamp coupons through its electronic benefits transfer program. Under the program, individual recipients' monthly benefits are recorded in a central computer file. Individuals then use "credit card" type cards with secret personal identification numbers to draw on these benefits and pay for their groceries. During fiscal year 1995, about 630,000 households participated in the electronic benefit transfer food stamp program. According to the Federal Electronic Benefits Transfer Task Force, the program could potentially cover over 10 million households.

— Medicare part B claims that were submitted and processed electronically jumped from 36 to 72 percent between 1990 and 1994, and further increases are likely. Medicare part B covers physician services, outpatient hospital care, medical supplies, and other health benefits, such as emergency ambulance service. The program cost $60 billion in fiscal year 1994, and, according to OMB, costs are expected to double over the subsequent 7 years.

Unfortunately, the same factors that are so important to streamlining federal operations—interconnected, often widely-dispersed systems; readily accessible information; and paperless processing—are also factors which increase the vulnerability of these operations and data. Specifically, the threats to agency systems and the potential for harm have increased because

— the move to more interconnected systems has provided greater numbers of individuals access to extensive databases of information through widely distributed networks of computers;

— agencies are placing greater reliance on electronic records, in some cases eliminating paper records; and

— intruders, including criminals, are becoming more skilled at defeating security techniques designed to protect computer systems and electronic information.

When systems are not adequately protected the potential for malicious and criminal acts is enormous. For example, by obtaining access to data files, an individual could make unauthorized changes for personal gain, such as diverting payments or reducing amounts owed on debts. Similarly, an individual could obtain sensitive information about business transactions or individuals, which could then be sold or used for malicious purposes. By obtaining access to computer programs, an individual could make unauthorized changes to these programs, which in turn could be used to access data files or to process unauthorized transactions, such as improper payments. Also, an intruder could eliminate evidence of unauthorized activity, thus, significantly reducing the likelihood that such activity would ever be detected.

Further, in an inadequately protected network environment, an agency's operations could be sabotaged from remote locations by altering or destroying critical data and programs, or by introducing malicious code, such as viruses, to damage or congest system operations. Significant damage could also occur as a result of accidental errors and deletions by authorized users. Regardless of the individual user's intent, in today's high-speed, highly automated, and interconnected computing environment, thousands of transactions could be erroneously processed or enormous amounts of data could be destroyed or disclosed before an agency detected the damage.

In addition to access control risks, computer facilities andelectronic media can be damaged or otherwise rendered unusable by fires, floods, contamination, and other man made and natural disasters. If an agency does not have adequate contingency plans and preparations for such unexpected events, it may be forced to suspend critical operations or it could lose data and software that are difficult and costly, or even impossible, to replace.

The need to protect sensitive federal data maintained on automated systems has been recognized for years in various laws and in federal guidance. The Privacy Act of 1974, as amended; the Paperwork

Reduction Act of 1980, as amended; and the Computer Security Act of 1987 all contain provisions requiring agencies to protect the confidentiality and integrity of the sensitive information that they maintain. The Computer Security Act definessensitive information as "any information, the loss, misuse, or unauthorized access to or modification of which could adversely affect the national interest or the conduct of Federal programs, or the privacy to which individuals are entitled under the Privacy Act, but which has not been specifically authorized under criteria established by an Executive Order or an Act of Congress to be kept secret in the interest of national defense or foreign policy."

The adequacy of controls over computerized data is also addressed indirectly by the Federal Managers Financial Integrity Act (FMFIA) of 1987 (31 U.S.C. 3512(b) and (c)) and the Chief Financial Officers (CFO) Act of 1990. FMFIA requires agency managers to annually evaluate their internal control systems and report to the President and the Congress any material weaknesses that could lead to fraud, waste, and abuse in government operations. The CFO Act requires agency CFOs to develop and maintain financial management systems that provide complete, reliable, consistent, and timely information. Under the act, major federal agencies annually issue audited financial statements. In practice, such audits generally include evaluating and testing controls over information security.

In accordance with the Paperwork Reduction Act of 1980, OMB is responsible for developing information security policies and overseeing agency practices. In this regard, OMB has provided guidance for agencies in OMB Circular A-130. Security of Federal Automated Information Resources." Since 1985, this circular has directed agencies to implement an adequate level of security for all automated information systems that ensures (1) effective and accurate operations and (2) continuity of operations for systems that support critical agency functions. The circular establishes a minimum set of controls to be included in federal agency information system security programs and requires agencies to review system security at least every 3 years.

Responsibility for developing technical standards and providing related guidance for sensitive data belongs primarily to the National Institute of Standards and Technology (NIST), under the Computer Security Act.OMB, NIST, and agency responsibilities regarding information security were recently reemphasized in the Information Technology Management Reform Act of 1996.

Our objectives were to (1) provide a general overview of the adequacy of federal information security at major federal agencies based on reported information, (2) identify and categorize the most significant information security weaknesses reported, (3) identify the general causes of reported weaknesses, and (4) assess OMB' efforts to oversee agency information security practices. Toaccomplish these objectives we analyzed the results of our evaluations of computer-related controls at five major agencies since June 1993.

These agencies included the Internal Revenue Service and the U.S. Customs Service, which are both part of the Department of the Treasury; the Department of Education; the Department of the Army; and the Department of Housing and Urban Development. Weper formed most of these assessments as part of our financial statement audits at these agencies. While such audits focus on the security of the data supporting the financial statements, they include evaluations and tests of general controls that affect a significant segment of the agencies' computerized operations.

A list of GAO reports and testimonies that address the adequacy of information security at federal agencies is provided at the end of this report. We supplemented reviews of our own audits with an analysis of 149 other reports on major federal agencies to determine if information security weaknesses had been reported and, if so, what types of weaknesses were reported. The reports we reviewed resulted from independent audits by agency inspectors general issued between September 1992 through March 1996, and from agency self assessments required under FMFIA for fiscal years 1994 and 1995. The agencies covered included the Departments of Agriculture, Defense, Education, Energy, Health and Human Services, Housing and Urban Development, Justice, Labor, Transportation, the Treasury, and Veterans Affairs; the General Services Administration; the National Aeronautics and Space Administration; the Social Security Administration; and the Office of Personnel Management. Together, our analyses covered the 15 major departments and agencies that are responsible for spending or safeguarding the largest amounts of federal resources. In total, these agencies accounted for over 98 percent of all federal outlays during fiscal year 1995.

We based our analyses almost exclusively on reported findings. Although we spoke with inspector general audit managers at several agencies to clarify information that had been reported, we did not assess the quality or completeness of any of the inspector general audits or agency self assessments covered by our survey.

To augment information included in reports on individual agencies, we met with members of the steering committee of the Federal Computer Security Managers Forum, an information-sharing group established by NIST, and we reviewed various OMB and NIST documents, as well as related laws.

To obtain information on OMB's oversight efforts, we met with officials from OMB's Office of Information and Regulatory Affairs (OIRA), Office of Federal Financial Management, and Resource Management Office branches responsible for overseeing programs at 11 of the 15 agencies included in our review. In addition, we met with senior information resource management officials and security program managers at five agencies to discuss their interactions with OMB and other agencies responsible for providing guidance and assistance regarding information security issues. These five agencies are the Departments of Agriculture, Health and Human Services, Treasury, and Transportation and the Office of Personnel Management.

Our review was performed in Washington, D.C., from July 1995 through May 1996 in accordance with generally accepted government auditing standards. We requested written comments on a draft of this report from the Acting Director of OMB or his designee. OMB's Deputy Director for Management provided written comments on a draft of this report. These comments are discussed in the "Agency Comments and Our Evaluation" sect. Recent audits show that weak information security is a serious government wide problem that is putting major federal operations at risk.

Between September 1994 and April 30, 1996, serious weaknesses were reported for two-thirds of the agencies covered by our review, and for half of these agencies the weaknesses had been reported for at least 5 years. A fundamental cause of these weaknesses is that agencies have not implemented security programs that provide as systematic means of assessing risk, implementing effective policies and control techniques, and monitoring the effectiveness of these policies and techniques.

Of the 15 agencies included in our review, serious information security control weaknesses were reported for 10 from September 1994 through April 1996. The two most commonly reported weakness indicate fundamental deficiencies in the ability of agencies to protect federal information and the continuity of federal operations. The first was poor access control, which increases the risk that an individual or group could inappropriately modify or disclose sensitive data or computer programs for purposes such as personal gain or sabotage. The second most commonly reported weakness was inadequate disaster planning, which increases the risk that an agency will not be able to satisfactorily recover from an unexpected interruption in critical operations. Many of the identified weaknesses have remained uncorrected for years. Of the 10 agencies with reported weaknesses, FMFIA reports for 5 showed that the problems had remained uncorrected for 5 years or longer.

Examples of reported problems include the following:

— Estimates by the Department of Defense indicate that attacks on unclassified computer systems and networks are a serious and growing threat to our national security, including Defense's ability to execute military operations and protect sensitive information. Defense data indicate that Defense may have experienced as many as 250,000 attacks in 1995 and that the number of attacks is doubling each year. Successful attacks by outside intruders have shut down systems and corrupted sensitive data. However, estimates based on tests conducted since 1992 showed that less than 1 percent of attacks on Defense's systems were detected and reported. Although no summary costs have been developed, Defense officials estimate that the cost of such incidents is at least tens of millions of dollars per year.

— During our audit of the IRS' fiscal year 1995 financial statements, we found that, as reported since 1993, controls over sensitive information were inadequate.

Although corrective actions are under way, as detailed in previousreports, IRS could not ensure that the confidentiality and accuracy of taxpayer data were protected and that the data were not manipulated for purposes of individual gain. Specifically, (1) controls did not prevent users from unauthorized access to sensitive programs and data files, (2) numerous users were allowed powerful access privileges that could allow circumvention of existing controls, and (3) security reports used to monitor and identify unauthorized access to the system were cumbersome and virtually useless to managers for monitoring activity. In addition, back-up and recovery plans were inadequate to provide reasonable assurance that IRS service centers could recover from disasters.

In June 1994, we reported a variety of computer-related control weaknesses at the Customs Service, including that thousands of internal and external users had inappropriate access to critical and sensitive programs and data files. In May 1995, the Department of the Treasury Inspector General reported that despite attempts to correct the problem, the weaknesses continued to exist.

— In June 1994 and June 1995, we reported that controls over the Department of Education's Federal Family Education Loan Program (FFELP) did not adequately protect sensitive data files, application programs, and systems software from unauthorized access, change, or disclosure. These controls are critical to Education's ability to safeguard FFELP assets, maintain sensitive loan data, and ensure the reliability of financial management information about the program. The Department reported that FFELP had $77 billion in outstanding loan guarantees as of September 30, 1994.

— The Department of Health and Human Services (HHS) first reported the lack of a formal, well-coordinated system security program in its Administration for Children and Families in its fiscal year 1990 FMFIA report. In December 1995, HHS reported that the Administration still had not implemented fundamental computer security program elements such as risk assessments and independent reviews of contingency plans for sensitive systems supporting this $17 billion dollar per year program.

— The Department of Justice first recognized automated data processing security as a weakness in 1985. Although Justice reported in February 1996 that it has made department wide security improvements, it also reported that some components had not completed and tested continuity of operations plans, developed policies for computer and telecommunications security, or conducted required risk assessments of component computer systems.

— In March 1995, the Department of Agriculture's Inspector General reported that controls over access to computer software programs and data were inadequate to prevent unauthorized activity at the Department's National Finance Center. The Center processes billions of dollars in payments and sensitive information for itself and other agencies, including payroll, retirement savings, administrative and travel payments, and property management information.

— In March 1995, the Office of Personnel Management Inspector General reported that federal retirement program assets were "highly vulnerable to loss or misuse" because of electronic data processing weaknesses, primarily excessively broad user access privileges, related to systems that maintained 2.1 million annuitant files and generated $36 billion in benefit payments during fiscal year 1994.

Serious information security weaknesses may also exist for some of the five agencies for which no weaknesses were reported. This is because audit reports at one agency specifically stated that computer-related controls had not been reviewed as part of the audit. Also, audit managers at two other agencies said that their computer audit capabilities were limited, and they could not readily determine what, if any, work they or their contractors had performed in this area.

For the 10 agencies with serious reported weaknesses, auditors made 90 new recommendations for specific corrective actions in reports issued from September 1994 through May 1996. In addition, these reports referred to numerous recommendations made in prior years that had not yet been fully or effectively implemented.

Although most agencies have reported actions initiated or planned to correct their weaknesses, a recurring condition reported in GAO, inspector general, and FMFIA reports is that agency actions, while resulting in some improvement, are not completed promptly and do not adequately address identified problems. Recent audits at IRS, Education, and Customs all found that, while some improvements had been made, corrective actions at those agencies had been repeatedly delayed or were incomplete.

As with Defense, the costs of agencies' information security weaknesses cannot be determined because agencies generally do not keep summary records of security violations or account for the cost of responding to such violations. In addition, due to poor controls and lack of user awareness, it is possible that many violations are not being detected or reported.

Security Programme Management

A well designed and managed security program with senior-level support is essential for ensuring that an agency's controls are appropriate and effective on a continuing basis. In this regard, managing information security is similar to managing risks associated with other aspects of agency operations. The program should establish a process and assign responsibilities for systematically (1) assessing risk, (2) promoting user awareness of security issues, (3) developing and implementing effective security policies and related control techniques, (4) monitoring the appropriateness and effectiveness of these policies and techniques, and (5) providing feedback to managers who may then make adjustments as needed. Such a program can provide senior officials a means of managing information security risks and the related costs rather than just reacting to individual incidents.

Without a well designed and managed program, security controls may be inadequate; responsibilities may be unclear, misunderstood, and improperly implemented; and controls may be ineffective or inconsistently applied. Such conditions generally result in insufficient protection of sensitive or critical resources and, conversely, may result in disproportionately high expenditures for controls over low-risk resources.

Individual audit reports describe varying causes for specific control weaknesses at individual agencies. However, in our reviews of information security controls, we found that the major underlying factor was lack of a well managed information security program with senior management support. For example, in May 1996, we reported that Defense had not established a comprehensive computer security program and had not assigned responsibility for ensuring that such a program was implemented. As a result, Defense information security policies were dated, inconsistent, and incomplete; user awareness was insufficient; and security personnel were inadequately trained.

Similarly, in August 1995, we reported that IRS had no proactive, independent information security group that was systematically deployed to review the adequacy and consistency of security over IRS' computer operations. Instead, IRS was addressing information security issues on a reactive basis. In June 1995, we reported that information security weaknesses at Education resulted from the Department's overall weak security administration and failure to develop and implement key policies and procedures. Several of the inspector general audit reports that we reviewed also indicated that agency managers were not taking the steps needed to ensure that controls had been implemented and were operating properly.

To gain an additional perspective on the causes of poor controls, we met with selected members of the steering committee of the Federal Computer Security Managers Forum, an information-sharing group established by NIST. These officials said that additional support from senior management would allow them to establish more effective programs. According to forum members, a lack of management support can result in inadequate resources devoted to information security, a situation that limits the ability of security program managers to address security needs proactively.

A number of factors can contribute to the perception of a lack of senior management support for information security. First, as with other types of internal controls, senior managers may view security efforts as impediments to the efficient accomplishment of the agency's mission. This is because security controls cost money to implement and monitor, and, generally, they diminish the ease with which systems and data can be accessed and updated.

In addition, some senior managers may be unaware of the full range of threats and vulnerabilities that must be considered when determining what level of information security is adequate. Others may not have the data they need to make informed decisions. As a result, they may want to adopt information technology for new applications without adequately considering the related risks, or they may be unwilling to strengthen security over existing procedures.

A comprehensive security program can help senior managers maintain an appropriate balance between operational efficiency and security by systematically and continually fine-tuning policies and control procedures through a risk assessment, monitoring, and feedback cycle. As agency systems become more interconnected and open to large numbers of outside users and as more sophisticated technical controls become available, the effort needed to manage agency systems and monitor the effectiveness of related controls will become more complex and more time-consuming. The benefits of better service and lower processing costs should far outweigh the cost of these additional security efforts. However, it will be important for senior managers to recognize the security challenges involved and to help their organizations successfully meet these challenges. OMB has participated in a variety of efforts to develop government wide policies regarding federal information security, and it recently issued an updated version of its central guidance to agencies on minimum automated information security program requirements.

OMB has also monitored agency efforts to address recognized security weaknesses or potential weaknesses related to individual agency programs or systems. However, OMB has not proactively attempted to identify and address the underlying causes of these problems, which often are rooted in the design and management of an agency's overall information security program. In addition, the depth and scope of OMB's monitoring efforts have varied significantly from one agency to another.

Although security program management is primarily the responsibility of agency managers, under the Paperwork Reduction Act, OMB is charged with overseeing the use of federal information resources, including providing direction and overseeing the "privacy, confidentiality, security, disclosure, and sharing of information." OMB oversees and guides agency operations through its three statutory offices, which are primarily responsible for setting policy, and its five Resource Management Offices (RMO). which are primarily responsible for examining agency budget issues and overseeing agencies implementation of government wide management policies. The Office of Information and Regulatory Affairs (OIRA) is the statutory office responsible for establishing government wide information resource management policies, including those related to information security, and assisting the RMOs in overseeing agency implementation of these policies.

OIRA's information security oversight efforts are conducted primarily by its Information Policy and Technology Branch, which employs 10 individuals who regularly deal with government wide information resource management issues. Three of these individuals haveroutinely spent a significant amount of their time on information security issues.

Over the last few years the Branch has participated in various projects to address cross-cutting information security issues as part of its overall responsibility to establish information resource Management policies.

These include efforts to (1) develop federal policies on the use of cryptography, (2) define the federal role regarding the security of the national information infrastructure. assist the General Services Administration in developing telecommunications security requirements, and (4) explore security issues related to electronic commerce. However, the Branch's most basic and comprehensive accomplishment regarding federal agency security practices was developing an updated version of OMB Circular A-130.

Issued in February 1996, to clarify guidance to agencies on managing information security as they increasingly rely on open and interconnected systems. Like the previous version, issued in 1985, establishes a minimum set of controls that are to be included in federal automated information security programs. These include assigning responsibility for security, developing a system security plan, screening and training individual users, assessing risk, planning for disasters and contingencies, and reviewing security safeguards at least every 3 years. It also requires agencies to clearly define responsibilities and expected behaviour for all individuals with access to automated systems and to implement security incident response and reporting capabilities.

OIRA obtained significant input from agency managers, NIST, and the Computer System Security and Privacy Advisory Board, including written comments from over 27 organizations and individuals, before issuing the final version. The senior information resource managers and security program managers that we met also generally agreed that OIRA had done a good job of developing and communicating guidance regarding information security and responding to their individual requests for clarification of guidance. To assist in overseeing agency practices regarding information resource management, including security, analysts in OIRA's Information Policy and Technology Branch communicate frequently with RMO program examiners to (1) help ensure that the examiners are aware of high-risk or problem areas that affect the agency programs and (2) provide technical assistance to the RMOs, sometimes at the request of individual examiners.

The Branch also attempts to maintain an understanding of agency practices through informal discussions with agency personnel and participation in various conferences and meetings. For example, the Branch's primary information security policy analyst estimates that he has made six to eight presentations at individual agencies per year and numerous presentations at professional conferences and meetings, such as those of the Computer System Security and Privacy Advisory Board. He has also routinely participated in the Federal Computer Security Managers Forum, which is sponsored by NIST and meets approximately every 4 to 6 weeks. At Forum meetings, he has the opportunity to talk directly with the individuals who are responsible for administering agency security programs.

However, OIRA does not systematically monitor agency compliance with OMB information security guidance or assess the effectiveness of agency information security management practices that are fundamental elements in the agencies' ability to effectively deal with information security risks and identified weaknesses.

The most recent effort to methodically gain a relatively detailed overview of agency practices was completed in 1992. That effort involved a series of visits at each of 28 agencies by a team of OMB, NIST, and National Security Agency representatives. According to a January 1992 letter to the Director of OMB from the Computer System Security and Privacy Advisory Board, the visits were enthusiastically received and resulted in greater awareness on the part of senior officials, which, in turn, resulted in increased management support for agency computer security programs.

Despite the apparent success of the 1992 visits, Information Policy and Technology Branch officials said that they have no plans to repeat the effort because it was very resource intensive. They said that as a result, no systematic visits to agencies were currently planned and that any future efforts along this line would address a range of information resource management concerns in addition to security.

Engaging the services of contractors on a limited basis would be one means by which OMB could supplement its staff resources and periodically take a closer look at individual agency practices. Information Policy and Technology Branch officials told us that OMB has not customarily used contractors to assist in carrying out its oversight responsibilities. At GAO, we have found that engaging contractors to assist on individual projects can be a cost-effective means of expanding our ability to review agency operations, especially in areas such as information security where very specific and often highly technical expertise may be needed.

Information Security Practices

We met with branch chiefs and program examiners responsible for examining programs at 11 of the 15 agencies covered by our review and found that their attention to information security varied. Examiners for all but one agency said that they considered information security during their examination of agency budgets and programs to some extent, although examiners for eight agencies said that they only did so when it had been highlighted by agency management or in audit reports as a problem. These considerations were generally limited to monitoring agency progress in correcting recognized problems and did not involve examining an agency's information security program or the effectiveness of agency security practices in general. For example, the RMO branches overseeing the Departments of Agriculture and Education and the Office of Personnel Management all said that they had paid special attention to security issues associated with certain systems or facilities because weaknesses had been recently reported.

The program examiners and their branch chiefs said that information security is usually not closely examined because it is only one of many issues demanding their attention. The number of program examiners responsible for each agency varied from about 5 for the Department of Education to about 30 for the Department of Defense.

There were a few cases where known problems were receiving virtually no attention from the RMOs. Most notably, the representative that we spoke with about the branches that oversee the Department of Defense said that the program examiners there almost never considered problems related to information systems, including security, because such issues did not seem to have a significant budget impact compared to other issues and programs. He emphasized that due to the Department of Defense's size and variety of programs, the Defense examiners had to be very selective in deciding which items merited examination. Also, a long-standing problem regarding a lack of disaster recovery planning at the Department of Veterans Affairs (VA) appeared to have prompted little interest from the RMO branch responsible for overseeing the Department, although other security issues were considered.

Officials in several branches indicated that they were becoming increasingly sensitized to the significance of information security due to recent operational issues within their agencies. For example, the VA Branch Chief said that VA's efforts to streamline its processes by accessing needed information in other agencies' systems had raised a number of concerns about the security of shared data and the related legal requirements. Similar concerns were expressed by the branches overseeing system modernization projects at the Department of Agriculture and the Health Care Financing Administration because these projects would result in increased accessibility of sensitive information on individuals.

Despite the increasing importance of information security, few of the program examiners said that they had any significant experience or expertise in dealing with information systems or related security issues. Most said that due to their lack of expertise, they depended largely on OIRA to help them understand the issues and assess related agency actions. Most of the branches said they had good working relationships with OIRA, as well as the other statutory offices within OMB, and that when they needed technical assistance, it was available. Also, some branches had informally designated an individual with some experience in examining systems-related issues to review these issues and to serve as a resource for other examiners in the branch.

Two of the branches we visited each had a relatively experienced individual to assist in the branch's examinations. These individuals were very familiar with their agencies' information processing operations and appeared to have performed a much more comprehensive review of information security than had been performed by other branches.

OMB provides no formal training to the RMO program examiners regarding information systems management and related security issues. Each summer, OMB provides several days of seminars on issues of interest to examiners. However, only a few hours are devoted to topics handled by OIRA, including information resource management issues, such as system development issues and security.

Officials in the Information Policy and Technology Branch believe that ad hocon-the-job learning is more effective in increasing the expertise of program examiners than a more formal program of training or awareness sessions would be. This is because the examiners can be overwhelmed by the volume of information available to them, and they are more likely to absorb information that is immediately useful. However, one branch chief said that there are few on-the-job learning opportunities regarding security issues because his branch devotes little attention to such issues.

To effectively oversee and influence any activity, it is essential to have meaningful, reliable, and routinely available information on the operations being examined. However, the documented information that OMB routinely obtains on the design and effectiveness of agency information security programs varies significantly in quality, quantity, and usefulness.

Officials in OIRA's Information Policy and Technology Branch said that they routinely obtain annual internal control assessments required under the Federal Managers' Financial Integrity Act (FMFIA) and strategic information resource management plans. Since 1985, OMB Circular A-130. Also, the Computer Security Act requires each agency to include a summary of its information security plan in its strategic information resource management plan that it submits annually to OMB. However, these documents vary significantly in level of detail and were of ten of little value for oversight purposes.

Our review found that the FMFIA reports tended to contain very cursory information that made it difficult to precisely understand the nature of the weakness reported. Similarly, most of the security program summaries were very brief, and, in most cases, they only described very general agency goals and policies, with little information on the effectiveness of the program or on planned improvements. Further, the reporting formats varied considerably among agencies.

The RMO branches that we met with said that they attempted to obtain whatever information was available on the programs they examined, in addition to the agency budget documents that were the starting point for their examinations. However, most RMO examiners said that they did not routinely seek out information on or review agency security programs and that any investigation of security issues that they made was almost always prompted by issues raised by management or auditors.

Most examiners said that they relied primarily on inquiries of agency officials and related documentation in examining agency programs, including any security issues that they were aware of. However, they also said that they used audit reports, usually issued by agency inspectors general and by GAO. Several examiners noted that such audit reports were useful both in providing them an independent assessment of agency operations and in strengthening their ability to encourage agency actions. Also, several of the branches said that their examinations benefitted from good working relationships with agency inspector general officials, who would alert them to key inspector general reports and other issues. We found that, for the most part, at least one examiner in each of the branches we met with was familiar with the information security weaknesses that had been reported in inspector general, GAO, and FMFIA reports for their agencies. However, some examiners were unaware of related detailed reports that had been issued on these weaknesses.

Until recently, independent audits of information security practices were performed largely at the discretion of inspector general offices and GAO and in response to congressional interest. As a result, OMB analysts and examiners could not rely on such reports being routinely available. However, program examiners at some agencies said that they have begun to review annual audits performed under the CFO Act as a means of monitoring agency control weaknesses, including those related to information security. These audits are discussed further in chapter 4 of this report.

Two relatively new developments can serve to improve and facilitate OMB's ability to oversee and influence the effectiveness of agency information security programs. One is an expansion of independent information security reviews prompted by financial statement audits required under the CFO Act. Another is the recently established CIO Council, which can serve as a forum for addressing government wide information security issues and raising security awareness.

Information Security Controls

Although Inspector General offices and GAO have reviewed information security at federal agencies on a selective basis for decades, audits performed under the CFO Act promise to make such independent audit information more routinely available at all major agencies. Generally, CFO Act audits are required to include an evaluation of the auditee 's internal controls, including information security controls. Such evaluations can assist OMB and the Congress in their oversight roles and serve as useful tools for agency managers.

In the early 1990s, selected segments of federal operations became subject to annual financial statement audits by agency inspect or general offices under the CFO Act. In 1994, this audit requirement was extended to all major federal entities by the Government Management Reform Act (Public Law 103-356). As a result, the percentage of federal expenditures that is audited has been steadily growing, and, by fiscal year 1997, about 98 percent will be covered by such audits.

The primary responsibility for monitoring information security programs rests with agency managers who must routinely assess their programs and adjust policies and practices as needed. However, independent audits, such as the CFO Act audits, can be useful to OMB because they provide an objective evaluation that may identify weaknesses that were overlooked by agency self assessments. For example, IRS did not report its information security weaknesses in its annual FMFIA report until after independent audits had identified the weaknesses.

Although the reviews of computer security controls associated with CFO Act audits pertain to financial management systems, they usually cover a significant portion of each agency's operations. This is because program and financial systems often are supported by common data centers and communications networks that are subject to the same general controls. For example, personnel responsible for makingneeded changes to software are likely to follow the same set of procedures for controlling such changes regardless of whether they pertain to a financial or non financial system.

Similarly, the adequacy of a disaster recovery plan for a large data center is likely to affect the security of all of that center's operations—both financial and non financial. Also, programmanagement systems often are the source of many detailed financial transactions and, therefore, are included in the auditor's review. However, there are significant aspects of some agencies' operations involving sensitive computerized data that are not likely to be covered by financial statement audits.

Examples include medical records and certain types of data supporting law enforcement operations. For this reason, it is important for OMB, as well as agency managers, to coordinate their reviews of CFO Act audit reports and their reviews of other information security assessments, such as self assessments conducted in accordance with FMFIA and OMB CircularA-130. When viewed together, these audits and assessments may provide a more comprehensive view of agency information security and allow OMB and agency officials to identify gaps in review coverage. The awareness and use of CFO Act audit reports as a means of identifying information security weaknesses varied among the OMB analysts and examiners that we spoke with. This is understandable since audits of many agency programs have not been required until recently, and the routine availability of annual financial audit reports is relatively new. OIRA officials told us that they had not viewed these reports as a source of information on agency compliance with federal policies, because they did not realize that information security reviews were generally included in financial statement audits.

However, they said that in the future, they would obtain CFO audit reports from OMB's Office of Federal Financial Management, where they are routinely received from agencies. The awareness of RMO program examiners was mixed. Most were aware of the CFO audit reports that affected the programs they were responsible for examining. However, a few were unaware of significant information security problems that had been reported.

Index